Cover: An original oil painting by
Renaud deVitry - December, 1967
which was entitled "Jesus Saves".
Author Photo: by Erin deVitry

JESUS SAVES

A 'Through the Bible in a year' daily devotional

Renaud deVitry

WESTBOW
PRESS®
A DIVISION OF THOMAS NELSON
& ZONDERVAN

Scripture taken from the King James Version of the Bible.

Scripture taken from the Holy Bible, NEW INTERNATIONAL VERSION®. Copyright © 1973, 1978, 1984 by Biblica, Inc. All rights reserved worldwide. Used by permission. NEW INTERNATIONAL VERSION® and NIV® are registered trademarks of Biblica, Inc. Use of either trademark for the offering of goods or services requires the prior written consent of Biblica US, Inc.

WestBow Press books may be ordered through booksellers or by contacting:

WestBow Press
A Division of Thomas Nelson & Zondervan
1663 Liberty Drive
Bloomington, IN 47403
www.westbowpress.com
1 (866) 928-1240

Because of the dynamic nature of the Internet, any web addresses or links contained in this book may have changed since publication and may no longer be valid. The views expressed in this work are solely those of the author and do not necessarily reflect the views of the publisher, and the publisher hereby disclaims any responsibility for them.

Any people depicted in stock imagery provided by Thinkstock are models, and such images are being used for illustrative purposes only. Certain stock imagery © Thinkstock.

ISBN: 978-1-5127-4077-6 (sc)
ISBN: 978-1-5127-4078-3 (e)

Library of Congress Control Number: 2016907019

Print information available on the last page.

WestBow Press rev. date: 05/18/2016

IN GOD'S IMAGE

(1:26)   And God said, "Let us make man in our image…"

New Year's Day again! As we have been made in God's image, New Year's Day is a "creation" day for us, a day to begin again creating a new earth in which to live. Last year still didn't bring perfection, so I begin again to bring order into my life, wherever it is still "without form, and void; and darkness…" (1:2). I want my life to truly be in God's image, so some New Year's resolutions are in order. To be in God's image, I want to be faithful in the very smallest things, to eradicate sin from my life as God's Holy Spirit prompts me, not giving in to the initial temptations that lead to sin. Then I can say, as Paul did, "Be ye followers of me, even as I also am of Christ" (1 Cor. 11:1), making others in Christ's image. Instead of finding fault with others, let us root it out of ourselves, and "Let your light so shine before men, that they may see your good works, and glorify your Father which is in heaven" (Mt. 5:16).

<u>My resolutions:</u>

_____

_____

_____

_____

_____

A modest man never talks about himself.

WALKING WITH GOD

(5:24)   And Enoch walked with God: and he was not; for God took him.

"Walking with God" has grandness to it: not "run" or "hang around" with God, but "walk with God". If God condescends to walk with us where we walk, we must put aside our desires and walk with Him. "Can two walk together, except they be agreed?" (Amos 3:3) Obviously not. Jesus said, "Take my yoke upon you, and learn of me" (Matt. 11:29). Being a "true yokefellow" means walking together in the same aim. God is not in a hurry, or anxious about missing the "deal of the century". He has a purpose, and if it means he must go to the cross, he takes it in stride. Enoch was not a flashy preacher, but he didn't flinch from saying the hard truth, either. "Behold, the Lord cometh with ten thousands of his saints, to execute judgment upon all, and to convince all that are ungodly among them of all their ungodly deeds which they have ungodly committed, and of all their hard speeches which ungodly sinners have spoken against him" (Jude 14-15). When we walk with God, in the same yoke, we feel acutely the reproaches that fall upon him. Wherever God goes, we must go, and that will finally take us to be with him in heaven. God has a place, next to him in his yoke, for each of us. Enoch is remembered for faithfully walking with God at a time when "ungodly sinners" were walking contrary to him. If you want to go to heaven, you had better learn to walk with God. Read God's word, agree with it, obey it, and walk with God.

Power comes from sincere service.

THE ALTAR

(8:20)   And Noah builded an altar unto the Lord.

The first thing that Noah did upon leaving the ark was to build an altar unto the Lord. When we read it, we think it seems the proper thing to do, as thanksgiving to God. It was not to have a feast with his family, because it was a burnt offering, completely burnt up. God had not instructed him to do it, but it seems logical, since there were plenty of the clean animals, and only pairs of the unclean. Noah, and all the godly people before him, had learned from Cain and Abel's offerings that blood sacrifice was pleasing to God, and so Noah began the new generations of man with a sacrifice, not of leftover food, but of blood, and that from the clean animals. When all the offerings were finished, the altar would remain as a reminder of God's salvation for the human race, not of Noah's offerings upon it. The altar became, especially during and after Moses' time, the place of sacrifice, to offer animals' blood for man's sins. Finally, Jesus came as the real savior of mankind, he himself being the priest, the sacrifice, and the ark of deliverance. Now, "we have an altar, whereof they have no right to eat which serve the tabernacle" (Heb. 13:10). Again, the sacrifice being done, we have only the cross and the empty tomb as our reminders of God's gracious salvation for man. We have nothing to give back to God, except our "bodies a living sacrifice" (Rom. 12:1) to God, and the "sacrifice of praise to God continually, that is, the fruit of our lips, giving thanks to his name" (Heb. 13:15). The altar is our meeting place with God after *his* sacrifice.

**The fear of the Lord is the beginning
of knowledge** (Pr. 1:7)

WHITE LIES

(12:13)   *"Say, I pray thee, thou art my sister".*

Is it necessary, at times, to sin? If we tell a "white lie", is it excusable for some higher purpose? A story like this hits us all the more because Abraham is the "father of faith". He repeats it again (20:2), and then his son Isaac (26:7) does the exact same sin. Isaac's son Jacob deceives his brother Esau, and then (27:12) his father Isaac; (in fact, he only cheats Esau, but learns deceit from his mother, who learned it from her husband!). All of these cases ended in the liar becoming more prosperous, so we may almost be led to believe it was "God's will". Rather, it is God's will to prosper us and, even when he promises blessing to us, we don't trust him to bring it about. Abraham later thought he again had to "help" God, and had Ishmael through Hagar. But, it wasn't God's plan, and Isaac has been opposed by Ishmael through history, in their descendants. David once wrote (Psalm 25:21), "Let integrity and uprightness preserve me, for I wait on thee". Abraham, the "father of faith", faltered here, but his wife Sarah is to be commended as a real "mother of faith". She "obeyed Abraham, calling him lord" (1 Pet. 3:6), even when her own life and purity were jeopardized, as she knew God was her real Lord and could be trusted. We can judge Abraham for beginning a "generational sin", but are we pure from the same sin? Do we trust God enough to get us visas into countries that are not open to the gospel, or do we resort to "white lies"?

Honesty is the best policy.

BOOTING THE BONDWOMAN

(17:17) *"Shall a child be born unto him that is an hundred years old?"*

Abraham's laugh was of mixed emotions: he was delighted and rejoiced at the prospect of having a son in his old age through Sarah, his own wife who was also ninety years old. But he also wanted his own works to stand: Ishmael was a product of his own ingenuity, to try to "help" God. "Oh, that Ishmael might live before thee" (17:18). God promised that yes, he would bless Ishmael because he was Abraham's son, "but my covenant will I establish with Isaac" (17:21), the son of *promise*, not of the *flesh* (Gal. 4:21-31). A year later, and fourteen years after Ishmael's birth, God blessed Sarah with her own son, Isaac. Sarah tolerated the bondwoman and her son until Ishmael mocked her son Isaac when he was weaned. Her response: "Cast out this bondwoman and her son, for the son of this bondwoman shall not be heir with my son" (21:10). Paul quotes this in reference to the Jews who persecuted the new "Christian" believers, making this piece of history apply to God's promise, as superior to religious bondage. There was no miracle to Abraham having a son through a young bondwoman, but God's promise was fulfilled when it was humanly impossible for his wife to have children. God's promise of salvation is another human impossibility, and if the bondwoman is not cast out, there is the danger of her taking some of the credit for bringing about God's promise. Today, those who follow Islam or Judaism, or any other religion of works, are sons of the bondwoman. Only God can save, not man's best efforts.

It is not fitting...for a slave to rule
over princes! (Pr. 19:10 – NIV)

Remember Lot's Wife

(19:17)   *"Escape for thy life; look not behind thee…"*

God is serious about sin, and he knows it will kill us. Lot's wife had some second thoughts about the sinful place that was about to be destroyed. She turned back first in her heart, then she lingered behind, and then she turned back and her sin destroyed her life. We are easily lulled into a peaceful coexistence with sin around us. What used to shock us soon becomes commonplace, until we can accept it as normal. Lot's "sons in law" apparently were not as concerned as we are that their espoused wives were nearly raped by the Sodomites the night before, in an attempt to appease their lust. Talk of the city being so evil that God was now going to destroy it seemed like "mocking", so they stayed and died, instead of being saved. "Escape for thy life" is an urgent cry for immediate action and "he that hesitates is lost". Even Lot "lingered" as he and his family had second thoughts about going, and they had to be pulled along by the angels. The sons-in-law probably "slept in" and died in their sleep. Lot's wife didn't sleep in but neither was she obedient to God. Jesus is empathetic: "Remember Lot's wife" (Lk. 17:32). Flee for your life away from sin, and don't ever look back or it will seem good again. If you live in Sodom, you have only a few choices: remain there and be busy preaching righteousness, as the salt of the earth (Matt. 5:13), or flee from it! If you are double minded, you will be a salt pillar that has lost its taste.

**…If the salt have lost his savour,
wherewith shall it be salted?** (Mt. 5:13)

MADISON AVENUE MARKETING

(23:20) ...made sure unto Abraham for a possession...

By this time, Abraham was a man of great wealth, with all sorts of possessions. So, why spend a chapter of Genesis telling how he bought a field with a cave in it? Outwardly, it seems he just needs a place to bury his wife, but he makes a big deal about paying money for it, instead of taking it as a free gift. The reason is that this is to be the first possession of a piece of land within the promise of God. Like Jesus' parable of the treasure in the field, Abraham saw something more than a gravesite for his dead wife – he saw the actual possession of a small piece of the land God promised him. Salesmen call it the "foot in the door" method: once your foot is in the door, the door is open. Later, (25:23) God speaks about Abraham's grandsons, saying "the elder shall serve the younger". Here is another promise of God from which we can learn another effective sales technique. Jacob was born with God's "silver spoon in his mouth" but didn't know it, or didn't trust God. So, he used the "tongue in the cheek", or "kick a man when he's down" method (also called the "stab in the back" method when used against your own brother!) Esau should have countered with the old "door in the face" method, but he wasn't very smart in marketing, like his brother. Still, God has a better way. When he came to purchase us, he left the Holy Spirit as his "earnest", or down payment on us (Eph. 1:14). All we have to do is to complete the transaction with the good old fashioned "Jesus in the heart" method, after repenting of all our other methods.

A bird in hand is worth two in the bush.

WOMEN AT THE WELL

(24:17) "...Let me, I pray thee, drink a little water of thy pitcher..."

There are some interesting parallels between this story and that of Jesus and the woman at the well (John 4). Ultimately, both stories are a picture of salvation. It is God's pursuing love that comes to find the bride. Jesus came as the servant of the Father, seeking a bride, which is the church. The servant came for the father (Abraham) to find a bride for his son Isaac. In each story, the final decision seems to be the woman's willing choice to follow, but behind the scene is God's careful preparation of people's hearts and of circumstances. Both Jesus and the servant went looking, but asked the women for a drink as a sign of openness. Both said "I will not eat" until finished. After asking for a drink, Jesus and the servant are the ones who truly have something to give. When they reveal their identities, the women run to tell others to come. We can sense the special and purposeful, even selective love of God: we are not here by chance, but are lovingly chosen and finally persuaded to come to him. We are not, in the end, "daughters of the Canaanites", but of the chosen family of God, of the family of faith, and we are bought already with Christ's blood. We also claimed we "have no husband", but were entangled with many other unfulfilling loves. Knowing that God has done all for us, we also must be willing to "go with this man" (v. 58), to "entertain strangers" (Heb. 13:2), to wait on God, like the servant, and to worship God in spirit and truth, resulting in a willing bride for Christ.

I have planted, Apollos watered, but
God gave the increase (1 Cor. 3:6)

UNDER A CURSE

(27:13)   And his mother said unto him, "Upon me be thy curse, my son..."

A person must be very sure he is right before pronouncing this, or else willing to lose all for what he wants to gain. Abigail's similar statement to David (1 Sam. 25:24) is made out of complete selflessness, like Paul (Romans 9:3) and Moses (Exodus 32:32) in their intercession for Israel. Judah (Genesis 43:9) and Rebekah in the above passage were convinced that they were doing the right thing, and willing to pay the consequences if not. But, in contrast, look at the sad and foolish pronouncement of the Jews at Jesus' crucifixion: "His blood be on us, and on our children" (Mt. 27:25) would be their national curse, if God held them to it. Shamefully, some say he did, and that it was acutely felt in the Holocaust. Truthfully, His blood is on all of us, and our sin is responsible for Jesus' death. But, praise God, Jesus did much more when he said "Father, forgive them, for they know not what they do" (Luke 23:34), and he "redeemed us from the curse of the law, being made a curse for us" (Gal. 3:13). God's curse is not a light thing: it means eternal torment in Hades. Be sure you know this before rashly taking a curse upon yourself! The only way it can be lifted is through humility, with the result of repentance and faith in Christ. The Jews were convinced that they were right to crucify Jesus. They were not right – they were wrong, and all who persist in rejecting him will receive what they requested: his blood will be upon their hands on Judgment Day. What about you and me? If we neglect his taking of our curse, we will pay for it.

**Christ hath redeemed us from the
curse of the law...** (Gal. 3:13)

STAIRWAY TO HEAVEN

(28:12)   ...*he saw a stairway resting on the earth,*
          with its top reaching to heaven (NIV)

Jacob dreamed this as he fled from his brother Esau, after deceiving him. It was not something he "dreamed up", but a personal encounter with God who sought him first, when he was not even seeking God. God used it to offer him the relationship he already had with Abraham and Isaac, and to reaffirm his covenant with them. The image is reminiscent of the tower of Babel (Gen. 11:4), but that one was built out of man's rebellion against God, after the flood. Was God afraid that they might actually reach heaven? He didn't destroy the tower or the people but simply did not allow them to continue by confounding their language. Without God as the head, and without acknowledging our true sinful state and helplessness to attain heaven, any man-made religion of trying to reach God in heaven is doomed to destruction. The tower remained as a monument to futility. Jacob had a vision of the true stairway to heaven, by which he was able to communicate with God, and when the real "Jacob's ladder" to heaven came in the person of Jesus Christ, the right foundation was laid, which is Christ himself. God showed his approval this time, again by language, on the day of Pentecost. Jesus is the one and only mediator between God and man. As he told Nathaniel, "ye shall see heaven open, and the angels of God ascending and descending upon the Son of Man" (John 1:51). By this, he identified himself as the true stairway to heaven, and the only way to reach God.

The man who...climbs in by some other way,
is a thief and a robber. (Jn. 10:1 – NIV)

WWF – Wrestling With Father

(32:28)   *...for as a prince hast thou power with*
           God and with men, and hast prevailed.

Jacob wrestled with God and <u>won</u>?! Are you kidding? What does this mean? Jacob had a strong personality, and certainly had wrestled with men and had won, but a great fear of facing his death preceded this episode. God creates us all with certain character traits which can be used for good, or will turn us to bad. All of the wrestling with men was to prepare Jacob for this time of wrestling with God. But how can a man "win" when he wrestles with the One who made him? Not even Satan could win against God. But God sets a standard for us, and trains us against men, so we will pass his test. Abraham wrestled with God about Sodom, and he won, as God wanted him to, but Sodom was still destroyed. Jacob wrestled with God and won, but left with a hip out of joint, a broken man. Winning God's way is coming to a place of submission to God. I have wrestled with men and with God, and it has formed me into a certain kind of person, because God designs us to win, and to be broken. As Jacob wrestled with his fear of death, and came out facing it instead of running away, he became a conqueror, "For when I am weak, then am I strong" (2 Cor. 12:10). That is the secret of winning when we wrestle with God, and that is why Satan can never win! We strive with God in prayer but, like Jacob, we only win when we say, "I will not let thee go, except thou bless me" (32:26). Submission is the realization that "the less is blessed of the better" (Heb. 7:7).

Power comes from sincere service.

A LAW UNTO THEMSELVES

(34:7) ...which thing ought not to be done

Here is a good story of how our conscience will work along with God's standard of the law. When we hear the law, such as the Ten Commandments, our hearts agree with it. At the time of this story, there was not yet a set of commands from God, but everyone agreed that the adultery of Shechem was wrong, and marriage was not the solution. "Should he deal with our sister as with an harlot?" (34:31) No! Even without a law their conscience is made to judge against wrong actions. Later, God made a law saying, "There shall be no whore of the daughters of Israel" (Deut. 23:17), and concerning the Philistine people, "Thou shalt make no covenant with them, nor with their gods" (Ex. 23:32). But now, even before the law came, these men said this "thing ought not to be done". Though we may be appalled at the angry actions of Simeon and Levi, still they correctly condemned Shechem's act of adultery and were not "bought off" with money, to marry the daughters of the land. Does our conscience also recoil in anger and horror at sin? Or, do we just settle down and marry with sin when it is threatening to take over our pure minds? The world is once again waiting for men like John the Baptist, whose preaching of the law will bring conviction. When the law is preached, the conscience agrees, saying "...which thing ought not to be done!" Dinah's name means "judgment", and God allowed the righteous anger of Dinah's brothers to bring judgment upon Shechem and his people. Ten commands are all that lingers...

A man's best friends are his ten fingers.

THE MALTESE FALCON

(37:19) "Behold, this dreamer cometh."

In the movie <u>The Maltese Falcon</u>, Humphrey Bogart says, "It's the stuff dreams are made of" when he sees otherwise nice people ready to kill for power or money. In Joseph's case, it was not the dreamer who had the problem, but those who were jealous of his dream and ready to kill him. Was Joseph wrong to tell the dreams to them? If he had not, possibly he wouldn't have been sold as a slave, but then neither would the dream have been fulfilled. When God gives us a dream, it will come to pass without our help. Jesus was considered to be a "dreamer" also, and was scorned by his own brothers, and by jealous Jews, who later had him killed. But, nothing could keep him from seeing his dream fulfilled. For Jesus too, being sold for 30 pieces of silver and other treacheries were all part of the plan of God. If you have a dream from God and don't have pride in your heart about it, then don't be afraid to tell it to others. We may be considered as dreamers to those who have not "tasted of the heavenly gift" (Heb. 6:4), but we should tell them the story anyway, even if it makes them jealous. We also may be put in jail, and suffer many things before the dream comes true, but it surely will come true! The rest of the world is chasing after a "Maltese Falcon" that is a counterfeit of the real treasure, and are killing and stealing for something that will not last, and will prove to be worthless. If you see a dreamer coming, be wise enough to say, "If it be of God, ye cannot overthrow it" (Acts 5:39), instead of trying to kill the dreamer.

"It's the stuff dreams are made of".

DON'T DESPAIR

(39:21)   But the Lord was with Joseph.

For many of us, maybe most of us, if only a fraction of the evil were to befall us which happened to Joseph or Job, we would be tempted to "curse God, and die" (Job 2:9). And, if left to ourselves, that is exactly what we would do. "But the Lord was with Joseph", and that makes all the difference in the world. If you have any thought that maybe you could be as gracious to brothers who sold you into slavery as Joseph was, think again. It is only the grace of God that keeps any of us from giving in to bitterness when things go wrong. Each time Joseph went through another unjust treatment, "the Lord was with Joseph" (39:2, 21-23, 41:37), and God promises to be with us in any similar trying situations. The hero of the story is not Joseph, but the Lord, who performs all things for his own good pleasure, and if we could just remember that we would never be frustrated. God's plan is not that the circumstances should destroy us, or even harden us, but to let the life of Christ be formed in us, and to transform us into trophies that others can admire. We can't help but love Joseph for his great heart of forgiveness, but we must see it is God's great forgiving heart that made him like that. Despair may lead to insanity, but God's will is that we continue in our faith in him who never fails.

Faith is the continuation of reason.

HAUNTING GUILT

(42:21)   *"We are verily guilty concerning our brother."*

Before forgiveness can mean anything to us, there must be a confession of guilt. Joseph heard his brothers say this among themselves, but not to him. Of course, Jesus forgave us before we were ever born but it takes some kind of admission of guilt before that forgiveness can be applied to us personally. A guilty conscience will haunt us until we make things right by going and asking forgiveness. But, God's way is that forgiveness should precede the admission of guilt, and lead the guilty party to repentance (Romans 2:4). Judas had a guilty conscience and said, "I have betrayed the innocent blood" (Matt. 27:4), but he never went back to ask Christ for forgiveness, and died by hanging himself, a tormented man. By now, Joseph was a powerful man who could have had his brothers killed if he chose not to forgive them. But forgiveness is a measure of greatness. "While we were yet sinners, Christ died for us" (Romans 5:8). Joseph had already forgiven his brothers, and they were dumbfounded when he said, "I am Joseph" (45:3). Like the woman at the well, who had a guilty conscience and then heard Jesus say, "I that speak unto thee am he" (John 4:26), all Joseph's brothers could do was to await their punishment, and then to be stunned by Joseph's unconditional forgiveness. One day, all men will "look upon me [Christ] whom they have pierced" (Zech. 12:10), and will know their guilt. A man must see himself lost and full of sin before he can cry out to God for mercy and forgiveness. Joseph's brothers had thrown him into a pit, but it was they who had really fallen into it, and guilt will prove that to us, too.

Whoso diggeth a pit shall fall therein (Pr. 26:27)

SPEECHLESS!

(44:16)   What shall we speak? ... God hath found out the iniquity of thy servants.

Speechless! "What things soever the law saith, it saith to them who are under the law: that every mouth may be stopped, and all the world may become guilty before God" (Romans 3:19). Just as a checkmate in chess, this is where sinners must be brought before seeing they are hopelessly lost and guilty before the Judge of all the earth. The only hope is mercy, and that can only be given when true sorrow unto repentance comes (2 Cor. 7:8-11). A police officer may pass by an offense if he sees true humility, and that the person agrees he deserves punishment, but never will he "let off" one who continues to maintain his innocence, or gives excuses when he has been caught "dead to rights" in his rebellion. Joseph had no desire for revenge, but he did want his brothers to feel the guilt of their sin and to despair that any escape from punishment was possible. God arranges elaborate circumstances in our lives, also, that we might repent with tears for our sins. We will stand speechless before a holy God on the judgment day if we have not yet repented and received forgiveness by Christ's blood. God will never show mercy to one who is not repentant, and has not seen his hopeless condition and utter guiltiness for his sins, and the need of Christ's blood. In the parable of the wedding banquet, the king asked how a man had entered without wearing wedding clothes. "And he was speechless" (Matt. 22:12). Unless we arrive before God in the "robes of righteousness", washed in Christ's blood, we too will be ashamed, speechless, and cast out.

**When words are many, sin is not
absent ...** (Pr. 10:19 - NIV)

HOW OLD ART THOU?

(47:8)　And Pharaoh said unto Jacob, "How old art thou?"

A simple search of ages reveals a lot about people's lives. Jacob answered Pharaoh that he was 130 years old as he entered Egypt. He and Esau were born when their father Isaac was sixty (Gen. 25:26), and together they buried him when he died at the age of 180 (35:28-9), making Jacob 120, which was just ten years before coming to Egypt. Joseph was thirty when he stood before Pharaoh (41:46), just prior to seven years of plenty, and probably the same year Isaac was buried, if they were now beginning the third year of the famine, with five more years to come (45:11). Counting back to his birth, this means Joseph was born when Jacob was ninety. That was after 14 years of service for his two wives (30:25), and just before six more years of service for the herds (31:41). Benjamin, then was born when Jacob was 96! (That makes Benjamin's birth nearly as miraculous as Isaac's birth when Abraham was 100!) Why don't we hear of this, except that a repeat miracle is no longer a miracle? All his descendants received the blessings of Abraham's faith. It appears that Jacob had all his children between the ages of 83 and 96 (after his first seven years of service to marry Laban's daughters). And, it is just about as certain that Jacob deceived Isaac for Esau's blessing when they were about 75 years old(!), unless Esau's grudge (27:41) takes place over several years. So, maybe you <u>can</u> "teach an old dog new tricks" – Jacob was 96 years old when he "got saved"! [Compare 28:20-22 and 35:1-9]

You can't teach an old dog new tricks.

BEYOND FORGIVENESS

(50:20)   *Ye thought evil against me, but God meant it unto good.*

This story goes far beyond forgiveness, and far beyond good triumphing over evil. For those who like happy endings, who can beat this one? Most stories have the "good guy" win, but how many have the bad guys also winning? Any religion worth its salt has good triumphing over evil, but only God's own heart could come up with forgiveness for our enemies while they are still enemies. Joseph was a very good example or type of Christ, who also forgave his "brothers" who sold him to be killed, as they hated him. Both Joseph and Jesus saw past the evil that was done to them by close friends, and saw God's purpose in the suffering. "Beyond forgiveness" means blessing those who are persecuting you, to the point of giving your life for someone who is laughing as he is killing you. Who can love that much? Only God can, and those who have his Holy Spirit living inside them. Interestingly, Joseph's brothers never did say, "we were wrong, please forgive us", at least not to Joseph. Their only concern was to save their own wicked skins. That is how we are, but "while we were yet sinners, Christ died for us" (Romans 5:8). Islam can only understand evil for evil, and forgiveness in exchange for prayers, or some other work. But the true Christianity is having the completely free and undeserved grace of God given to us because God has seen and accepted the sufferings and prayers and death of Christ in our behalf. That is something new and far beyond forgiveness, that God offers.

Mercy triumphs over judgment! (Jas. 2:13 - NIV)

CIVIL DISOBEDIENCE

(1:17)   But the midwives feared God

Because they feared God, they disobeyed the command of Pharaoh to kill the Hebrew males as they were born. How does this fit with Peter's command (1 Peter 2:13), to "submit yourselves to every ordinance of man for the Lord's sake"? Even today, if a person follows the orders of a superior and it goes against a higher law, or a law of the conscience, the person will be prosecuted, though he "was only following orders". We are expected to exercise our own judgment in such matters and to make proper decisions, even if an evil king orders us to do something that is morally wrong, and threatens to punish or kill us if we disobey. The point is that "the midwives feared God". Their fear of God was greater than their fear of the king. "By the fear of the Lord men depart from evil" (Prov. 16:6). But, how can we be "rightly dividing the word of truth"? (2 Tim. 2:15) Can we take this scripture and others like it as proof texts for civil disobedience in other areas? This is one of the hardest areas of the Christian life, trying to discern the will of God in questionable circumstances. Again, the point comes down to simply fearing God, and being ready to "suffer for well doing" (1 Peter 3:17). God will be the final judge of our actions, and we must fear him more than man when it comes to such a decision. Mahatma Gandhi, though not himself a Christian, used this principle to gain the independence of India, through civil disobedience. Should we not, as Christians, be ready to suffer persecution, jail and death to see God's kingdom be established? Let the fear of God, beginning of wisdom, guide you.

**The fear of the Lord is the beginning
of wisdom** (Pr. 9:10)

WHIPPED INTO LIFE

(5:4)   *"Get you unto your burdens"*

This pronouncement of Pharaoh is the general idea of the world concerning our predicament. Since Adam's sin there has been a curse upon man and his work (Gen. 3:17-19). Man is so far from the grace of God that he feels almost more secure under some taskmaster than to be free to simply worship God for his goodness. The sad condition of the gospel preaching today is that people leave the bondage of sin, to be enslaved now to some "good works" to try to gain God's favor. When the grace of God appears, like Moses who came to deliver Israel, the biggest problem is in convincing men that they are really about to be set free. When slavery was abolished in America, slave owners kept their salves in bondage through the bondage that was in their minds. We have a slave mentality that makes us feel we must do something to earn freedom. When the salvation story comes to us, we become even more in bondage, feeling we have no right to go free, and the bondage of the Pharisees is much harder than that of sin. We almost get angry at God for sending a savior, saying "it was better before I was saved". But, the true grace of God will set us completely free from all burdens. Satan doesn't mind if we leave the bondage of sin, as long as we become in bondage to religious works, which still lead to destruction. My brother once told me we must be "whipped into life", but life is much more than a whipping.

Wise men never sit and wail their loss.

FICKLE FINGER OF FATE

(8:19)   *"This is the finger of God"*

What tipped them off? "The magicians of Egypt did so with their enchantments" several times (7:11,22, 8:7), but this time they saw they couldn't fake the miracle of God. Magicians can make a rabbit "materialize" out of a hat, but it is only really that they trick our eyes by sleight of hand. Only God can create something and these magicians knew that. David spoke of the creation (Psalm 8:3) of the heavens (moon, stars & planets) as the "work of [God's] fingers", but after he created man sin entered the world. So, it seems that every other reference to the "finger of God" has to do with his judgment against sin. God gave the Ten Commandments "written with the finger of God" (Ex. 31:18) as his standard of judgment. When he brought judgment upon Belshazzar, he again wrote on the plaster wall with what appeared as "fingers of a man's hand" (Dan. 5:5), and when Jesus was asked to judge the woman who was caught in adultery, he "with his finger wrote on the ground" (John 8:6). An interesting parallel to Moses and the magicians is seen when Jesus is accused: "He casteth out devils through Beelzebub" (Luke 11:14-20). His answer is, "If I with the finger of God cast out devils, no doubt the kingdom of God is come upon you!" A comedy show years ago joked about giving the "flying fickle finger of fate award", but God's finger is not fickle; he dispenses justice in accordance with his commandments. It is man who is fickle, because sin has blinded his mind. But when God's judgment comes on a nation as it did upon Egypt, wise men will acknowledge their sin and say finally "this is the finger of God", or perish (fickle Pharaoh's fate).

God heals and the doctor takes the fee.

THE BLOOD

(12:13) 　*"...and when I see the blood I will pass over you."*

The greatest of all plagues is coming: the end of the world and the final judgment, and eternal torment for those who don't survive. And the only point of separation from "the sheep and the goats" will be the blood. "The Lord doth put a difference between the Egyptians and Israel" (11:7). Why? It is based only on their faith and obedience about the blood. Not good works, not good looks, not good intentions, but the blood. The same will be true on Judgment Day. Never mind arguing, if you don't rid your house of leaven (sin) and put the blood of Christ on your doorpost (heart), you will be destroyed. Ignorance is no excuse: most of the Egyptians died (firstborn) without ever hearing about the blood. So, it is not a matter of having to willfully reject Christ before perishing – a loving God punished unsuspecting babies for their parents' unbelief (killing them, but not sending them to Hades) to show his sovereignty and righteousness. Do we think he will now lightly pass over those who have not the blood of his son's sacrifice? Now, it won't be for the ignorance of the heathen, but for the unbelief of "Christians"! "His blood will I require at thine hand (watchman)" (Ezek. 3:17-21). Yes, the heathen are lost without Christ's blood. Sincerity won't save them without repentance and the blood of Jesus. Like the "innocent babies" in Egypt, multitudes of Muslims, Hindus, atheists and even many "Christians" will die and miss Heaven for their sins, not having the blood. Who will tell them? We must!

"This is my blood of the new testament" (Mt. 26:28)

THE ONLY REAL HERO

(14:13)   "Stand still and see the salvation of the Lord."

God alone is the hero of the Bible. We look so hard to see a hero, a man who doesn't fail God, but we all do. The Bible is the story of God, not of any great men. Israel saw the miracles in Egypt, parting of the Red Sea and so many other miracles, and yet they continually turned their backs upon God. The Bible is God's story, not man's. Man's history is one of only sin and failure, with God's glorious acts of salvation when man comes to his end. At the Red Sea there was nowhere else to turn but to God. But how soon they turned back to murmuring and sin! Still, God remains faithful to his people. Man has nothing to boast in, except God himself. If we have any righteousness, it is due to the salvation of God. Only shortly after the Red Sea Rescue, "…they tempted the Lord, saying, Is the Lord among us, or not?" (17:7). Psalm 107 shows man's continual backsliding, each time things start to go well. Pride and self-reliance is the reason, and man's nature is to forget God. Prosperity, or even just having bread and water, is not the sign of "the Lord among us", and only pride would murmur to demand from God. When Israel became proud, God humbled them, and finally turned to Gentiles. The church was born, and then the "Roman Catholic" church became powerful and rich. So, God raised up the new "protestant " church, but each time a segment of it became proud or rich, God allowed another one to emerge. Why should we think we are any different? We will stand if God is our only hero and standard.

Thou shalt have no other gods before me. (Ex. 20:3)

MURMURING AGAINST GOD

(16:8)   "Your murmurings are not against us, but against the Lord"

Like Ananias (Acts 5:4) "Thou hast not lied unto men, but unto God".
Solomon said (Prov. 14:31), "He that oppresseth the poor reproacheth
his Maker". Jesus asked Paul (Acts 9:4) "Why persecutest thou me?", and
explained in a parable (Matt. 25:40), "Inasmuch as ye have done it unto
one of the least of these my brethren, ye have done it unto me". When
we speak against parents or authorities, we are despising God's authority,
and murmuring against pastors or husbands is murmuring against God.
God told Samuel (1 Sam. 8:7) "they have not rejected thee, but they have
rejected me." Jesus said (Luke 10:16) "He that despiseth you despiseth me;
and he that despiseth me despiseth him that sent me." (See also Rom. 13:2
and 1 Thes. 4:8). Hosea became a picture to all of Israel and Judah of their
rejection of God. His wife left him as the Jews had left God. But Gomer
was not rejecting her husband: she was rejecting God, wanting to be her
own boss, and out from being under any authority. A police officer doesn't
feel rejected when someone ignores his orders – he just writes up a ticket
and lets his superior authorities take charge. If you are separated from a
wayward spouse, take this to heart: divorce is rejection, but it is sadder for
the one who has left his or her covenant promise. Continue to try to bring
your spouse home, and be a model of faithfulness. The murmurings are
not against you, but against God. We have been guilty of the same, many
times, and God continues to forgive and woo us back to our covenant
with him. Be content with pleasing God, and let him change the hearts
of those who offend you.

The issue is righteousness, not happiness.

JURASSIC PARK

(19:22)   "...sanctify themselves, lest the Lord break forth upon them"

We have been brought up with only part of the truth. The statement "God is love" (1 John 4:8) is true, but God is also a consuming fire (Heb. 12:29). The description of God in this chapter sounds more like a movie called "Jurassic Park". God told Moses (19:23) to "set bounds about the mount", like the high voltage electric fence that kept the dinosaurs in control. "The voice of the trumpet, exceeding loud: so that all the people that was in the camp trembled" (19:16) is like the roar of the T-Rex. God is not some "Jurassic Park" to be visited by children on a field trip, in the safety of sealed car, but he will be much more fearful than a T-Rex on Judgment Day. Our only electric fence on that day will be the protective screen of Christ's blood to "sanctify ourselves". In Job 40 and 41, God showed Job that if he couldn't survive a fight with "behemoth" or "leviathan" (which might well be dinosaurs!), how could he stand to face the wrath of the God who made them? Man today has a fearful fascination with "velociraptors" and dinosaurs of the past, because he doesn't want to think of the impending wrath of an angry God. He is not some "nice grandpa", but is more like our worst nightmare of we have to face him in our sins. When the King of kings, the "T-Rex of all T-rexes" comes to "devour his adversaries" (Heb. 10:27), there will be no escape. If we think some electric fence can keep God in a zoo, we'd better return to a healthy fear of God and forget that plan. We need to sanctify ourselves with the blood of Christ, who forgave those who injured him on the cross, but will not forgive an insult to the spirit of grace (Heb. 10:29).

An injury is much sooner forgotten than an insult.

WITCH HUNTING

(22:18) *"Thou shalt not suffer a witch to live".*

Are we talking about the "wicked witch of the west", the kind that rides on a broomstick? If there are good and bad witches, should we drop houses on the "black magic" witches and honor the "white witches"? Or are all witches simply different degrees of the same sin? Maybe you don't even believe in witches, but whatever they are, God obviously does. "Witch hunts" became popular in America a few hundred years ago, and many witches were burned at the stake to pay for their sin. But, it's been a long time since I've heard of a son being killed for striking or cursing his mom or dad, or for kidnapping (21:15-17). God gives a death penalty for most of the Ten Commandments, and truthfully, we all have to die because of sin in general. God hasn't changed his mind: death is still the penalty to be paid for sin. But who will kill the witch? "He that is without sin among you, let him first cast a stone at her (John 8:7). This is not to deny God's righteous judgment on witches, but to make us all consider, as we see people executed as capital punishment for some crime, how many times we should have died already for our sins. We can all get very loud in the midst of a mob crying out for blood when a death penalty is due, but if someone in the crowd began to call for blood for all of our capital offenses, would we quiet down? Witch hunts are great fun for non-witches, and for Pharisees, but are these same men and women ready for justice when they, or their own families, are caught in a capital offense? Let us all learn to repent for our own sins, and leave judgment to God.

Obedience alone gives the right to command.

ACCORDING TO HOYLE

(26:30)   "...according to the fashion...showed thee in the mount."

I was in a Catholic Church chapel while reading this morning and was noticing how many of these furnishings of the temple are still being used. There's an altar, a lamp, and a small "tabernacle". In most Catholic churches there is also a laver and incense, and something called a "monstrance" (to show the body of Christ – like showbread). But there are also a lot of other things not "according to the fashion" as shown to Moses, like statues, pictures and a big "crucifix", and even what things they have are not according to the plan. When Jesus came, he was the reality of all these parts of the tabernacle, and his life and death made an end of their significance, as only shadows of the real. If we hope to ever understand the gospel, we must stick to the original blueprint, the Bible. We cannot present the gospel and hope for any real and lasting results unless we stick to the pattern given by God; just as in carpentry, we write "pattern" on one piece, and always refer back to it for our standard. When we lose the standard, we are left to groping about to find the substance of what we believe. The pattern for Moses was the original – that which was "showed thee in the mount". Trying to return to the shadow through some vague recollection of what the pattern was before is worse than going backwards, if we still have the original pattern and just refuse to refer to it! We must return to the pattern in our hands and throw out the traditions that are contrary to it, no matter how much we like them.

**Remove not the ancient landmark, which
thy fathers have set.** (Pr. 22:28)

DRESS CODE

(28:2)   And thou shalt make holy garments...for glory and for beauty."

The way we dress expresses who we are, and we dress in different ways for different functions. Most people would not dare to come without proper dress to see the king, yet Mahatma Gandhi came with simple Indian dress to meet with Mountbatten, who was the viceroy of India. He was making a statement of who was really the host of whom, as England was the guest of India. Still, we dress the king or the priest in beautiful clothes to express "glory and beauty" for them. Aaron was a priest to represent the tribes of Israel before God, and he wouldn't dare to dress haphazardly before God when his (and their) life depended upon it. God dressed Adam and Eve in the skins of animals, because only the blood of a sacrifice could clothe the ugliness of their sin. Even our clothing in heaven will not be acceptable if it is our own works – it must be "garments of righteousness" (Isa. 61:3, 10) which is the blood and righteousness of Christ. For a priest, his "glory and beauty", expressed by holy garments, must also be a reality in his inner life, because God alone is the real judge of glory and beauty. Jesus Christ is our high priest who alone shows true glory and beauty on the inside and outside, because he is God's express image. It doesn't matter if a priest's garments show glory and beauty to man, as that would only be a vain show, unless it is understood he is representing Jesus. Rather, these holy garments remind the priest to be holy, "that he may minister <u>unto me</u>", says God (28:1). We are "a royal priesthood"; and our holy garments? "Let it not be that outward adorning...of putting on of apparel" but the glory of Christ within and speech that glorifies God.

Language is the dress of thought.

THE TORTOISE AND THE HARE

(31:13)   "I am the Lord that doth sanctify you."

We all like the story of "the tortoise and the hare" because we believe "victory belongs to the most persevering". The Sabbath rest is an insult to the intelligence of the man who tries to work his way to heaven. Since God created the world in seven days, we continue to make calendars with "weeks" of seven days. There is no "natural" reason for it, as with a day (24 hours for the Earth's rotation), a month (lunar cycle), or year (Earth's cycle around the sun). But man, like the tortoise, continues to plod along seven days a week, trying to make ends meet, and to win the "human race". This work-a-holic attitude affects how we think of spirituality, too. But God put a death penalty for Sabbath breakers to remind us it's "not by works of righteousness which we have done, but according to his mercy he saved us" (Titus 3:5). Maybe the hare was right, after all! We should work hard for six days, but we need a rest, too, not just for our tired bodies, but as a sign or reminder to us that God alone can save us. But man in his wisdom has forgotten why we even have seven day weeks. If he takes a day off at all, it is just to have fun, but not to spend it thanking God for saving him. Or else, he uses it to catch up and get ahead of the rabbits who might be ahead of him, and to prove to God how hard he works at being good. The point is, we don't persevere at obeying God's commandments, and on Sabbaths "to obey is better than sacrifice" (1 Sam. 15:22). Only God really perseveres in his love for us until "it is finished" (John 19:30), and "He that endureth (in faith) to the end shall be saved" (Matt. 10:22).

Victory belongs to the most persevering.

TRIVIAL PURSUITS

(33:1)　...Leave this place...and go up to the land I promised... (NIV)

A simple command, but it took forty years to complete it; too many conflicting interests and fears, too much concern for earthly things. God gave us a command, too, "Go ye into all the world and preach the gospel to every creature" (Mark 16:15). After 2000 years it still hasn't been completed. We're too concerned with being a PhD in religion, or about being beat up or persecuted by "giants", or fighting over who gets credit when somebody "gets saved", or who's boss, or where our next meal will come from. If our eyes are on the goal of "the land", of being in Christ ourselves and getting others to know him, all these other pursuits will fall into place. If we get sidetracked with too much concern for these things, the job will never be finished. By way of contrast, we read later "so the people were restrained from bringing" (36:6). Imagine if this were our attitude towards the great commission! If the church worldwide would ever become so consumed with the work before us, it would be done in no time, but we are all consumed with other pursuits, and each generation wanders in the wilderness for 40 years, and dies without completing the work. The picture of the work of Bezalel and Oholiab (see next entry) shows that we can begin many things and complete them all if we have a mind to work, and a single purpose in mind, toward which all of the work is directed. Let us put aside trivial pursuits, and with a singleness of purpose complete the work that is before us of preaching the gospel.

He who begins many things finishes nothing.

MASTER CRAFTSMEN

(35:31)   And he hath filled him with the spirit of God...

Bezalel, along with Oholiab, was chosen by God and was filled with everything needed to do his commission. He was filled first with the Spirit of God, then also "in wisdom, in understanding, and in knowledge, and in all manner of workmanship...". Finally, both were filled with the ability to teach others (35:34). God's works are perfect, and when he involves people in his work, he puts his spirit into us to enable us to do his work perfectly. The work done by these master craftsmen would glorify God for as long as their work endured, and even long after, as we read of their precision in the pages of Scripture. When God told Noah to build an ark to preserve the human race from the flood, we read in a few paragraphs the details of how it was to be constructed. But, how could Noah be sure it would float, or hold all the animals, or withstand the tidal waves of a worldwide catastrophic flood? Only the spirit of God could give him the skill and knowledge to complete the task. Likewise, for the tabernacle and its furnishings to be what God envisioned, Bezalel and Oholiab needed the mind of God to see what God's instructions meant. Paul explains how this can happen, saying "God hath revealed them unto us by his Spirit" (1 Cor. 2:10-16). When God sent Jesus to preserve the human race from sin, he filled him with his spirit, and all that was needed to do the work. Each of us is given ability to complete the tasks "which God prepared in advance for us to do" (Eph. 2:10 – NIV), and by his spirit we can enjoy the work and teach others as master craftsmen. "Do you see a man skilled in his work? He will serve before kings; he will not serve before obscure men." (Pr. 22:29 - NIV)

Honest labor bears a lovely face.

SEEING EYE DOGS

(40:36)   *When the cloud was taken up... the children of Israel went onward....*

Only blind people can really appreciate what it means to be guided by the eyes of another. Seeing Eye dogs are trained to be seeing eyes for people who have no sight. In dense clouds or storms, airplane pilots can fly by the instruments instead of "flying by the seat of their pants" as they had to in the early days (gravity telling them when they were right side up). Israel in the wilderness was spiritually blind, and though Moses was a great man he could lead Israel only by being in close fellowship with God. The pillar of cloud and of fire was God's visible presence to the nation of Israel, and God meant for them to lean completely upon him for guidance. Just as a blind man grows to trust his Seeing Eye dog as he continues to daily guide him safely through traffic and other hazardous situations, so the Israelites were led as sheep by a shepherd. But Moses was not that shepherd – God was. Moses, for all his greatness, was a blind man, too, if not for God's Presence with him. He said, "If thy Presence does not go with us, do not send us up from here." (33:15 – NIV). Israel was not to look to Moses but to God for their guidance and leadership, and we must not look towards any man, no matter how "spiritual" he may be. We are to "fly by the instruments", not by our feelings, but by faith in the one who sees the end from the beginning. The whole Bible is a revelation of God to us, so that we may cease to trust in our own eyes, or the leadership of any man, and look to God. If God gets up and moves, we had better get up and move with him, or be lost.

**And if the blind lead the blind, both
shall fall into the ditch.** (Mt. 15:14)

FATNESS

(3:16)   ...all the fat is the Lord's.

When the Scriptures speak of "fat" or "fatness" it means something like prosperity or extravagance: "...and let your soul delight itself in fatness" (Isa. 55:2) speaks of God's blessing on his saints, as they hunger for his righteousness; but when Israel lusted and tempted God in the wilderness, "...he gave them their request; but sent leanness into their soul" (Psalm 106:15). If "all the fat is the Lord's" and "The earth is the Lord's, and the fullness thereof" (Ps. 24:1), then he can give it to whomever he chooses. God's desire is to bless his saints with fatness, but we must first acknowledge our sin before him. An offering of sacrifice should make us feel the cost of our sin and bring godly sorrow for that sin. An ungodly prosperity doctrine has swept over the churches of today, which is idolatry and covetousness. God blessed Abraham, Job, Solomon, David and many others with riches and "fatness", but not because they set their affections on it! (Col. 3:2) It was the same sin of covetousness that caused Satan and even Adam and Eve to fall, so God speaks much about the "deceitfulness of riches". "It shall be a perpetual statute...that ye eat neither fat nor blood" (3:17), but when God chooses to bless us, it is another matter (Deut. 32:14, Neh. 8:10). Until Christ died on the cross it was a sin to drink blood, but he instituted the "Lord's supper" on the night he was betrayed, and said, "This is my blood" (Mark 14:24), as he told his disciples to drink the cup. Only those who understand their sin, and the cost of Christ's blood to pay for it, can partake worthily of his blood. If we are truly done with sin, let us prove it by a right attitude.

**For the love of money is the root
of all evil.** (1 Tim. 6:10)

PYROMANIA

(6:13)   The fire…shall never go out.

"The fire shall ever be burning upon the altar" means several things. It means "…my sin is ever before me" (Ps. 51:3) and requires an acceptable sacrifice; but also, that the blood of Christ is always there to take away my sin. People say "ignorance is bliss", but God says true happiness comes only through the fear of the Lord, and "the fear of the Lord is the beginning of wisdom". So, ignorance is not bliss, but knowledge of the truth brings true joy. Israel had joy whenever they walked in the truth, but wrath and judgment when they rebelled. Fire on the altar was a daily reminder of their tenuous relationship to God, based upon observance of the law. The good news is that Christ fulfilled the requirements of the law for us. That is something to be shouted from the rooftops! For us, the fire on the altar never goes out – Christ's blood is always there to cleanse us from our sins. But, for the disobedient, the fire will also never go out, as they "shall be cast into outer darkness: there shall be weeping and gnashing of teeth" (Mt.8:12). The fire on the altar will be either a comfort or a terror to those who see it. If we are wise, we will walk in the fear of God and learn to depart from evil, and preach the good news to all who will listen. "For our God is a consuming fire" (Heb. 12:29), and that, too, should be a source of comfort to us. He destroys the wicked, but he burns up the chaff in the lives of his saints, as well. The fire on the altar reminds us daily to choose life, not death. If you are rebellious still, you have cause to weep, but…

Laugh if you are wise.

A Portion For The Meek

(7:35)   This is the portion of the anointing of Aaron...

There is a certain portion that goes along with each office appointed to men, as there is a portion of inheritance that goes with being born into a family. In India, the caste system has kept the priesthood class as a privileged and very rich class for thousands of years. Others are kept from ever reaching any kind of jobs or status through this same oppressive system, which has made the self-appointed priest's office into an inheritance. Inheritance is more important than appointments (Heb. 1:1-9), and Jesus was both "appointed and anointed" as a son and a priest. Aaron's sons lost their lives through their disobedience (10:1), and their portion was passed on to younger brothers. Question: How can a poor man, of low caste and no position, ever hope to attain a better inheritance? Answer: By being born again into God's family! Our portion may never be in this life, but it is a promised inheritance to those who are "in Christ". The Aaronic priests got no inheritance of land in this life, but their daily needs were all met. Even Moses, who was greater than Aaron [his older brother] never received any inheritance of land in Israel. Moses, called the deliverer of Israel, "...was very meek, above all the men which were upon the face of the earth" (Num. 12:3), but his inheritance or portion was not in this world – at least not in his lifetime. The prodigal son's older brother (Luke 15:11-32) had his portion of "3 square meals a day", but the real blessing came to the prodigal son when he became meek through the circumstances that brought him to repentance. When we are broken and repent, and turn back to God, we also are heirs.

**Blessed are the meek, for they shall
inherit the earth.** (Mt. 5:5)

STRANGE FIRE

(10:1)　Nadab and Abihu…offered strange fire before the Lord.

They were told, "Ye shall offer no strange incense thereon, nor burnt sacrifice nor meat offering…" (Ex. 30:9). The only fire that was acceptable was one lit by God, whether on the altar of incense or the altar of sacrifice. Nadab and Abihu died without mercy for their presumptuous sin. "The fire shall ever be burning upon the altar; it shall never go out", fueled by continuous sacrifices by the Levitical priests. It is a picture, too, of eternal torment for God's enemies. God is a consuming fire – he sent fire to consume the first offering of the priests, which brought the fear of God upon the people. The very next verse shows Nadab and Abihu "offering strange fire" on the altar of incense, so God sent out fire to consume them! The same happened to the 250 men who offered incense not authorized by God in the rebellion of Korah (Num. 16:35). The altar of sacrifice was a shadow of Christ's sacrifice on the cross, and the incense altar is an example for us of our acceptable prayers before God, after the acceptable sacrifice of Christ has been completed. We can come before God with no other sacrifice than the blood of Jesus, and our prayers must be fueled with no selfish motives, no false doctrine or "strange fire" that is contrary to God's revealed way of salvation. The altar of incense is no place to offer sacrifice – our works will not suffice if we are not trusting solely in the blood of Christ. God will consume us with fire that will not be quenched if we try any other way.

Rashness and haste make all things insecure.

REWARD FOR LABOR

(12:7)   ...And she shall be cleansed from the issue of her blood.

From the time of Adam and Eve's sin our labor has been cursed. "In sorrow thou shalt bring forth children" and "cursed is the ground for thy sake; in sorrow shalt thou eat of it all the days of thy life" (Gen. 3:16-17): these were the curses on the labor of women and men because of sin. God's mercy brought forth a Savior, through childbearing, but God was careful to show that even the "travail" or "labor" of childbearing could not pay for any sins. We feel "the labourer is worthy of his hire" (Luke 10:7), but God, who says "if any would not work, neither should he eat" also says "a man is not justified by the works of the law, but by the faith of Jesus Christ" (2 Thes. 3:10/ Gal. 2:16). God finished creation's work with a day of rest, and pronounced "it is finished" when he was done with redemption. In Christ's birth, we see Mary's obedience to the above mentioned law fulfilled. The circumcision of Jesus was the first time he shed blood, as a sign that he would be the Lamb of God. After Mary's days of purification, she offered two pigeons or turtledoves in the temple, because she couldn't afford a lamb, but the real Lamb of God was there with her, to cleanse her from this and all other uncleanness, as God's fulfillment of all sacrifices. Jesus was "a lamb of the first year", though she was unaware of it and brought pigeons instead. There was nothing to save us in the blood of Mary's labor, bringing Christ into the world, and even that labor required a blood sacrifice. The only acceptable labor was done by Christ on the cross, and our labor is to "believe on him whom he hath sent" (John 6:29).

Without labor nothing prospers.

ESCAPED AS A BIRD

(14:4)   ...two birds alive and clean, and cedar wood, and scarlet, and hyssop...

Compare this with another passage: "Our soul is escaped as a bird out of the snare of the fowlers" (Ps. 124:7), and we could make several associations. The birds are living souls: one is mine and the other is Jesus'. Cedar wood may be the cross (or the doorposts of the Passover). Hyssop is for cleansing, to dip in the blood (Ex. 12:22 & Ps. 51:7). The scarlet wool is for the blood of the lamb. The running (or living) water is for the Holy Spirit giving life, and for cleansing away the stains of sin. Taken together, we see a picture of salvation. One soul (bird) must be killed in an earthen vessel (14:50), signifying the life of Christ in an earthly body. By the death of one soul, another can be set free and not suffer the punishment, but it must be covered with, or dipped in, the blood of the one sacrificed. We, as the living bird, identify with Christ's sufferings, being taken with the cedar wood (carried by Isaac for his sacrifice), the scarlet and hyssop. We are dipped in the blood of Christ, washed with clean water, and set free, but with the remembrance of what we narrowly escaped. Sprinkled seven times shows the completion of the work – no more sacrifice is needed (Heb. 9:19-22).

"Let the water and the blood, from thy wounded side which flowed, Be for sin the double cure: save from wrath and make me whole."

Rock of Ages, cleft for me, let me hide myself in thee.

POETIC JUSTICE

(17:11)　For the life of the flesh in the blood...

In a large sense, life is communication (John 17:3), and since all life comes from God, we die if we lose touch with him. Blood is the medium by which life is carried to every part of the body, and as blood pressure becomes very low, life begins to ebb away. Since man became cut off from having communications with God, only God could re-establish it. He chose some universally observable things to make truth plain to us. "The heavens declare the glory of God; and the firmament showeth his handiwork" (Ps. 19:1). Parents show authority and relationship, and hopefully love. Pictures communicate to us, and "a picture is worth a thousand words". Blood is such a picture, being universally observable: we all have the same red blood flowing in our veins. "Blood brothers" are bound by a very real picture, in their bloods being mingled. It means "my life for your life, as your blood is flowing in me". Blood transfusions are even plainer, as the act of giving blood actually means life for the recipient. Without blood, we die. Just as God made the first blood sacrifice, to cover Adam and Eve with its skin, so Christ's blood communicates life to us. Marriages also die from a lack of communication: "...and they shall be one flesh" (Gen. 2:24), but the life of that one flesh is in their blood covenant, and in their faithfulness to communicate in all things. God gave us a picture to portray his love for us – how can two become one? "This is a great mystery, but I speak concerning Christ and the church" (Eph. 5:31-2). Marriage is a blood covenant, and Christ is our example of how much God loves us, and how much we must love our spouses, even to the point of death.

A picture is a poem without words.

DEATH DEFYING DAREDEVILS

(20:9)   He has cursed his father or his mother.

A common complaint of children today, when they are feeling angry or frustrated, is "I didn't ask to be born!" When they grow older the attitude becomes "The world owes me a living", as they curse their mother or father, and blame them as the reason for all their problems. It's a lame statement, as nobody else, including their parents, ever asked to be born, and it indicates their heart attitude about God. It is like Adam's statement to God that the fault for his sin was "the woman whom thou gavest to be with me" ("I didn't ask for her!"). One may say today "Why am I judged guilty for Adam's sin?" but again, even when we sin, God extends his mercy to us, as well as to Adam, through Christ's blood. If we die in our sins and miss heaven, it is not Adam's fault, or our parents' or God's fault. It will be our own fault for not repenting and trusting in the blood of Christ for our sins. In effect, we all have the same choice as Adam had, to say "yes" to the tree of life (Christ) and "no" to sin. God will hold us responsible, and nobody else. Would you dare to curse your father or mother? Would you dare to curse God? (24:10-16). You would be stoned to death under the old covenant with only yourself to blame. And God, who knows "the thoughts and intents of the heart" (Heb. 4:12), knows whether we have cursed him in our hearts, regardless of whether or not we have spoken it with our mouths. Would you be bold enough to admit your sin and confess it to God, and trust in Christ's blood alone? Only then can you ever be made righteous with God. Would you dare to doubt this is all true? Then you have despised God's word and refused his only offer for you.

We are each responsible for our own happiness.

EYE FOR AN EYE

(22:14)   ...he must make restitution...and add a fifth of the value to it. (NIV)

Like so many of God's laws, restitution is the name of the game, here even adding a fifth to it as an extra incentive to stop. The basic idea is "eye for eye, tooth for tooth" (Ex. 21:24, Lev. 24:20). The Old Testament counterpart of the "Golden Rule", this rule was simply to keep retaliation from getting out of hand. Equity is the rule, so that feuds do not result. But this was not given to promote retaliation, only as a limit for fairness' sake. Shylock, in Shakespeare's "Merchant of Venice", demanded a pound of flesh, as all legalists would do. Jesus changed the emphasis by stating we should "turn the other cheek" instead of striking back, and "do to others as you would have them do to you" (Lk. 6:31 - NIV), because the old law also says (19:18) "love thy neighbor as thyself", and not simply "eye for eye". Selfish and fearful men today say "do unto others before they do unto you": hurt them before they hurt you. Or, another twisted proverb: "If you love something, let it go: if it comes back it is truly yours; if it doesn't, hunt it down and kill it!" Today, wars are fought over small issues that escalate each time the retaliation is more than equity merits. We all have a sense of justice, an imprint of God's nature as we are created in his image. God gives us another option besides retaliation, or "eye for eye", and that is forgiveness. "And forgive us our debts, as we forgive our debtors" (Matt. 6:12), and if we don't forgive, God cannot forgive us. Here is real equity if you want it! Do you want to be forgiven by God? Then forgive others – don't seek retaliation. If God retaliates, who can stand?

An eye for an eye makes everyone blind.

IN GOD WE TRUST

(25:20)　"What shall we eat the seventh year?"

God is here anticipating the question that naturally will arise when we are forced into a place of trust. Will we trust God, or continue to trust in our own strength and wisdom? If God is so interested in giving a Sabbath rest to the land, isn't he much more interested in preserving us, his people? Regarding God's law to "not muzzle the ox when he treadeth out the corn" (Deut. 25:4), Paul asks "Is it about oxen that God is concerned? Surely he says this for us..." (1 Cor. 9:9-10 – NIV). Likewise, God's command to let the land rest is also for our benefit, so that we may learn to put our confidence in him. Our trust in God grows out of his faithfulness. It is not that God becomes faithful to us in response to our faith. God is the initiator of even our faith. "For by grace are ye saved through faith; and that not of yourselves: it is the gift of God: not of works, lest any man should boast" (Eph. 2:8-9). Our confidence in God is built upon seeing his faithfulness. Can we trust him to sustain us for a whole year if we obey his command to let the land rest? That will depend upon where we really put our trust. "In God we trust" is written on the U.S. dollar, but do we trust God when the money runs out? Faith is both the gift and the means of getting the gift! "Have no confidence in the flesh" (Php. 3:3) as Paul had. Instead, "Beloved, if our heart condemn us not, then have we confidence toward God" (1 John 3:21). If you are trusting in yourself, you have reason to fear. Be confident in God, and let your trust in people lead them to be trustworthy.

Confidence: You get it by getting it.

AGE TO WAGE

(27:2)   "...to dedicate persons to the Lord by giving equivalent values..." (NIV)

How do you measure the value of a person? The basis here seems to be on their strength for work, so that a man is valued at 50 shekels at age 20 to 60, but only 5 shekels at age 1 month to 5 years, and 20 shekels from age 5 to 20. After 60 years, he again drops off to 15 shekels, down from 50 just a year before. Of course, in this estimation, it is honoring to the elder men not to have to pay so much. But, there is an interesting correlation to how we value men in our society today. Sixty or sixty-five is considered retirement time for many, and "over the hill" for most youngsters. However, it is when men have finally reached a stage of maturity, and their experience should be paid much more than the young, who have only youthful energy. "The glory of young men is their strength: and the beauty of old men is the gray head" (Prov. 20:29), because wisdom usually comes with experience, and with gray heads. Instead, we have "old folks' homes" filled with unwanted grandfathers, and problems of "euthanasia" instead of "honor thy father and thy mother: that thy days may be long upon the land which the Lord thy God giveth thee" (Ex. 20:12). It is usually not until we ourselves reach the age of wisdom that most of us will realize that "the flesh profiteth nothing" (John 6:63) – we are more than bodies, and our souls and spirits will live forever. If we value our elders so little that we would kill them to make room for our "free time", then God and our children will not be guilty to do the same to us. Begin early to learn from elders.

Age measures also experience.

REPLACING A BUTTON

(1:17) ...these men which are expressed by their names...

Reading the book of Numbers makes me feel, at first, like I'm "just another number to God". Especially today, when a person is known by his social security number, punches in at a time clock to work, and is told he must produce more results or, "you could be replaced by a button!" If even evangelism gets reduced to the number of people who make "decisions", then something is wrong with our understanding of God. We're not stamped out with cookie cutters, but each one of us is a product of the unfathomable imagination of a creative God who takes time to design each snowflake, and has made no two people exactly alike. Rather, to us, his blood-bought saints, he speaks words like "Before I formed thee in the belly I knew thee" (Jer. 1:5), and "...I have called thee by thy name; thou art mine" (Isa. 43:1). Try to imagine a God who knows the number of hairs on your head! God created us with a purpose: not to be a number, or to be one of countless meaningless and mindless bodies to fill up space in his church or in heaven. Each of us is a unique expression of God's creativity. God doesn't want to destroy any of what he has created in each of us, but to make us fit for heaven by taking the sin out of us. He makes all things good, and when man turned bad through sin, God still made a way to redeem us. We're not from a big bang, or from an accident of nature, and if we see others as being God's special creation, we will spend our lives to see that they become children of God. We will take the time to learn how to unlock their hearts and open them to the Savior. God creates all of his redeemed creatures through us, his saints.

**All good things which exist are
the fruit of originality.**

YOU LIE, YOU DIE

(3:10)   ...and the stranger that cometh nigh shall be put to death.

The Levites were set apart for the temple service, and no others could even approach without dying. Maybe a parallel verse is the words of Jesus, "And a stranger will they not follow, but will flee from him: for they know not the voice of strangers... All that ever came before me are thieves and robbers: but the sheep did not hear them." (John 10:5, 8). There are many ways to break the 10 Commandments, and this "stranger" is one form of a liar. Satan is the father of lies and of all those who follow in his deceitful ways. He, and all liars who try to come into God's presence by some other way, will be destroyed. Jesus is "the way, the truth, and the life" (Jn. 14:6), and all others are of "the wrong way, the lies and the death". Beware of any who come with deceitful smiles, but are not the true priests of God. God made a provision for those who were not of the Levites to be brought near without being put to death. These were "Nazirites" by way of a vow (6:1-21) but, as soon as they sinned, even by just being near a dead body, all their past righteousness was nullified. This is another picture that we need a priest who is perfect, not beset with sin, as our mediator. All our righteous acts are cancelled because of our sin. We make a vow of separation to God and we break it, because we are (in our own strength and righteousness) children of the father of lies. Even our most righteous acts will not get us a place in God's presence. Only Jesus, who is truth, can approach God's presence, and we can come only through him. Broken vows are lies, and we cannot charm God into accepting us.

Compliments are only lies in court clothes.

SPIRIT OF JEALOUSY

(5:14) ...[if] the spirit of jealousy come upon him...

Undoubtedly, the most destructive thing a marriage can suffer is adultery, but just as bad is the "spirit of jealousy", when a husband or wife suspects the other of adultery. Since marriage is based on mutual respect and trust, how can we deal with this, to prove one's innocence without destroying respect and trust? This chapter shows God's way, and a few points from which we can learn. First, the couple should <u>go together</u> to the priest with an "offering of jealousy". The last verse shows why: "then shall the man be guiltless from iniquity, and this woman shall bear her iniquity" (if it turns out she is guilty). If not, what would be the man's (implied) iniquity? Probably his unjustified feeling of jealousy! If not properly handled, this could still destroy the marriage, as what wife wants to live with a suspicious and untrusting husband? A godly suggestion is given here: let them deal with this doubt <u>as a couple</u>, giving an "offering of jealousy" to an impartial priest, <u>assuming</u> the woman's innocence first, so the offering will be for his jealousy. When the whole curious "bitter water that brings a curse" ceremony is finished, the woman will be vindicated by the fact that she is now able to conceive still by her husband (of course, after enough time is gone to prove the conception is not by another man!). The last important condition: an innocent woman will show no ungodly unforgiveness for her husband's jealousy, which must now be laid to rest to save the marriage. Similarly, the same principles should be used if it is the wife that is jealous and suspicious of her husband.

Anger is cruel... but who can stand before jealousy? (Pr.27:4 – NIV)

COMMUNION WITH GOD

(7:89) ...he heard the voice of one speaking unto him from off the mercy seat...

Here is the end product of all the activity involved in the making of the tabernacle and its furnishings: communion with God. The tabernacle was completed prior to this (Ex. 40:33-35), but apparently this was after the glory of the Lord subsided enough for the priest to enter. Also, no one would dare enter until the Lord directed him to do so. This comes just after the longest chapter of the Pentateuch in which all the offerings of each tribe are listed to give equal credit to each, which was to show God's gracious acceptance of the gifts, and meticulous care in enumerating them. The listing of the gifts over twelve days is nearly reminiscent of "the twelve days of Christmas" song, which repeats itself throughout the twelve days. Now, Moses has a special place to meet with God as advocate for Israel, and mediator between God and man. This was the unique way that God showed his presence and nearness to his people. It may be that the voice speaking to him was that of the Son of God, the eternal Word, or it may be the Father, but certainly by the New Testament times it is only Jesus Christ who speaks to us, the time for prophets being past (Heb. 1:2). The perfect tabernacle is now his own body, and every other picture of the tabernacle finds its fulfilment in Christ, which the writer of Hebrews points out at great length. For the Jews, though, the voice speaking to Moses from between the cherubim was the culmination of all their labor on the tabernacle, and a sign of God's favor on them, coming now as the presence of God on earth in one meeting place.

Speak that I may know you.

LOVE DIED FOR YOU

(10:29)   ...come thou with us, and we will do thee good...

Doing good, like doing evil, is contagious: "Whatever goes around comes around." Sin and death, by the act of one man, "came to all men" (Rom. 5:12), so that it doesn't now come to us naturally to do good to others. We tend to do good only to those who first do good to us. We are fortunate that God, who initiates all things, is good (Ps. 100:5). He didn't respond to man's sin with judgment, but paid the price of blood that he could be merciful, and he commands us to follow his example. "...While we were yet sinners, Christ died for us" (Rom. 5:8). "Hereby perceive we the love of God, because he laid down his life for us: and we ought to lay down our lives for the brethren" (1 Jn. 3:16). "Beloved, if God so loved us, we ought also to love one another" (1 Jn. 4:11). Moses is here practicing the principle given to Abraham: "I will bless thee... and thou shalt be a blessing... and in thee shall all families of the earth be blessed" (Gen. 12:2, 3). We can practice this, too, and see others won to Christ, by choosing to always act and react in love, just as Moses was an example to this man who was not an Israelite. Jesus said "Love your enemies" (Mt. 5:44). If we can love our enemies, it will be easy to love our friends, and our enemies will see the love of God in us. Anybody can throw back a spear when one is thrown at him. David chose not to, but rather to honor Saul as his anointed king, though his life was always in danger (1 Sam. 18:11, 19:10). We will show by our actions if we are the children of God (Matt. 5:45), or children of the devil (John 8:44), so die to yourself and ...

Be good to all and treat all kindly.

WE SAW THE GIANTS

(13:33) ...we were in our own sight as grasshoppers...

When God speaks a word to us, we had better obey it! There will always be plenty of circumstances around to haunt our thoughts and to turn us from immediate, complete and joyfully willing obedience, but God's word is supreme. When the word of God comes, the Holy Spirit comes and convicts us in our conscience that is God speaking. Once the word comes, we are responsible to obey, or we will be tormented in our thoughts until we do. The Israelites were defeated in their minds without even facing the "giants", and were tormented with thoughts that they would be eaten alive for dinner, like grasshoppers. God will never command us to do anything that he does not give us the grace and power to accomplish, with or without giants. The devil will cause the simplest act of obedience, even something as small as saying "I forgive you" to someone who has hurt us, to loom up as a mighty giant in our thoughts, to keep us from walking in joyful submission and obedience to God. Soon, our conscience will keep us awake at night until we do the act of obedience to God's word. It will no longer be the thought of the "giant", but the agony of disobedience that will bother us. Samuel told King Saul "...to obey is better than sacrifice... for rebellion is as the sin of witchcraft, and stubbornness is as iniquity and idolatry. Because thou hast rejected the word of the Lord, he hath also rejected thee from being king." (1 Sam. 15:22-3). If you can't sleep at night, you don't need sleeping pills, but an act of obedience. If your sleep is filled with nightmares of giants, repent, or face a real nightmare on Judgment Day.

It is our thoughts which keep us awake.

IS GOD SHORTHANDED?

(14:21)   But as truly as I live, all the earth shall be filled with the glory of the Lord.

God answered Moses' unbelief, saying "Is the Lord's hand waxed short? Thou shalt see now whether my word shall come to pass unto thee or not" (11:23). Certainly it will! When God promises to bring his people into the Promised Land he will do it, regardless of their unbelief, or their stubborn wills. God doesn't require our cooperation to do what he wills, but he does demand it, and it is our privilege to be his fellow workers. Today, the land of promise is the whole world, and we are commanded to go in and possess it for God's kingdom. Will we do it? If not, he will simply pass by us and use those who are willing. God is sovereign, and he does what he says, not for Israel or for us, but for his own Name's sake. Our unwillingness in the face of God's "Great Commission" (Matt. 28:18-20) shows a much deeper problem. Are you really sure <u>you</u> will go to heaven? Again, if heaven is now considered as the Promised Land, how will we get there? The giants to conquer are our own sins, and unbelief is in rejecting Christ's sacrifice and trying to go in by our own works, as the Israelites presumptuously tried to do (14:40-45). To go to heaven, we need God's presence, and the ark is now Jesus in our hearts. If we have died to sin and believed in his blood, we will not only go to heaven, but will "boldly go where no man has gone before", to bring God's eternal gospel to the lost. God swore it would happen, and it will. "As truly as I live" – "because he could swear by no greater, he sware by himself" (Heb. 6:13). God will surely do it, but if we don't help, we will be rejected, at least for that privilege.

Will you be God's hands?

BEND OR BREAK

(17:5)   ...and I will make to cease from me the
murmurings of the children of Israel...

The sign God chose to use was the rod of Aaron which budded, signifying life. When God's anger was aroused before this, he killed those that murmured, but now he made a sign, to keep others from stubbornness and rebellion. A living rod will bend, whereas a dead and dry one will break. By analogy, those who are yielded to God will not snap when pressure comes, but will be like a bow in the hands of an archer, resilient and usable. Those who are "stiff necked" and resistant will be broken. Tall palm trees bend instead of breaking, when strong storm winds blow. Aaron's rod not only was able to bend, but actually "brought forth buds, and bloomed blossoms, and yielded almonds" (17:8), just as we will produce fruits like peace, longsuffering and meekness, instead of murmuring, envying and strife, if God's Spirit is in us. A sure sign of being stiff necked is when we begin to murmur. <u>Question</u>: Was Aaron really in any way better than the others? No! He also spoke against Moses, and could have just as easily deserved a death sentence, but God spared him, maybe just as a picture to others of God's authority. We are all under the authority of somebody, and murmuring shows the first sign that we are in rebellion. Even Moses grumbled against God, and disobeyed by striking the rock with his rod in anger. If you are in authority, walk in meekness, being submitted to God. If you are under authority, be willing to bend, or you will be broken. God is not bound to forgive those who rebel.

It is better to bend than to break.

CAMEL FILTERS

(21:23)　And Sihon would not suffer Israel to pass through his border…

Too often, wealth can become the stumbling block to clear thinking. All that Israel asked of this king was the right to pass through his land, not even taking as much as a drink of water. If it is true that "the fear of the Lord is the beginning of knowledge", then Sihon must have been a little short on the wisdom end, as he didn't fear God. In India, rich Hindu and Muslim families pay large bribes to have their children educated at Christian-run schools, but become enraged if the children are taught from the Bible and want to follow Christ. How stupid! Money can buy education, but it can't but wisdom. "It is easier for a camel to go through the eye of a needle, than for a rich man to enter into the kingdom of God" (Matt. 19:24). All that Israel asked was for their camels to pass through Sihon's border, and he couldn't even do that. "Ye blind guides, which strain at a gnat, and swallow a camel" (Matt. 23:24); he "restrained" the camels! Imagine, having money to buy education and straining out Christ like a gnat, and swallowing the camel of the pursuit of riches through education. How easy it would have been for the rich man to give crumbs to Lazarus, but he stumbled over his love of wealth and perished. Americans die of cancer by smoking "Camel cigarettes", so they try to keep their destructive habit by changing to "Camel filters". They still die of cancer, though it may take longer. Neither eyes of needles, nor strainers nor camel filters can filter out the love of money, the idolatry that leads rich men to destruction.

Wealth and wisdom do not mix.

LOVE THAT TAKES?

*(23:19)   God is not a man, that he should lie; neither
the son of man, that he should repent.*

When God makes a covenant with us, he can be trusted to keep it.
Marriage is "until death us do part" unless someone fails to keep the
covenant. If it is based on the modern concept of "as long as we both shall
love", there is sure to be a divorce in store if love is only a feeling. God's
love means commitment: once he has set his love upon Israel, he won't
change with feelings. Balaam is a picture of man's selfish love, unfaithful
and changing with every new offer. Even when he was talking only to
the true God, he could hear "Thou shalt not go with them" (22:12),
and still go back to God for a second opinion, thinking God was just as
changeable as he. He could actually hear the living God talk to him, and
yet he continued to "seek for enchantments" and to flirt with "rewards of
divination" (24:1, 22:7). God's true love for his people is everlasting and
expressed itself through giving, even to the point of the death of his son,
Jesus. Balaam's love was expressed through his habit of taking whatever
he could get away with as he continued to struggle against God's love for
Israel and even for him, as he rebuked him through his donkey. Today,
"making love" is an idea or expression that encourages people to commit
adultery. One 'Beatles' song says "and in the end, the love you take is equal
to the love you make". But love is not sexual promiscuity, which is selfish
and taking. True love is expressed in what we can give freely for the good
of the one we love. Balaam's counsel (31:16) instead led Israel into adultery
(25:1). Beware of counterfeits, and of wolves in sheep's clothing!

"All (true) love shared is good"

COMMON SENSE

(25:2)   ...and the people did eat, and bowed down to their gods.

These chapters recount some of the senseless sins from Israel's history. Solomon, noted for his common sense and great wisdom, said "But whoso committeth adultery with a woman lacketh understanding" (Prov. 6:32), but Solomon himself fell into sins of idolatry by his hundreds of marriages to heathen wives and concubines. These people fell in the same way (25:1-2) through adultery and a lack of "common sense". Then, a man was bold (or stupid) enough to bring one of these women to the camp while people are weeping over their sin! Moses recalls the times of Korah's rebellion (26:9), the sins of Er and Onan (26:19), Nadab and Abihu's "strange fire" (26:61) and the rebellion of all Israel when faced with "giants" (26:65). It seems we don't really learn from our past mistakes through "common sense". Several chapters later, God says that a husband may nullify any vow made by his wife when he hears about it and disagrees with her decision (30:13). Because we are all prone to sin, God made provisions for the weakness of the flesh by sending Christ to die for our sins. But also, as women are the "weaker vessel", God made the husband responsible for the final decision in the wife's choices. If she goes against "common sense" by making or breaking vows, or by breaking God's commandments, the husband will be judged if he allows it, as in Adam and Eve's sin. In today's all too common divorces, the husband or wife who wishes to reconcile should simply say "For what it's worth, I don't want a divorce". It would be common sense to at least <u>say</u> it, and be on record as taking a stand for marriage (and possibly saving it!)

Common sense is not so common.

PASSING THE TORCH

(27:18)   *Take thee Joshua... a man in whom is*
          the spirit, and lay thine hand upon him.

Regardless of how great a man is, or how big his ministry, we all must die. If all we have done is to continue bearing fruit, someone faithful must be entrusted with carrying it on. Even men as great as Elijah, Paul or even Jesus himself, had to train and pass on to Elisha, Timothy, and Jesus' disciples, what they had worked for, or all would have been for nothing. Joshua was chosen, not "out of thin air", but as one who had already proven faithful and filled with the spirit of God. We don't just lay hands upon one who wants to be filled with the spirit, but also to acknowledge the anointing that is already upon a person. Jesus spent all night in prayer before selecting his twelve disciples, and we need direction from God to do the same. Moses prayed (27:16-17) that God would choose Israel's new shepherd, instead of assuming that Joshua or Caleb should be the one, and God answered. Moses was great because God chose to make him great, and since he was only a servant to God's plan, God chose who should follow him. In God's service, we must remember this, lest we become proud and begin to think "this is <u>my</u> ministry". Nobody is indispensable – Moses' sin caused his "thorn in the flesh": he could not enter Canaan. So, God prepared Joshua. We will also die; whom are you preparing to take your place? We should constantly be working ourselves out of our own jobs, preparing others to take our places. Soon we must "lay on hands" and pass the mantle on to another generation.

> **...entrust to reliable men who will also...**
> **teach others...** (2 Tim. 2:2 – NIV)

WHEN JUDGMENT COMES

(31:3)   ...Arm some of yourselves unto the war...and avenge the Lord of Midian.

The notion of a "holy war" brings to mind several thoughts from scripture. First, we may think that only in the Old Testament did God pronounce judgment on the heathen (Ps. 9:17, 79:6), since "God would never punish those who haven't heard of him", but in the New Testament we read of "blazing fire" as God judges "those who do not know God" (2 Thes. 1:8). The reason: God says they <u>knew</u> him but willfully <u>forgot</u> him (Rom. 1:21). The Midianites were descended from Abraham through his second wife Keturah, so the vengeance against them is for willfully forgetting God, and trying to seduce Israel away from God. Secondly, when judgment comes against the ungodly, it is only after judgment begins "at the house of God" (1 Peter 4:17). God dealt strongly with Israel, and punished them severely for their sins, before he commanded them to attack the Midianites. A third idea is that "as no one is discharged in time of war, so wickedness will not release those who practice it" (Eccl. 8:8 - NIV). God was punishing the wickedness of the Midianites, and those who stand with God have to fight his battles against his enemies. We are also in a spiritual war that started in heaven (Rev. 12:7), and continues as long as life remains on earth. The battle rages on, day and night, and the enemy will not let up on his attacks. There is no discharge for us, no laying down of weapons to take leave or vacation. Everyone is on one side or the other, and we can only fight or defect to the other side, except for the possibility that our prayers may turn those opposed to God back to faith and obedience to him, to turn them from his wrath.

Error tolerates, truth condemns.

LOVE THAT KILLS?

(33:53)   *...I have given you the land to possess it.*

How could God give the land inhabited by the Canaanites to the Israelites, when it belonged to the Canaanites? Because "The earth is the Lord's, and the fulness thereof" (Ps. 24:1), but the land was given with a catch to it: "I have given you the land to possess it". If Israel wanted it, they had to go and get it. For God to <u>give</u> the land meant he had to first <u>take</u> it from the Canaanites. Does this sound consistent with the fact that God is love (1 Jn. 4:8)? Or else, if God didn't take the land but sent Israel to take it, is that in harmony with love, on the part of God or Israel? Was it a good thing for Israel to go in and kill and plunder to possess the land? God alone can judge that. The greater commandment, more than loving our neighbor as ourselves, is to love God with all our heart, soul, mind and strength. If we know it is God who commands us to kill, even though it be our own son, we must love God enough to be willing to obey him. But, one may ask, if God is love, how can he bear to kill anyone, let alone to send them to an eternal punishment?!? The answer is in God's sovereignty, and his jealous love for those upon whom he has set his love. <u>Unfair?</u> Well, that jealous love is offered freely to any and all who will simply confess their sins and come to God by faith in Christ's sacrifice. Any other religious act that does not come on this basis will be viewed by God as equal to the most evil crime, as we have rejected the love he has shared in the person of Christ. If you want to love God, begin with receiving his love.

All love shared is good.

THE LOTTERY

(34:13) ...This is the land which ye shall inherit by lot...

God knows well the covetous nature of man, and gave specific rules to govern the inheritance of land given to the tribes of Israel. A lottery was used to exclude the choice or will of man, in dividing the land of Canaan. "The lot causeth contentions to cease" (Prov. 18:18), but notice how the same lottery system today has done more to highlight the covetous nature of man. In America, for instance, the lottery is a way to become a millionaire overnight and it has evolved into an elaborate system of gambling. People who have little money may gamble away a whole paycheck, and lose it all in the hopes of getting rich. What God used to eliminate greed became a means for greed. Consider also the daughters of Zelophehad (Num. 36). God gave a fair judgment for them because of the problem of the inheritance changing hands after marriage. In India today, the dowry system has again highlighted the greed of man, as oppressive dowry demands cause people to even kill innocent brides for the love of money. Zelophehad's daughters saw ahead that even marriage to men they loved could end up in land being passed on to another tribe, so God had them marry within their own tribe. No man-made system can extract greed from the hearts of men. Only the Spirit of God can make my wicked heart love God more than unjust gain. Jesus bought us with his blood, but man is more interested in casting lots for his clothes. Only God's Spirit can deliver us from the idolatry of a greedy heart.

**For the love of money is the root
of all evil.** (1 Tim. 6:10)

BIG

(2:21)   A people great, and many, and tall as the Anakims…

Moses told Israel, "The Lord your God hath multiplied you, and, behold, ye are this day as the stars of heaven for multitude" (1:10), but God has never been interested in numbers, as he is in character. This huge nation was now afraid to go against the nation of giants. God was not at all asking them to depend on their numbers, nor their height (as compared to giants, but said, "Dread not, neither be afraid of them. The Lord your God, which goeth before you, he shall fight for you" (1:29-30). The only quality God is interested in is faith in him, and that is a gift from him, too. Joshua and Caleb had it, even in their old age. David had it and killed a giant, even as a small lad. Even the quantity of faith is not as important as its being the real item. "If ye had faith as a grain of mustard seed…" (Luke 17:6), Jesus said, you could do anything, as your faith is not in yourself but in a great God. Today, a group may become great, many and tall as giants in the eyes of the world, but it will not make them right with God, unless their trust is in the blood of Christ and not their own numbers or righteousness. Great nations and great religions have come and gone, and God is not impressed. Because God has accepted the blood sacrifice of his own son, all who approach him must come on that basis. At one time, Constantine declared that Christianity was the world religion, but unless each person's faith was in Christ's blood, the numbers were meaningless. Although Christianity, or Islam or Hinduism might become the greatest in number in all the world, God will still save us only by faith in Christ's blood. In God's sight, quality is Christ himself, living in us.

Quality is more important than quantity.

CHOOSING COMPANY

(4:6)   Keep therefore and do them; for this is your wisdom…

'Say unto wisdom, Thou are my sister; and call understanding thy kinswoman' (Prov. 7:4). You are judged by the company you keep so choose wise and good friends. God gave his people the Ten Commandments to keep them from judgment, and to give them a standard of righteousness that would glorify him through their lives. If we choose to keep company with God, his people and his holy law, this will be "your wisdom and your understanding in the sight of the nations, which shall hear all of these statutes, and say, Surely this great nation is a wise and understanding people." If you keep company with lawbreakers or idolaters, unless it is to teach them the right way, you will soon become like them. "For all the men that followed Baal-peor, the Lord thy God hath destroyed them from among you" (4:3). Boaz said to Ruth, "Blessed be thou of the Lord… thou followedst not young men, whether rich or poor… for all the city of my people doth know that thou art a virtuous woman" (Ruth 3:10-11). We must be more concerned, however, with how God will judge us, than with people. Jesus was judged by the Pharisees based upon the company he kept: "…they say, Behold a man gluttonous, and a winebibber, a friend of publicans and sinners. But wisdom is justified of her children" (Mt. 11:19). God judges not by appearance, but by the heart; not by company, but by fruit. Like Jesus, we can only safely keep company with "sinners" if we keep company daily with God's commands. Abraham kept company with God and "was called the friend of God" (James 2:23), but "a friend of the world becomes an enemy of God" (James 4:4).

You are judged by the company you keep.

GOD'S LAMENT

(5:29)   *Oh, that there were such an heart in them, that they would fear me…*

"…and keep all my commandments always, that it might be well with them, and with their children for ever!" "Oh, that there were", but there was not! Rather, "The heart is deceitful above all things, and desperately wicked: who can know it?" (Jer. 17:9). This speaks about my heart (and yours), even on my very best day. This was spoken just after Israel had said for the first time "All that the Lord hath said will we do, and be obedient" (Ex. 24:7-8). Moses immediately sprinkled blood on them, showing that blood alone – blood of the covenant, and ultimately only Jesus' blood – could wash away our sins. This is God's heart being expressed – he who is "not willing that any should perish, but that all should come to repentance" (2 Peter 3:9). God wants it to be well with us and our children forever, but our wicked hearts won't allow him to bless us. My heart wanders into sin so often! Like Israel, I <u>say</u>, but I don't <u>do</u> what is right. Our only hope is that a <u>new heart</u> would be given to us. That's the gospel! On the train today I spoke with Gursel, a young man from Turkey, now deceived by Sai Baba. When I asked about the Bible, he wouldn't read it because he said "it's been changed". Well, it's changed my life, and millions of other blasphemers and sinners, and if it is changed, what must the <u>original</u> have been?! The Bible alone can bring about a new heart in us, so the Lord can bless us. By it we learn the fear of God and his commandments, and are led to repentance. God laments over us in our sinful condition, but he doesn't leave it at that. Instead of leaving us there he provides us with all that is necessary to come to him with the kind of heart that he longs for us to have.

…the goodness of God leadeth thee
to repentance… (Rom. 2:2)

CARD SHARKS

(9:18)   I did neither eat bread, nor drink water, because of all your sins...

Imagine, if we could only have such a leader today: one who would fast and pray for the spiritual condition of the people he were governing. Instead, politics has become a great gambling ring, and nobody can fully trust a leader. Yesterday, in Srinagar, the leadership of a school again was awarded by court decision to a previous principal, while the people outside grow weary of the stench of politics. It is in all secular and church governments. The Christians, who should be fasting, praying and weeping for God to send revival and forgiveness to Kashmir valley, are fighting for power and filthy lucre, loving this world more than heaven. God, who is above all leaders, "shows no partiality, and accepts no bribes" (10:17 – NIV), while Christian leaders are becoming the worst in all the world at taking bribes and swindling money, and being "yes men" to corrupt men in higher places, for political and financial gain. Like clever gamblers in a poker game, we act like we are losing until we see our chance to win. We pretend to be victims of corruption, while we are holding the trump card that would release God's blessing to our valley of despair. Should not Christians be the first to repent of their sins, and then pray for the sins of other Christians, and to lead the way for the lost people to find hope in Christ's blood cleansing for their sins? We revere leaders like Abraham Lincoln, Gandhi or Moses, who fasted, prayed and laid down their lives for their own people, but God is withholding blessings until we do the same.

There is no gambling like politics.

DON'T ADD OR DIMINISH

(12:32)   Do all I command you; do not add to it or take away from it. (NIV)

Compare this verse with similar statements in Joshua 1:7, Proverbs 30:6 and Revelation 22:18; God is serious about what comes from him! The very next verse speaks about false prophets and how to judge them as such. Let them do signs and wonders - no problem; but what decides if they are false is this: "To the law and to the testimony! If they speak not according to this word, it is because there is no light in them" (Isa. 8:20). In the Bible, revelation of the word of God came "...precept upon precept; line upon line, line upon line; here a little and there a little" (Isa. 28:10). But not just anybody can be a prophet of God – He must be called and anointed of God, and <u>must</u> speak according to what has gone before, that God's word may be one revelation, all in total agreement. Jesus cannot be crucified, and then proclaimed as not crucified. Neither is salvation by the blood of covenant sacrifice, and later by works! Moses had no problem with more prophets: "Would God that all the Lord's people were prophets" (Num. 11:29). **But:** They had better not be <u>false</u> prophets, and "God doesn't like people putting words in his mouth – that's unsanitary" (a quote from Bill Cetnar). Neither can we diminish it – it says what it says, and "Heaven and earth shall pass away, but my words shall not pass away!" (Matt. 24:35). Only as God can Jesus say that, or he himself would be a false prophet. If you want to be a prophet, you had better be ready to submit to prophet rules! Any ***addition*** to or ***subtraction*** from God's word causes ***division*** in the body of Christ and ***multiplication*** of sin's problems. **Add thou not unto his words**

> **...lest he reprove thee, and thou
> be found a liar.** (Pr. 30:6)

TWINKLE LITTLE STAR

(16:18) Appoint judges…and they shall judge the people fairly. (NIV)

How important is honesty? If truth, honesty and fairness is important to you, are you honest and fair with others? Do you cheat on your taxes? If you are dishonest in hidden ways, or with "small" areas of life, can you expect to speak words of truth and life to others? Dishonesty is most evil in high places of authority. We choose judges based upon their ability to give fair judgments, as though in God's place. But, when they become corrupt, whole states and countries are affected. Especially in the church, people expect priests (which we all are!) to judge righteously, or where else on earth can they turn? "The Lord hath chosen thee to be a peculiar people unto himself, above all the nations that are upon the earth" (14:2). We consider famous people in movies, and in music, to be "stars", because they seem to be beautiful, or have "made it" in life. But God says truth, honesty, mercy and obedience (Micah 6:8) are the important things to him. Do you want to be a real star? Listen: "Ye are the light of the world…let your light so shine before men, that they may see your good works, and glorify your Father which is in heaven" (Mt. 5:14-16). "And they that be wise shall shine as the brightness of the firmament; and they that turn many to righteousness as the stars for ever and ever" (Dan. 12:3). When Lucifer, the dragon, fell, "His tail swept a third of the stars out of the sky" (Rev. 12:4), and when ungodly men pose as believers and speak false prophecies, they are "wandering stars", or falling stars (Jude 13), leading others to destruction. Do not be seduced by worldly riches. A 'star' in God's eyes is one who believes in Christ and leads others to him.

A truthful person shines like a star.

THOU SHALT NOT KILL

(19:6) ...he was not worthy of death, inasmuch as he hated him not in time past.

God's sixth commandment says "Thou shalt not kill". Does this mean not to kill mosquitos or flies, or animals that we intend to eat? What about killing fruits and vegetables by picking them, or killing microbes by the billions as we drink water? The meaning is "Do not murder", so Jesus can say "whoever is angry" without cause is the real transgressor. Or, one who intentionally kills for some sadistic pleasure is also a murderer. The point is: intention and anger are what make killing into murder, and God will judge these heart attitudes on the final judgment day. Otherwise, God would be guilty of murder when he sent the Israelites to judge the Canaanite nations. But God is the final judge. Then, how do we know, in a wartime situation, if we are killing or murdering? Or, how does someone (like Abraham with Isaac) know that he is hearing from God when told to go and kill someone (Canaanites, or Isaac, etc.)?!? Faith in the true God will be the criterion, and God's judgment day will reveal it all. Muslims go to "jihad", and Christians to "crusades", all hoping they are hearing from God. "The time cometh, that whoever killeth you will think that he doeth God service" (Jn. 16:2). Be careful, if you <u>think</u> God is telling you to go and kill someone (maybe like Hitler, or a doctor who performs abortions) even if it is to save others' lives. God will be the judge, and you had better be certain whose voice you hear. As Jesus told the disciples who wanted to call down fire from heaven, "Ye know not what manner of spirit ye are of. For the Son of man is not come to destroy men's lives, but to save them" (Luke 9:55-6).

Thou shalt love thy neighbor as thyself. (Mt. 19:19)

MYOPIA

(22:6)   Do not take the mother with the young. (NIV)

God has given us the ability to make wise choices. A man who is hungry doesn't have to kill a mother bird along with the young, or the eggs, but should satisfy his hunger, and allow the mother to continue to bring forth life. God's commands are logical: don't kill fruit bearing trees to build siege works in war time (20:19-20) – they will sustain you later. Our choices should not simply be for what is expedient now, but with a view to the future. Similarly, a case is given of a rebellious son (21:18-21), who will not listen to his parents. His "pleasures of sin for a season" (Heb. 11:25) are more important to him than an impending judgment of being stoned to death. Through "lust of the flesh" a man will commit adultery with another man's wife (22:22), being more concerned with present pleasure than righteousness and God's judgment. His one moment of pleasure is the cause of torment for the husband and wife, and himself, and it will lower God's standard of righteousness in the land in which he lives. We make choices that will affect our future and the future of society. "If you are not part of the solution, you are part of the problem." A person who continues in sin, not listening to God, his parents, or even his own conscience, will finally arrive in Hades. He can hardly blame God or anyone else, as he has chosen to continue to rebel against God. It will be the final place of "being your own boss", as God gives that one over to the eternal pursuit of selfishness, in torment. Myopia, or short-sightedness, does not lead to Utopia.

We choose that which we wish continued.

FLASHBACK!

(24:18)   Remember that you were slaves in Egypt, and the Lord redeemed you. (NIV)

Isaiah 51:1 says "Look unto the rock whence ye are hewn", and David said "He brought me up also out of an horrible pit, out of the miry clay, and set my feet upon a rock, and established my goings" (Ps. 40:2). Remember: it hasn't been so long since we were lost and without hope. It will help us make godly judgments, and not to condemn people for the sins they continue to do, often in ignorance. If I get angry when somebody steals, lies, gets angry at me, commits adultery, or disobeys my orders, am I perfectly without fault in the same area (even now, after becoming a Christian)? It's good to remember: we were also bondmen, bound to sin, and free now only by God's grace. What place do we have to judge and condemn others, when we have been guilty of the same sins (Rom. 2:1)? A "bondman" is a slave, and we were slaves bound to sin. Though now we have been made free, "If you think you are standing firm, be careful that you don't fall!" (1 Cor. 10:12 - NIV). We could, through our hardness and unforgiveness, be brought back into bondage! Remember where you came from, and the wind of pride will be taken out of your sails. Be an encouragement to one another, instead, and grow together in the grace of God. It cost God the blood of his Son to redeem us, so remember that we now belong to God, and glorify him in your body (1 Cor. 6:20).

**Remembering the past helps us
to not repeat the past.**

THE LORD YOUR GOD

(28:58)   If you ...do not revere this glorious and awesome name... (NIV)

The distilled essence of sin is "self-righteousness", and the entrance requirement for heaven is that we joyfully bow the knee to the lordship of Jesus Christ. Pride is the ugliest of sins, but it disguises itself in so many packages that attempt to appear humble. "Self-realization" and "self-help" ("The Lord helps those that help themselves") are commonly quoted quips of the spirit of this world that seek to turn us from submission to God. God helps those who <u>can't help</u> themselves! Only God can say, without being accused of a lack of humility, "I am the first, and I am the last; and beside me there is no God" (Isa. 44:6). If we think we can do anything at all to gain Gods favor, or to earn entrance into heaven, the problem of pride will be there. The only "self" God is willing to allow into his presence is "the crucified self", and even this we cannot do ourselves (try it!).Pride, self-will and unbelief are broken when we finally bow our knees in humble adoration of the crucified savior, and say with Thomas, "My Lord and my God" (Jn. 20:28). Flesh and blood, or man's intelligence (Matt. 16:17) can never reveal this truth to us; it comes by revelation of God, so that pride can never say, "I figured it out". I have nothing to offer God but my sin, my "self", to be crucified with Christ (Gal. 2:20, 6:14). The humble man will admit this, but the uncrucified religions of the world will still seek to offer some kind of good works to God, in hopes of salvation. "Self" is still alive, like the "Terminator", with its last breath and energy crawling to assert its ability, its will to live. Only death on the cross will do. "Self" is still lord, and won't be crucified without a fight.

A modest man never talks of himself.

SWIFT JUSTICE

(30:14)   ... the word is very nigh unto thee, in thy mouth, and in thy heart...

We expect justice to be swift and final when it is in our favor, but if we are the guilty parties, we wish it could be delayed. Martyrs in heaven cry out, "How long, O Lord, holy and true, dost thou not judge and avenge our blood...?" (Rev. 6:10), but unclean spirits are more likely to say "Art thou come hither to torment us before the time?" (Mt. 8:29) Those who are scoffers say "Where is the promise of his coming?" (2 Pet. 3:4) not fearing the judgment of God on those who reject the gospel. How will God give a fair judgment on the last day, and separate "his sheep from the goats"? Abraham said, "That be far from thee to do after this manner, to slay the righteous with the wicked...Shall not the Judge of all the earth do right?" (Gen. 18:25). Yes, he surely will, and then his righteous judgment will not delay. But, if we are so concerned with swift judgment, so is God. If delay of justice is injustice, then delay of obedience on our part is disobedience. "Today, if you will hear his voice, harden not your hearts" (Heb. 4:7). Now that God has poured out his judgment against sin upon Jesus, he "now commandeth all men everywhere to repent" (Acts 17:30). We don't have the option or luxury to put off the decision, because if we say "no" or even "sometime later", we are really saying "no" to God's command to repent. The answer to the sin problem is the blood of Christ, and delay in turning back to God is now simply seen as rebellion. Salvation is simple enough for a child to be saved, because "the word is very nigh unto thee". His delay in judgment is mercy, but he will not always wait for obedience, and justice will be swift.

Delay of justice is injustice.

WHEN GOD IS NOT AMONG US

(31:17)   Are not these evils come upon us because our God is not among us?

Not just in battles, as with the Amalekites (Num. 14:42), and against Ai (Joshua 7:5), but in all that we do, if God is not with us we will be defeated and lost. Evils are befalling America today: crime, recession, divorce, abortions, drugs and alcoholism, pornography, homosexuality, empty church buildings becoming mosques and temples (see 2 Tim. 3:1-9). Instead of continuing in worse sin and going to other gods to find "enlightenment" and "peace", we should come to our senses and say "are not these evils come upon us because our God is not among us?" Then, how do we get God to come back among us? God's answer is [2 Chron. 7:14] turn back to God and he will return to you! The United States has turned *as a nation* from the God of our fathers, and no military might will ever bring us blessing again. We need a national revival! Jesus has been betrayed again for a paltry sum of money. We may go on, as Israel did for forty years, doing empty sacrifices in a temple called "Ichabod…The glory is departed" (1 Sam. 4:21), but soon the Roman army will come and overrun the country that has crucified its own God! And yes, His blood will be upon us and on our children (Matt. 27:25) – is it not already? "Come now, and let us reason together, saith the Lord" (Isa. 1:18). Let us repent of our adulteries and abortions and shedding innocent blood. Our wars today are not for righteousness as much as to save a way of life that has left behind the God who gave us all of the blessings. May God grant us repentance!

**The fool hath said in his heart,
There is no God.** (Ps. 14:1)

SUPER HERO

(33:27)   *The eternal God is thy refuge, and underneath are the everlasting arms.*

The real greatness of Israel, or of Moses, was only the presence of God with them. Clothing makers would have us believe that their product of clothing can make us into a new person, if we would only try to believe in the clothes to do so. We all know that "a book is not judged by its cover", but there is some truth in this that points us back to Christ. We are "clothed with righteousness" (Ps. 132:9) when the blood of Christ covers our sins, just as God clothed Adam and Eve with skins of some innocent animals as a blood sacrifice. If anyone dares to try to enter God's wedding feast without the proper wedding garment of Christ's blood, he will be thrown out. Just as a policeman in uniform is suddenly transformed into a man of authority, so the authority of Christ transforms us as we are clothed with him. Clark Kent wouldn't think of being "Superman" without first changing his clothes, and neither would any other self-respecting super hero. Jesus told the disciples to "stay in the city until you have been clothed with power from on high" (Luke 24:49 - NIV). If we have any hope of being superheroes like Moses or the Apostles, we need the same clothing of the Spirit of God. When the eternal God is our refuge, we are no longer going in our own strength. One of God's daughters was once afraid to fly in a large airliner across the U.S. until she thought "underneath are the everlasting arms". She became at peace as the refuge of Christ clothed her with his presence. Elisha put on Elijah's mantle and became a new man. Let us go out, clothed with the armor of light, and give the world some real life superheroes, clothed with Christ.

The clothes make the man.

STUMBLING STONES

(4:6)   What mean ye by these stones?

God has "dared" to place himself in history to verify the truth of the gospel. Altars and stones have been left behind for archeologists to dig up, as well as for future generations, who will see and ask questions. The Bible is an intricate picture of God's dealings in history, not cluttered with extraneous stories, but rather a masterpiece with Christ as the centerpiece, and every other story and person and thing setting off the beauty of Christ. "These stones", taken from the bottom of the Jordan River, were one more tangible proof for the future generations that God does truly act in the affairs of men. "These all died in faith, not having received the promises, but having seen them afar off" (Heb. 11:13). As exciting as it was to cross the Jordan and pick up stones from its bottom, these people still died without seeing the promised Messiah. But for them, as it is for us today, "Distance lends enchantment to the view." We look with admiration at these miracles from afar, just as these people looked ahead to the coming of Christ and we all look with amazement at God's perfect plan as it unfolds. Noah's Ark, far from being a myth from our remote past, was referred to by Christ himself (Matt. 24:37), and by Peter (2 Pet. 3:6), and by the writer of "Hebrews" (Heb. 11:7), being common knowledge to them. History is a panorama of God's gracious dealings with sinful man. The Ark of Noah waits to be discovered in God's time, when men will say "What does this ark mean?" Along with the stones, the ark waits to cry out the praises of God (Luke 19:40) from history.

Distance lends enchantment to the view.

WANTED: EXPERIENCED PERCEPTIONIST

(6:25)   *And Joshua saved Rahab the harlot alive, and her father's household...*

Our experience with God on Judgment Day will be like this, depending upon our perception of who Jesus is. If he is Lord of heaven and earth, and the Son of God who died and rose again for my justification (Rom. 4:25), I will bow before him and enter heaven, but the man who perceives him as only a prophet, but not God, will find the same loving Savoir to be his enemy. God does not change his mind, but commands us to do so. Rahab the prostitute perceived the spies as men of the true God (2:9-10), and so her family was saved in the destruction of Jericho. A trial or misfortune will become a good thing (Rom. 8:28) if we perceive God's hand in it, and we will gain experience instead of becoming bitter. When Joshua met a man with a drawn sword, and asked "Art thou for us, or for our adversaries?" (5:13), he replied "Nay". Joshua perceived him as an appearance of God, and worshiped him. Israel's success or failure depended entirely upon their spiritual perception of God's authority. Later, Joshua made a mistake in his perception of the Gibeonites, and "made peace with them" (9:15). He had been deceived by appearance to compromise with those God had told him to destroy. From this, we learn how to deal with sin. When we compromise with sin, and are tricked into dwelling at peace with what is contrary to God, we learn a bitter lesson, unless we remain in the cloud of deception. As a last example, Joshua said "Put your feet upon the necks of these kings" at the end of a battle (10:24), perceiving them as they truly were: enemies of God who would bring a snare to Israel if allowed to live. Perceive, and be militant against sin.

Experience depends upon perception.

THE DAY THE SUN STOOD STILL

(10:13)   *So the sun stood still in the midst of heaven…*

Okay, science students, put on your thinking caps! When God does a miracle, the world of science is turned on its ear. The thought of stopping the sun and moon in the heavens seems to be one of the most mind-bending miracles in the Bible. Of course, it is the earth that would have to stop rotating for the sun and the moon to appear to stop, and that would mean probable changes in gravity, tidal waves, and a host of other catastrophes. Unless, of course, the Creator of the universe is behind it (who else could be?) God, who created all things, put physical laws into motion to govern the harmony of the universe, but he is still in charge. For a miracle to take place, God can and will suspend laws of physics to do what seems to us impossible. But then, who can explain how he created matter out of nothing? How did Jesus walk on water? Is anything impossible for a God who had no beginning? If you can wrap your mind around someone juggling ten balls at once, is it possible that our Creator and Sustainer can juggle the whole universe of stars, planets and galaxies in harmony with each other? And why should stopping the earth for a day be a show stopper for such a Supreme Being? In the 1951 Sci-Fi movie "The Day the Earth Stood Still", Klaatu and his robot come to earth to stop the earthlings from their destructive direction. Certainly the world would take notice if such a U.F.O. came to earth to stop us in our tracks, but I doubt it would make the world literally stand still. God's purpose for miracles is that we would take notice and stop our destructive habits of sin. When Joshua heeded God's prompting and prayed, it was truly the day the earth stood still.

Be still, and know that I am God. (Ps. 46:10)

WAR HORSES

(14:11)   As yet I am as strong this day as I was in the day that Moses sent me.

I got a newsletter last week from Lenna Belle (Grandma") Robinson, now about 91 years old, and leaving Korea after thirty years there as a missionary. At 91, is she ready to quit? No way! "Starting a new life in the U.S.A. – Hope to join Youth With A Mission, being the Lord's recruiter!" Caleb also was no quitter: he was ready to fight giants then, at 40, and was ready now at 85. Moses died at 120, yet "his eye was not dim, nor his natural force abated" (Deut. 34:7). If God has a work for us to do, he will strengthen us for it until it is done. "For which cause we faint not; but though our outward man perish, yet the inward man is renewed day by day" (2 Cor. 4:16). [Read also Isaiah 40:31]. Wait on the Lord! He will renew your strength, too. We get old, and in our minds we faint and become weary (Heb. 12:3), long before we are supposed to, and our bodies respond with weakness and fear. Let us be like Caleb, "Strong to the finish". Others feared and "made the heart of the people melt" (14:8), but people like Caleb and Lenna Belle encourage the weak and weary to press on. Caleb had a promise from God and, since he was still alive, felt God was as able as ever to fight through him. If God is our strength, we also will remain strong. Contrast this with the thoughts expressed, probably by David, concerning old age: "Cast me not off in the time of old age; forsake me not when my strength faileth. For mine enemies speak against me... Saying, God hath forsaken him'" (Ps. 71:9-11). Our promise from God is the same that he gave Joshua: "I will not fail thee, nor forsake thee" (1:5). God's old war horses never die: they will live forever.

**But they that wait upon the Lord shall
renew their strength.** (Isa. 40:31)

RED IN THE FACE

(15:63)   *Judah could not dislodge the Jebusites, who were living in Jerusalem. (NIV)*

What an embarrassment for the capital of God's kingdom! When we are embarrassed it shows on our face, and as long as we have a pure conscience, we will continue to blush at our shame when confronted with it. When we lose the ability to blush, it is a sign of how deep in sin we are. A drunkard's face is also red, but not from shame. It is the long term effect of alcohol. If America today is embarrassed about a president who (for instance) commits adultery, he is only the face of the country that wears the pride or shame of the collective mass of voters. He is the president, and we must pray for him, to guide his decisions. If America does wrong, the president wears the shame, before the nations. India, once the "crown jewel" of the British Empire, now has its own problems, but is still beautiful to look upon, with Kashmir as the beautiful head, Delhi as the heart, Kerala as the feet that bring the gospel, and a train of children at her hand in the northeast. Srinagar is the beauty spot on Kashmir's face, and the place where India blushes. In Srinagar itself, a city torn by militancy and forced submission by the Indian army, the church is the only hope of "saving face", but the church is embroiled in the politics of the school system, and in legal battles between Christians, a shame before the public. Today, the "Jebusites" are not some heathen nation, but our own sins of selfishness and pride. Mordecai told Esther "For if you remain silent at this time, relief and deliverance for the Jews will arise from another place" (Esther 4:14 - NIV), and what a shame it will be if God allows someone else to bring peace to Kashmir, because Christians are at war!

Man is read in his face.

GOD'S PROMISES

(18:3)   How long are ye slack to go to possess the land...?

"The Promised Land" sounds so mysterious, so far away, like "Never Never Land". In fact, our promised land is eternal life in heaven, which sounds like the place of Peter Pan, where time is banished, so that nobody ever grows old, and which borrows a lot of the descriptions of heaven (more precious than gold, etc.) To the Israelites, the land "flowing with milk and honey" (Ex. 33:3) [cream and sugar, today?], was all real, and all undeserved: "all the land which he sware to give unto their fathers", and "There failed not aught of any good thing which the Lord had spoken unto the house of Israel; all came to pass" (21:43,45). It was also "a land for which ye did not labour" (24:13). If this is all true (and it is), how long will we wait to take possession of these promises? God does not lie: what he says, he will do. Salvation is of the Lord (Jonah 2:9), we did nothing for it. All we can do is to go and possess the land (our own souls, and those of others as they believe the promises of God), and thank God for what he has done. The Israelites would not go in because of their fear of the giants, and now the next generation had conquered much of the land, but still seven of the tribes had not received their inheritance. The land had been conquered, so what remained to do? Joshua, Like Jesus, had paved the way by conquering the nations, but for the Israelites to take possession, they had to believe God's promises, and in his strength go in and defeat the tribes that still occupied the land. If we believe God, how long will we wait to take our inheritance?

**...Through faith and patience inherit
the promises.** (Heb. 6:12)

REFUGEE CAMPS

(20:2)   "...appoint out for you cities of refuge..."

The point of all of God's laws is for justice, and the idea of cities of refuge is a natural outcome of that. Injustice will breed hatred because people lose faith in the system of justice, and then ultimately in God. So, when a person is killed, someone is certain to be angry, and may kill the person who killed his friend, but the problem is that someone will also be angry enough to kill him if the man did it by accident, and really is not guilty. God's will is for justice and peace to follow instead of a chain of angry murders. The "Hatfields and the McCoys" are an example of what happens when people don't quickly solve disputes. A city of refuge is not to allow guilty criminals to get away, but for people to get a fair trial when they have done a sin without any forethought, or even desire to do evil, like an accident. "The death of the high priest" prefigures Christ, as his death pays the penalty of our sin, since he died in our place. A city of refuge will allow tempers to cool and people to think clearly before they also compound the problem through angry retaliation. There is also a great need today for a similar place of refuge where people can find justice being upheld. Political asylum is given to people like Salman Rushdie who may have done a sin against others, so that they may be given justice. Hatred must be combatted with forgiveness, which is much more appropriate if we understand how many times God has forgiven us our sins. Hatred is the cause of wars in all the world, and "...peacemakers...shall be called the children of God" (Matt. 5:9).

It is injustice which breeds hatred.

UNITED STAKES OF A MIRACLE

(22:12)   The whole congregation... gathered... to go up to war against them.

Civil war is so much in our hearts, we are ready at the drop of a hat to assume the worst about our closest friends and family, as soon as something <u>appears</u> wrong. Why not rather love, and assume there must be a logical reason for their actions? Why must we be armed to the teeth and ready to kill before we even <u>ask</u> why it is that people do something? Canaan was conquered by dividing it first in half, and the beginning of the problems of Israel came long before the "divided Kingdom". Sin is in our hearts, and as good as it is to fight for purity in our worship, we must be careful against becoming "police" of others' consciences. Here, an altar was built for the very purpose of preserving unity, and nearly led to civil war through a misunderstanding. It must have taken a lot of humility to back down and not go to war, when these men realized they had been mistaken. Too often, people continue to make war, even after realizing the folly of their quick tempers, because they want to prove "I was right". I once read a plaque that stated, "No matter how much a man criticizes his wife's judgment, he never questions her choice of a husband". The United States of America continues to be a miracle to the world of unity in diversity ("E pluribus Unum": out of many, one), but the Civil War was fought to preserve the union, with 620,000 deaths before it became truly united. Incredibly, both sides were fighting for freedom, and fought bravely and fiercely to win. The stakes are high for such a daring proposition to work, and the grace of God alone heals the wounds of that misunderstanding.

United we stand, divided we fall.

HEAVEN'S HEROES

(3:10)   *The spirit of the Lord came upon him.*

Where do heroes come from? The real ones seem to show up just when they are needed, seemingly out of nowhere. Children watch their heroes on movies, or in comic books, and dream about a day when they might be heroes. Or, maybe they read about heroes in the Bible and ignore their faults, but hope to emulate their good points. The "fearful, and unbelieving" (Rev. 21:8) are made equal in the eyes of God, as those who will never be heroes (7:3), nor will they inherit heaven. Real heroes may have many faults, but being fearful and unbelieving are not among them. Some may even be fearful, but overcome the fear by believing they are in the right. We don't necessarily have to trust in ourselves, but can be confident in God's protection over us, which will make us overcome fear. Samson is usually pictured as a massive, muscular man, but he may well have been just a little "pipsqueak" who had the spirit of God upon him to do his feats of strength. Otherwise, why such surprise (16:5) at his might? There is no mention of his size, but simply "the spirit of the Lord came mightily upon him" (14:6). Some heroes trust in themselves, and go fearlessly out to win battles, but in God's eyes, the real heroes are those whose trust is in God himself. Otherwise, we would have to call Satan, Hitler and many other megalomaniacs, heroes. They may be heroes to their followers, but God will call them rebels and failures on Judgment Day. If you are trusting in yourself or your ability, the Spirit of God will never come upon you, and who wants to be among "the Heroes of Hades"?

"Self-trust is the essence of heroism" (?)

KILLING ME SOFTLY

(4:21) ...took a nail of the tent, and took an hammer in her hand, and went softly unto him...

Sisera, with nine hundred chariots of iron, was a fear to all of Israel, and yet he was not defeated by the strength of numbers of a mightier army, but by loving concern, which put him off guard; he fell asleep in peace, and was killed. Delilah also tamed Samson by charming him with love (16:4-22). These are not examples of real love, as the purpose was to deceive, but it shows the power of loving persuasion. What a sweet and delicate way to kill a man: Jael invited Sisera in, gave him milk to put him to sleep, and then drove a tent peg through his skull! What can we learn from this? First, this is how sin lulls us to sleep and finally destroys us. Immorality and drugs give us a false sense of peace and then lead us to the slaughter (Prov. 7:22, 24:30-34). On the other side, we must have this kind of hatred for sin, with no mercy. Sin tries to come in to find a comfortable place in our hearts. Jael never wavered: her intention, even when serving milk was to destroy this enemy. Like Jehu and the Baal worshippers (2 Kings 10:18-28), as he tricked them all into coming to be destroyed, so Jael saw a way to softly and gently lull Sisera to sleep and then kill him. There is no place for fellowship between us and sin – either it will kill us softly, or we must kill it. God said, "...thou shalt smite them, and utterly destroy them; make no covenant with them, nor shew mercy unto them." (Deut. 7:2). That must be our attitude toward sin: don't let it beguile you, or it will kill you. Rather, be like Jael and give a death blow to its head.

A Smith & Wesson Beats Four Aces.

GIDEON: THE MIGHTY WARRIOR

(6:12)   ...the angel of the Lord... said, "The Lord
is with you, mighty warrior". (NIV)

The King James Version says "thou mighty man of valor". Why should Gideon be thought of as a "mighty warrior"? He simply "was threshing wheat in a winepress, to keep it from the Midianites" when the angel of the Lord met him; nothing particularly valiant there, unless it was his defiance of evil. Mainly it is God's word, his confession over him that he is a "mighty warrior" that makes him mighty. Jerry Russell, the pastor who led me to Christ, and who started me on writing these daily devotions many years ago, once asked me to organize a prayer chain, and head it up, saying I was a man of prayer. Actually, his word of encouragement to me made me into a man of prayer. Although Gideon had doubts, fears and questions, God led him and made him great, using **dew**, a **drink** and a **dream**. "Putting a fleece" before God, he still doubted and asked for dew to fall the other way, like flipping a coin, then "best out of three!" to make sure. This was man-made, but God-executed. Next, God deals with fears by testing and showing men's hearts as they bow down to drink: are some watching for the enemy? Then take those men only (God-made, and man-executed). Finally, the questions are dealt with through a dream. We may be led to our own wrong interpretation, but here, even that is given by God (God-made and God-executed). Note that he fearfully tore down his father's altar and grove, in sheer obedience to God, before the Spirit of God came upon him (6:34). Valor may mean simply obedience to God when fear is still there. Trusting in God is the source of our real strength. "Lord, make me a man of valor like Gideon!"

Fear and courage are brothers.

The Lord Will Rule Over You

(8:23)   ...I will not rule over you, neither shall my son rule over you...

Most people would jump at such an opportunity. Gideon, however, knew it was God and not he who delivered Israel from the Midianites. Today there are too many who feel people need them as their leader, and they are "a dime a dozen". What the world needs is leaders who are truly submitted to God in their hearts, who don't fall to flattery and the inflated pride that follows it. Gideon was no more perfect than any of the judges, but this attitude is to his credit. He <u>did</u> judge Israel, but he knew it was God who enabled him to do so. It was not just pious rhetoric. He was wise and brave, defeating Midian with 300 men, but this was possible only because he knew it was God who was fighting for Israel. India and America and all countries need this kind of a ruler, whose trust is in God. This kind of humility will bring God's blessings. Gideon was a humble man, one who made peace whenever possible (8:2-3), instead of exalting pride. Like Gideon, we should always seek to give the glory to God and not take it to ourselves. He even spoke of his son's and grandson's generations, saying that God, and not they, would reign over Israel. When Israel demanded a king, God said "they have not rejected thee, but they have rejected me, that I should not reign over them" (1 Sam. 8:7). Gideon was right; but when his son Abimelech came along, he did the opposite of what Gideon had done: he killed men more righteous than he to take over leadership. The sad fact of history is that bad men take authority to themselves when they see the vacuum of hesitancy on the part of truly capable leaders. A good test for a leader is whether he can also follow orders.

Obedience alone gives the right to command.

KNOW YOUR GROUND

(11:27)   *...I have not sinned against thee, but thou*
            doest me wrong to war against me...

Jephthah took the time to ask the king of Ammon why the army came to fight against Israel. He sent messengers with his words of rebuttal against the king's accusations, before simply attacking him, for two reasons: to know the king's grievances, and to respond to them, so there would be no doubt as to who was really at fault. The result was that the Israelite army now went to fight with a boldness that was lacking before. They now saw the Ammonite attack as unjustified because Jephthah reviewed their history. This should be our strategy in spiritual warfare, too: first find out what grounds the devil has for attacking us, then review this in the light of God's dealings. If there are, in fact, legitimate grievances, we must clear them first (forgive, make restitution, repent of sins, etc.). Once we have a clear conscience, and know the ground we stand upon is already rightfully taken, we can now proceed boldly to war a good warfare. "Then the Spirit of the Lord" (11:29) will come upon us, and we will win in God's strength, not our own. There is a definite psychological advantage when we know we are in the right way, and the enemy knows that we can never win when we doubt. Be bold! Unfortunately, the story of Jephthah and his victory ends with the result of his vow: his own daughter is given in sacrifice to the Lord. Even his daughter is convinced that a vow to the Lord cannot be broken, and trusts that her father will fulfill his promise at her expense. Jephthah, true to his word, stands on the ground of his rash promise to God, and "keeps his oath, even when it hurts" (Ps. 15:4 – NIV).

**Be sure you know the condition of
your flocks.** (Pr. 27:23 – NIV)

FOOD TO EAT THAT YOU KNOW NOTHING ABOUT

(JN. 4:32 – NIV)

(15:7) ...yet will I be avenged of you, and after that I will cease.

This appears to be a prophecy of how Samson died, when he avenged his loss of eyesight by destroying many Philistines in his death. However, although most of Samson's life seems to be a selfish pursuit of revenge for personal reasons, there is a deeper drive in his heart. Samson was a Nazirite from his mother's womb and was dedicated to God. He was used by God to execute judgment on the enemies of his people. But, Samson was a real person with real faults, just as we are. God didn't just erase his personality to preserve himself a "perfect" Nazirite, but worked through his personality faults to bring about his own will. Samson made many mistakes, but his heart's desire was for God and his righteousness (Matt. 6:33). He hated unfaithfulness when he saw it in others, as can be seen many times in his anger when men solved his riddle by blackmail, his wife was given away, and she and her father were burned. He was in many ways a common and worldly man, going in to a harlot and taking personal revenge, but behind it all he was a man called by God. His final revenge was not simply a "kamikaze" attack, or a suicide, but the cry of a man who wanted to honor God even in his death. When a woman, for an evil plot, becomes a "human bomb" to kill Rajiv Gandhi, the world is horrified. But God alone, who judges the basic intents of man's actions, can judge between faithfulness to a conspiracy for political gain, and faithfulness to God. We may never be called to such an extreme decision, but God calls all of us to faithfulness in our commitment to him.

The deepest hunger of a faithful heart is faithfulness.

BUSINESS AS USUAL

(16:20)   But he did not know that the Lord had left him. (NIV)

"Let not...the mighty man glory in his might" (Jer. 9:23). We can argue over whether God leaves because of our sin, or if sin comes because God leaves, but when the Spirit of God is gone, we are bankrupt! God chose Samson from the womb, which argues strongly in favor of God being the cause. God came upon Saul, anointing him with his Spirit, and then left him, and he was miserably destroyed by evil spirits. God had his own purpose for Samson, and he used him mightily, though he was a carnal man. God will use you and me, but would we even notice if the Spirit left us?!? Like Samson, we would expect life to be "business as usual", but life without the Spirit of God, returning to the life we had before Christ came in to save us, is no life at all. When Jesus' disciples were once asked if they wanted to leave with others over what Jesus had said, Peter said "to whom shall we go? Thou hast the words of eternal life" (Jn. 6:68), but later, he tried to return to fishing after the crucifixion. Fortunately, God's promise to us is "I will never leave thee, nor forsake thee" (Heb. 13:5). Even when Samson's pride is humbled, his prayer is one of selfish revenge. But God used him, and God was glorified. Samson is such a picture of each of us: we are not spiritual people but, when God's Spirit "[moves us] at times" (13:25), we find we do spiritual things that amaze us. It is humbling but true that we are just like Samson. God uses me with all my faults. I'm not a great spiritual man. If I pray, if I fast, it is God's Spirit stirring in me. I want to be used more, not to sleep my life away, and to give God glory for every good thing that I may do.

**...he that hath not the Son of God
hath not life.** (1 Jn. 5:12)

A DINOSAUR LESSON

(21:3)   Why should one tribe be missing from Israel today? (NIV)

A nice time to stop and think about the consequences of their actions! The tribe of Benjamin nearly went the way of the dinosaurs and dodo birds as people reacted against their sin. God had a purpose in the whole episode, which was to teach them a lesson. One way to destroy sin is to destroy people, which God could do at any time, sending us all to outer darkness. But a better plan is to redeem us, and give us a hatred for sin so we won't do it again. Until this time, Israel had learned well how to stop sin by killing Canaanites. But, what do you do when sin is inside of you and your own people? Shall we kill all the bad people? Then we will all die and go to destruction. A major discovery for all of us is that we are all guilty before God. God could have continued to send plagues upon Israel each time they sinned, as he did in the wilderness, but learning by discovery has a more powerful effect. When my father beat me with a stick, it made me think twice before doing a sin again, but when he let me discover for myself the consequences of my sin, it made me start finding answers for the root of my sins. Israel could not merely ask God to make a new tribe of Benjamin, but had to learn by their mistake, and were made to find an answer. When we discover dinosaur fossils, it makes us consider why the great species of animals became extinct, and how we can keep whales, buffaloes and eagles from disappearing. But, more importantly, it teaches us to take responsibility for not only the preservation of animals, but also the human race. God's solution is not eradication, but redemption, and a better answer than killing our enemies is forgiving them, and leading them to Christ.

Discovery is one more way of finding answers.

RUTHLESS

(1:16)   Thy people shall be my people, and thy God my God.

Ruth's speech is like a prayer of salvation, or a marriage vow, one of unqualified dedication to Naomi, her people, and the true God, even ending with "until death do us part". This shows also God's love in accepting a Moabitess into the people of Israel [see Deut. 23:3]. Possibly, this applies to men only: an unconverted person (Moabite) cannot be one of God's people, but Ruth had a truly circumcised heart, and at a time when most of Israel did not! Obviously, Ruth didn't know of the prohibition, anyway. She always shows humility, in gleaning fields, bowing before Boaz, and obeying Naomi. Like a true convert should, she completely forsook all her family, her gods, her people, her life, and even where she should be buried, to follow the true God. Why? She had seen in their lives something worth dying for which she didn't see in her own people and gods. She was vowing allegiance to God and his people. This is a high mark for us as Christians: is our commitment to God this strong? We would do well to repeat this passage periodically to re-affirm our vow of covenant relationship to God. Instead of saying "Don't make me go there!" we should have Ruth's attitude "Don't make me ever leave you, God!" To say "Your God is my God" means God makes all the decisions, and we willingly follow wherever he goes, as a submissive wife, as "a helper suitable for him" (Gen. 2:18 – NIV). Boaz commends Ruth for her valor, in leaving all behind to follow God and his people, and for her discretion in not running after younger men (3:10). Let us be as "ruthless" as Ruth in our pursuit of following after God.

The better part of valor is discretion.

No Advocate

(2:25)   ...*if a man sin against the Lord, who shall entreat for him?*

Eli may not have been the most perceptive priest, judging from his treatment of Hannah as she prayed and wept (1:12-14), and he may not have been a model father, judging from the way his sons turned out, performing gross sins right under his nose. Even this little talk seems to be pretty "lightweight" when their immorality is the cause. But, Eli is spot on in his judgment of what is at stake. A judge will arbitrate and judge cases of man vs. man, but what if our case is against the judge himself? Who can appease his anger? The death of his sons is a chilling admonition to us as fathers, to take responsibility for our children's actions before they turn into serious threats to society. They certainly deserved God's judgment, but fathers should take charge much sooner than this to avert such a tragic end for their children. This passage shows the further damage caused by their sin: the previous verse states, "Ye make the Lord's people to transgress". Our sins affect others, too. These wicked sons caused God's worship to be defiled, and caused people to despise even the joy of bringing offerings. We, as Christians, are in the public eye, so what I allow myself to do will affect other believers, as Paul describes in Romans 14. My sin will cause others to fall into sin, because I don't live in a vacuum. But ultimately, my sin is against the Lord, the Judge of all the earth. That is the real problem of sin. Only Christ can stand as my advocate before his Father and intercede for my sins against him. Those who come without Christ's blood will find they have no defense attorney on Judgment Day.

**The king's wrath is as the roaring
of a lion...** (Pr. 19:12)

POPEYE'S SPINACH

(4:3)   Let us fetch the ark...that...it may save us...

These people were really out of touch with reality. The Ark of the Covenant was more like a good luck charm than the actual presence of God. Their trust was no longer in God, but in their own strength, and their delusion was that all they needed to win was a "pep rally". The ark was only an idol, since their hearts were not true before God. Today, the same tendency towards idolatry is our problem. People fight "with God on our side" when they are not on God's side. God demands repentance when there is sin, and will allow us to be defeated, even before unbelievers, if we continue in our presumptuous delusion of his favor when we are in deep sin. For many today, because they are "Christians", God must bless them, they think. We see in movies that all we need to do when the devil attacks us is to flash a Bible or a crucifix in his face, and he will run away in fear; but God, not the devil, is the big problem. We need to get back to God in our hearts. If there is a quarrel between Christians, which side will win if both are flashing all their supposed Christianity before each other, and before heathen courts? God wants repentance, not idolatry or self-delusion. The presence or absence of the ark was only an external picture of Israel's heart. "The glory is departed" (4:22) was true before the ark was taken. Today, the Christians in Srinagar are all sure that God is on their side, and that others are not true Christians. But who is ready to humble himself before God and say "The glory is departed"?

The worst deluded are the self-deluded.

PITY PARTY

(5:12)   ...and the cry of the city went up to heaven.

These were the Philistines crying, but to whom did they cry? Their god Dagon had fallen over twice and had its head and hands broken off when it was placed before God's presence in the ark, so certainly it could not answer them. In fact, it could not even cry for help when it fell over. "The cry of the city went up to heaven" where only the true God can hear. They are most to be pitied, who can only complain (Eph. 2:12). "Now we know that God heareth not sinners" (Jn. 9:31). Later, we read "and the people lamented" (6:19) when 50,070 men were killed for looking into the ark. Again, the prayers, if they could be called prayers, brought neither pity nor answer from God, although these were at least Israelites who cried out to God. But there was no response from God because there was no sign of repentance. Finally (7:2), "all the house of Israel lamented after the Lord", as they remembered how their relationship to God used to be. Now, their hearts are ready, and Samuel gives them a formula for repentance. The result was a revival, as idolatry was put away and people returned to their first love with God. Which of these do we want? Any heathen can complain and be pitied, but there will be no answer from God until they turn to the true God and admit they are bankrupt. Even if we are Christians, complaining and crying will not get a response from God, until we are ready to repent of our hardness of heart, and put the blame for our sad condition upon ourselves, and not on God. Do we want pity for our complaints, or do we really want to do business with God? He is ready when we are.

Those who do not complain are never pitied.

ANOTHER HEART

(10:9)   As Saul turned to leave Samuel, God changed Saul's heart… (NIV)

This idea of a new heart is prevalent throughout Scripture, as in passages regarding the new birth. Paul says, "Therefore, if any man be in Christ he is a new creature" (2 Cor. 5:17), and Ezekiel speaks of "a new heart and a new spirit" (11:19, 18:31, 36:26). Both Jesus and Peter use the phrase being "born again". All of this speaks of something outside of ourselves, done by God's own will and sovereignty. When Saul prophesied, it was because of the anointing of God, not anything he tried to do. But it was, apparently, something other than salvation in Saul's case, because it didn't last. To his credit, he showed some real fruit of the Spirit, as he "held his peace" (10:27), when despised by some troublemakers. He held his tongue and "answer[ed] not a fool according to his folly" (Prov.26:4); too bad he didn't continue in a humble spirit. When the Spirit's anointing was on Saul, he acted in a godly and conciliatory way, but when he began to see victory in battles, due to God's anointing, he let pride enter his heart, and was then back to his old heart, his natural self, excusing himself for sin. He became taken over by evil spirits through pride, jealousy, and disobedience to God, and finally committed suicide. His anointing as king was never a question to David, but the "other heart" given by God did not prevail. "Why?" we ask: the gospel, which results in the new birth, must be preceded by the law of God, to bring about conviction of personal sin, a disgust over those sins, and a willful turning from sin back to God as the Lord and Master. To overlook this in preaching the gospel will surely bring bad fruit, and only God can provide us with a new heart.

A new heart also will I give you, and
a new spirit… (Ezek. 36:26)

A HANDY AND HEADY ARMY

(11:7)   And the fear of the Lord fell on the people,
and they came out with one consent.

Saul began well as the leader of Israel's armies, and as the king. He was tall, strong and handsome, and while the Spirit of God was upon him, he commanded respect from all the people. His confidence was in God, so the people were confident in him. They had grown in confidence also from their victories as God's people under Moses, Joshua and the judges, and they learned by their mistakes that they would lose, no matter how skillful they were, whenever they turned away from faith in God. Saul began his army with 3,000 skillful men, and until today, Israel possibly has the most skillful and dedicated army in the world, respected and feared for their ability to do all they set out to do, but mainly because they are called "Gods people". Saul began as an almost timid and shy man, until "the Spirit of the Lord" came upon him, and he was "turned into another man" (10:6). But, along with his new found confidence came self-confidence, and the beginning of his downfall. He committed his first recorded sin, offering a sacrifice, which only a priest can do, and then offering a lame excuse to Samuel, refusing to take responsibility for his sin. Soon, he made more and bigger mistakes. We also can fall to pride, when God's Spirit gives us success. We may grow greatly in skill, in knowing God's word, and may use it as a sword that cuts and kills, if not used in the right spirit. Our confidence must always be in God, not in ourselves, or we will fall. Don't let your God-given skills go to your head, nor your confidence ever be in yourself. Be skillful hands, armed with God's word, confident in Christ, our head.

Skill and confidence are an unconquerable army.

To Obey Is Better Than Sacrifice

(15:22)   "Does the Lord delight in burnt offerings and sacrifices…?" (NIV)

Yes, he does, but not "…as much as in obeying the voice of the Lord". "The Lord" means "Lord of all, or not Lord at all", so if he is Lord, obey him, or don't call him "Lord" (Matt. 7:21-7). When going to God, "…be more ready to hear, than to give the sacrifice of fools" (Eccl. 5:1 – Compare Hosea 6:6, & Mark 12:33). David also wisely observed, after his adultery, and murder of Uriah, "…thou desirest not sacrifice, else would I give it: …The sacrifices of God are a broken spirit…" (Ps. 51:16-17). That was Saul's problem: he didn't have a broken and contrite heart. We are quick to <u>do</u> something when we want to please God, or parents or leaders. We love "penance", and we like to get a "caning" and get it over with: like a "band aid" on our putrefying sores of sin. And we like a religion that makes us pray, give sacrifices, or <u>do</u> <u>something</u>, so when we're done we can still be our own boss. But God doesn't work that way – he demands obedience, and no "maverick" attitudes will stand before his holiness. The only acceptable sacrifice is the blood of Christ, once for all sins. If that love of God doesn't break our hearts, certainly no sacrifice will be a substitute. Saul was a rebel, plain and simple, and the sacrifice he wanted to do was to look good to people, not to please God. Adam's sin also was the same kind of rebellion. "Witchcraft" and "idolatry" are in our hearts if we think we have a better plan than God's plan. Man needs God's grace to continue to break his stubborn will, or he will surely miss Heaven for his willful sin. God help us all to be obedient to the voice of the Lord and to his word.

Delight thyself also in the Lord. (Ps. 37:4)

WHO'S AFRAID OF WHOM?

(18:12)   And Saul was afraid of David, because the Lord was with him...

In many verses, David is fleeing from Saul "for fear of Saul" (21:10, 23:26). Three times in one chapter it is recorded that "Saul was afraid of David" (18:12,15,29). How can these both be true? It was because David first feared God and would not lift a hand in his own defense against God's anointed. He fled for his life, which was wise, but knew that God was his protector. David later said, "Let us fall now into the hand of the Lord, for his mercies are great; and let me not fall into the hand of man" (2 Sam. 24:14). God's anger is just, but man can act with insanity! So he feared Saul because he could not trust him. But Saul, on the other hand, had good reason to fear David "<u>because</u> the Lord was with him, and was departed from Saul" [Compare Lk. 12:4-5!]. Saul knew that God's Spirit and power were upon David, and he was a threat to him, as he feared losing his position as king. King Herod did the same and he killed innocent children to protect his kingship. The Jews feared Jesus, and later his disciples, and killed and persecuted them out of fear. We also may fear what man can do to us, but know this: if they are against us, it is because they fear us, "because the Lord is with us" and not with them. As David, let us love those who hate us, and we win! David had previously come against Goliath, who had no fear of God, and certainly no fear of David, and David had no fear of Goliath saying "Who is this uncircumcised Philistine that he should defy the armies of the living God?" (17:26). Let us fear only God, and not what man can do to us.

**The fear of man bringeth a snare: but whoso putteth
his trust in the Lord shall be safe.** (Pr. 29:25)

WHOLLY DEVOTED

(20:17)   *...for he loved him as he loved his own soul.*

David later lamented Jonathan's death, saying "thy love to me was wonderful, passing the love of women" (2 Sam. 1:26). Paul described marriage, saying "So ought men to love their wives as their own bodies" (Eph. 5:28), and David said that Jonathan's devotion to him was even greater than that. It is a picture to us of how great our devotion to God should be, passing all other loves. People are devoted to many "gods", and it is evident that only devotion to the true God will bring real and lasting reward, and fulfillment in this life. Jonathan loved David "as he loved his own soul", and we are told to "...love the Lord thy God... with all thy soul...and thy neighbor as thyself" (Luke 10:27). That amount of love should be there for our "neighbor", or even our worst enemy, as the parable of the Good Samaritan shows. If that is true, then how much more should our love for God be if it is with <u>all</u> your strength, soul and mind? True devotion is selfless and giving, even unto death as martyrs through the ages have done. Abraham was told to devote his "only son Isaac, whom thou lovest" (Gen. 22:2) to God, as a burnt offering. His devotion to God was such that he could be ready to give even his promised son back to God, which was more to him than his own life. Our faith and devotion to God flows from this kind of faith and devotion. It is not a slavish devotion out of fear of punishment, but a trust relationship of deep love that sees all fulfillment in perfect devotion to the God who first loved us. We have nothing to give back to God but a life and death that is surrendered to his purposes, trusting all into his hands.

All is holy where devotion kneels

HAND-IN-HAND

(23:16)   Jonathan... went to David... and strengthened his hand in God.

Jonathan displays such a different spirit from that of his father Saul, who had to strive continually to remain in his place as king. Jonathan saw correctly that we are all equal before God, and that God alone can choose who will have the right to rule. God establishes his kingdom in our hearts, and gives us each our necessary gifts to function together. When a king has to kill others to retain his place of authority, he has lost already. Jonathan had no desire to strive for a position as king, but to walk with David as fellow heirs of a kingdom not of this world. "Where your treasure is, there will your heart be also" (Mt. 6:21). Jonathan was able to walk hand in hand with David, not struggling to get ahead by his birthright as son of the king. In God's kingdom there is room enough for everyone, and the rule is "preferring one another" and not striving to be ahead. Saul was not able to submit to God, so he had to fight to make himself head over others. David chose to yield up his right to the throne, and even later, when Absalom challenged him for it. When we walk in submission to God we can walk hand in hand, and all are equal before God. David told Abiathar "abide thou with me" (22:23), as he said to others, "And every one that was in distress, and every one that was in debt, and every one that was discontented, gathered themselves unto him" (22:2). James explains, "For where envying and strife is, there is confusion and every evil work" (Jas. 3:16), but where there is a fear of God, and love for his kingdom, there is room for everyone to work hand in hand, and a king can walk equally with those in debt and in distress.

Let's go hand in hand, not one before another.

TRUE HUMILITY

(25:41)   *...let thine handmaid be a servant to wash the feet of the servants of my lord.*

"...before honour is humility", and "Pride goeth before destruction" (Prov. 15:33, 16:18). Abigail shines all the more through the shocking contrast with her husband Nabal. Her whole speech to David is a masterpiece of humility and grace. Nabal married a "virtuous woman" (Prov. 31:10), but didn't deserve her. She had the spirit of David, who wouldn't lift a hand to destroy Saul, God's anointed king who sought to kill him. David never thought of him as an enemy; though he could have, in a moment, ended his own problem of fleeing for his life, he would have lost a most important part of his own character that God was forming. David also speaks of himself as a "dead dog" or "a flea" (24:14, 26:20), and earlier as unworthy to be the king's son (18:23 - NIV). Abigail's words remind us also of John the Baptist who spoke of Jesus as "mightier than I, whose shoes I am not worthy to bear" (Mt. 3:11). Abigail goes further and says she wouldn't even be worthy to wash David's feet, but would feel privileged to wash even his servants' feet! What grace! Our thoughts recoil at the thought of her being married to one such as Nabal, and yet she was faithful to him to the end. She fully expected, after saving Nabal's neck, to go on as his wife, suffering silently, and unsung for life. But God rewarded her and David for their humility, and they married after Nabal's death. I love this story! Let us all be as Abigail as we live under cruel circumstances, "being destitute, afflicted, tormented; (of whom the world was not worthy)" (Heb. 11:37-8), and wait for God alone to vindicate the situation. Let humility be our beauty. "Lord, make me a servant in my heart".

**He that shall humble himself
shall be exalted.** (Mt. 23:12)

DESPERADOS

(27:1)   "The best thing I can do is to escape to the land of the Philistines" (NIV).

Saul had just spoken the second time that he was wrong, and said, "I will no more do thee harm", but David now says, "I shall now perish one day by the hand of Saul". He was no fool, to think Saul would now change, but knew Saul to be a desperate man. Even David was a desperate man, who nearly killed Nabal and all his men because he provoked him to anger. If David could be driven to such a point of thoughtless anger in his desperate situation, he knew Saul was capable of any evil, as he was not submitted to God in his heart. Saving Saul's life the first time had not changed his heart, so there was no reason to believe the second promise of safety, when he had broken his first. Actually, there was not even a promise given the first time, but only a plea for his own welfare (24:17-22). It was better to escape than to tempt a desperate man. Nabal was saved by his wise wife's intervention, until God himself brought punishment and justice, but nobody was there to intervene for David before Saul. Desperate men without the Spirit of God are not likely to be swayed, even by the most fervent pleas of an intercessor. Today, I'm going to Delhi to meet the bishop, in the hopes of seeing reconciliation in the Biscoe School situation, and that, hopefully, out of court. If he is not a desperate man, and is filled with the Spirit of God, he can easily resolve the situation, being a wise mediator, and will restore unity and confidence to the church of Srinagar. God's desire is to make men desperate for his kingdom, and not for the pursuit of a perishable kingdom. (See Matt. 11:12).

Tempt not a desperate man.

HOW ARE THE MIGHTY FALLEN!

(1:19)   "The beauty of Israel is slain upon thy high places..."

Driving to Ooty today, I saw a twisted, dead body of a man –hit and run- left on the highway. Six months ago, I saw a man with his head run over in an accident. These chapters show the same tragic irreverence for human life: Saul decapitated and hung on a wall; two groups of twelve men grab each other's heads and then simultaneously kill each other with swords; Asahel is run through with the back end of a spear, and people stop to look at him on the road; retaliations by killing in bed, and so on. Where is the dignity of human life? I'm appalled at the lack of it. "How are the mighty fallen!" Mankind itself is fallen from dignity, and will be cast unknown, unremembered into destruction, unless we take a hand in saving them. Isaiah cries out against the king of Babylon, "How art thou fallen from heaven, O Lucifer, son of the morning!" (is this possibly an allusion to Satan's fall?) Our greatness is only as we find our place in God's kingdom; rebellion will result in destruction: a total waste is what Hades is! God cares about us – do we also care for one another? Is a twisted body lying dead something to stare at, or to hang on a wall? We are all made in God's image (even Satan was made for good). No wonder David laments! The loss is to humanity, to so treat the dead bodies of those created to house God's Spirit. To senselessly kill each other in a choreographed death dance: we were made for more than that. Consider, and preach the gospel!

So God created man in his own image... (Gen. 1:27)

SADLY MISTAKEN

(3:8) *"Am I a dog's head...that thou chargest me today with a fault...?"*

There are different ways we deal with our faults, and until we do, neither God nor man will forget them. This verse shows a proud and defensive way, which lashes out at others instead of facing guilt. Abner showed, before he killed Asahel, that he didn't want to kill him, saying "Stop chasing me! Why should I strike you down? How could I look your brother Joab in the face?" (2:22 – NIV). His life may have been spared if he had confessed the whole story to Joab. We all carry "secret faults" (Ps. 19:12) from time to time, and may try by good deeds to make up for them, instead of confessing them to the offended parties. But unconfessed sins don't go away and bitterness begins to grow in the heart of the offended one. Abner may have thought all would be forgotten if he surrendered to David, but Joab carried the grudge, and killed him in the same way his brother was killed. God also will punish our sins according to justice: "eye for eye", unless it can be paid for by an equal price which God has determined. Now that Christ has died in our place, no other price will be accepted. If we come to God saying, "Am I a dog's head that you charge me with a fault, seeing all the works I've done?", God's wrath will still burn against our sin and there will be no escape from his judgment. Abner lost his life for having that attitude. An even worse scenario appears in the next chapter, when two men kill Ish-Bosheth in bed and expect a reward for it from David. Instead, David had these wicked men killed, as he did with Saul's supposed slayer (4:10). Jesus said, "A time is coming when anyone who kills you will think he is offering a service to God" (John 16:2 - NIV). Bad news on Judgment Day!

A fault confessed is half redressed.

A Gift Foot In The Mouth

(6:16)   ...and she despised him in her heart.

David's wife Michal had been through a lot with him, even helping to save his life, and she knew him quite well. She knew his character, and how well he had behaved before her father, Saul. But still, even after being brought back as David's wife, she now "despised him in her heart". He that is careful not to judge others "thinketh no evil" (1 Cor. 13:5). If someone does something that even <u>appears</u> questionable, we should assume at first sight that there is some good reason that we don't know about, instead of passing judgment. Michal was judged and made childless for life because of her rash judgment. How a person is moved to worship God in his heart or actions is to be judged by God only, so we should be careful about judging people for dancing or otherwise expressing emotion before God. David's offering of praise to God was acceptable to God, but despised by Michal, who was not in the place to judge it. It was not done for her, but for God. Sometime later, David chose to "show kindness" to one of Saul's surviving descendants (9:1), and to Hanun, son of Nahash, king of Ammon (10:2). "Don't look a gift horse in the mouth" means don't judge the quality or intention of a gift given to you (don't check if the horse has good teeth, if it was given as a gift!). Hanun did this, and was judged for it. Mephibosheth could hardly believe it, but he humbly and gratefully accepted David's offer, and received the grace of God through him. David, by the way, didn't judge Saul's family for their father's sins, and was blessed by God for it. Assume the best and not the worst about people, and be blessed by their gifts.

Judge not, that ye be not judged. (Mt. 7:1)

THE PERFECT CRIME

(11:27)   But the thing that David had done displeased the Lord.

No kidding! What an understatement! This was for adultery and murder, done to one of David's most faithful men, but necessary in the Bible, that we may know that any sin can be forgiven if we truly repent and turn away from sin, and pay back what we can. As soon as David repented (12:13), God had already forgiven him, as though to say, "I knew you would repent, but you will be punished still, though you won't die". Nothing surprises God. In fact, he knows it all before it happens, and in even more exact a statement, he pre-plans it for his own glory. So, how did this work for God's glory? First, it was David's "thorn in the flesh", to keep pride from ever again surfacing. Also, it shows that no matter how much God anoints somebody, it is still our nature to sin, if God removes his Spirit for a moment. If we are truly born again, we will repent and be broken. Third, nobody is so important that God won't hate our sin: nobody is indispensable! Fourth, there is no "perfect crime"; God sees it all, and will bring judgment sooner or later (better now, than on the Judgment Day!). Lastly, God is glorified because we see, as always, that only God is truly righteous, and not we. The Bible is a history of real people, but more than that it is about God. Nobody shines like God in the Bible, and man's sin is a constant reminder of that. God oversees all things and judges righteously. Maybe the only perfect crime is that the perfect Son of God suffered and died to pay for our crimes, so that we, the imperfect, could "get away with murder", and still be declared righteous because of his grace to all who will believe the good news.

Fear follows crime, and is its punishment.

LOVE TURNED TO HATRED

(13:15)   Then Amnon hated her ... more than he had loved her. (NIV)

That is what happens with feelings, when you let them rule your life. Amnon was only overcome with lust, not love, so it is wrong to elevate this evil act with such a good word. True love would never have forced itself on another. Amnon ruined Tamar's life by this act, which could have been redeemed had he married her. This is how our feelings go with all sin. We are strongly attracted by it, and it looks like something we really want to do, but in the end it brings revulsion, and separation from God. Then we hate it more than we loved it. We must learn from this process to overcome it, not to continually give in to its desires. Sin always ruins somebody. God gave us feelings that we must use for his glory, and love is only good in the context of marriage, not for adultery. God's love drove him to save us from ruin, not to ruin us. Satan tempts us, and then hates us and ruins our lives, having never wanted anything good for us. Our hatred against sin should be greater than our love for it. The stark contrast of Amnon's attitudes before and after his act make it all the more hideous. We are tempted to hate him, but be careful! God puts these real characters and situations in the Bible to show us the evil of our own sins, and to turn us back to reason. Like the spoiled child in George MacDonald's story of "The Wise Woman", we judge ourselves when we judge others. She shouted at the other girl who was copying her, and as she began to pull her hair, she found herself pulling her own! We must continue to hate sin and turn from it, and then we will be able to lovingly turn others from sin and back to God.

Love must be sincere. (Rom. 12:9 – NIV)

FAKING OBEDIENCE

(14:32) "...and if there be any iniquity in me, let him kill me".

In the next verse, Absolom "bowed himself on his face to the ground before the king", while his heart was planning to steal the kingdom away from his father David, and maybe even to kill him. Absolom "stole the hearts of the men of Israel" (15:6) – How? By an outward show of submission, while his heart was planning wickedness. Such treachery and trickery makes us sick, and how much more must it make God sick, who sees the evil in men's hearts daily! Sacrifice is an outward act, but obedience is a heart attitude. Anyone can pray, give alms, read scripture, bow in submission, and otherwise look holy on the outside, but only a heart change can remove the sin from our nature. Judas stated, along with the other disciples, that the "ointment might have been sold for much, and given to the poor" (Mt. 26:9), but such an outward sacrifice is only to make us look good before men if the heart is not right. He sold the Savior, since he couldn't profit from the ointment, and sacrificed a kiss, to look good to men. Absolom also won the people's hearts with his fake kisses. In his heart was no love, but revenge and lust for power. Our heart attitudes don't show until we act on them. His bowing "on his face to the ground" was a thin mask of deceit to cover his rebellious heart. He could "steal the hearts of men", but nobody can steal God's heart, who alone can judge men's hearts. When Hazael stood before Elisha, the prophet wept, knowing his wicked future, and would have wept before Judas and Absolom, had he been there. Jesus' sacrifice was acceptable only because of his obedience, and we will be judged by our hearts, not just actions.

**You are always on their lips, but far
from their hearts.** (Jer. 12:2 – NIV)

MAY THE BEST MAN WIN

(17:14)   *"The counsel of Hushai … is better than the counsel of Ahithophel".*

Clever men may use their cunning for evil or for good. The need today, as always, is not for more brains, but for wisdom that is submitted to God. Intelligent men discovered nuclear energy, but how we use it now is the important question. Will we serve humanity with it by creating nuclear power plants (and even then, will we take the time to make them safe), or will we make atomic bombs to escalate hatred and the lust for power in the world? Ahithophel was the wisest of counsellors to David, but he defected to Absalom's rebellion. Hushai was not as wise, but was better because of God's control of his life. "Now the serpent was more subtil than any beast of the field" (Gen. 3:1), but he was not the best. God made him and God cursed him for his wrong use of being clever. "The fear of the Lord is the beginning of knowledge, but fools despise wisdom and instruction" (Pr. 1:7). Clever men can gain power and worldly riches, but there is a day of judgment coming when their cleverness will not help them. Absalom was clever, but was motivated by evil desires, so David proved to be the better man, as he did with Saul. Solomon was clever enough to ask God for wisdom to guide Israel, but he was not the best. He excelled all others in the world for wisdom, and gained power, peace and prosperity through it, but he was not the best, as he made unwise choices that led to the division of Judah and Israel. Ahithophel was no doubt clever, but Hushai was submitted to God and to King David, even when David was apparently losing his kingdom. My prayer for the court battle over the control of the schools in Srinagar is "May the best man (or woman) win".

Clever men are good, but they are not the best.

BUT DEAD MEN

(19:28) *"All of my father's house were but dead men before my lord the king".*

...yet didst thou set thy servant among them that did eat at thine own table." Mephibosheth speaks for all of us before God. We are all "but dead men", deserving death for our rebellion against God, and it is only the grace of God that took us instead to eat at his own table, among those he loves. Ziba, his servant, is still fighting and conniving over some land, but Mephibosheth says, "Let him take all", because all his joy is in David being with him, and returned as king. God's grace alone can bring about this attitude in us sinners. We were all on our way to God's judgment, and lame from sin, unable to help ourselves. If we are still coveting and striving for something more, we have not been broken by the love of God. Mephibosheth's attitude is proof enough of a work of grace in his life. Jesus said, "It is better for you to enter life maimed or crippled" (Mt. 18:8 - NIV), Better for Mephibosheth than for Ziba, because as a lame man he sees his true state before God. Ziba is like Martha, striving for approval, while Mary sat at Jesus' feet. "Set your affection on things above, not on things on the earth, for ye are dead..." (Col. 3:2,3). Only when we see ourselves as truly dead can God raise us up to heaven. We were "dead in trespasses and sins" (Eph. 2:1), but now, "...reckon ye also yourselves to be dead indeed unto sin, but alive unto God..." (Rom. 6:11). True, we were accounted as dead men, but now we are to choose to reckon ourselves as "crucified with Christ", and yet alive to God (Gal. 2:20), and dead to sin.

Take the whole world, but give me Jesus.

CHASING THE GIANT

(21:17)   *"Thou shalt go no more out with us to battle..."*

David tried that once before, and it was the occasion of his sins of adultery and murder. Now, his own men said he should stay back, being the "light of Israel". This word is the beginning of the end for David, when he ceased to be the giant killer, and had to stay back after one (giant) tried to kill him. Death comes closer every day for each of us, regardless of whether we are weak or strong, rich or poor. We are all expendable, and will all die, no matter how many plans we think we must finish. Contrast this with Jesus' death: when he knew it was his time to die, he spoke of it plainly. When Peter said, "This shall not be unto thee!" (Mt. 16:22), Jesus rebuked him and "stedfastly set his face to go to Jerusalem" (Lk. 9:51), to his death. Like David when he was younger, and first faced a giant called Goliath, he "hasted, and ran toward the army to meet the Philistine" (1 Sam. 17:48). Death waits for nobody, and if we are afraid of it, it will take us by surprise. So, should we run towards death? To do so, if we are not prepared, is worse than suicide. There is no honor with God to die, as a pilot in a "kamikaze" raid, or in a "jihad", if our sins are not dealt with beforehand. On the "other hand", to shirk from death when we are afraid is a living death, and we may as well *be* dead. What is the solution? Jesus went steadfastly to his death because he knew he was about to conquer it, as David did with Goliath. When we confess our sins and our need of a Savior, Christ comes to live in our hearts, by faith, and we need not fear death. Death will not wait for us to get ready. We must do that before death comes, not when it overtakes us, and it is eternally too late.

Time and tide wait for no man.

THE BLUEPRINT

(23:5) "Is not my house right with God?" (NIV)

These "last words of David" are based upon a firm foundation: that God has "made with me an everlasting covenant, ordered in all things". In construction, a house is only as strong as its foundation, and a wise builder will never build without a plan. David is speaking of his whole life, his family and fortune, and their future security. His life was about to end, and his concern is with what will follow after him. Moses said, "Lord, thou hast been our dwelling place in all generations" (Ps. 90:1). Those who build without God in their lives are building on a foundation of sand (Mt. 7:26-7). They may amass great riches, but "a sinner's wealth is stored up for the righteous" (Pr. 13:22), and that is not wise planning. Each of us has a life to live, and we cannot blame the end of it on any other person, or on our caste, or religion, or sex, or financial status at birth. God will judge each of us for what we have done with the "talents" (Mt. 25:15) he has given us, whether one or many. Is *your* "house right with God"? How do you know? What plan is it based on, and are you sure you can trust the architect? Followers of Jim Jones years ago took poison and ended their lives because they trusted his words, but God will not blame Jim Jones for their deaths. They were personally responsible for having chosen to trust him. God has given "an everlasting covenant, ordered in all things" as a blueprint for each of us to build from. If we deviate from it, God won't be responsible for our consequence – we will. We should trust in the architect of all things, who has made us in his own creative image, and has made us our own architects, for better or worse.

Every man is the architect of his own fortune.

ONE SMALL REQUEST

(2:16, 20)   and now I ask one petition of thee, deny me not.

The "foot in the door" method always asks for "one small request", and Pandora's Box follows! When Bathsheba becomes the unwitting message bearer for Adonijah's treacherous request, Solomon wisely and rightly says, "ask for him the kingdom also" This is how Satan took the authority from Adam, by a small request, and attempted the same with Jesus, using three "small petitions" or temptations. Small petitions sound so innocent, but a wise man will expose the sin at its inception. A small court case in an obscure town is all that is needed to establish a precedent to overthrow a big law, or topple a government! Adonijah says "the kingdom was mine", showing his covetous attitude, and lack of repentance. Unrepentant sinners try to arrange "deals", and ask petitions, playing on emotions to get their evil ends. Haman's "petition" (Esth. 3:8-9) would have destroyed all the Jews, so Esther made her petition, and Haman ended as Adonijah did – killed for his evil request. "Deny me not" is how we try to get a commitment before we tell our "small request". So, James and John (Mk. 10:35) ask Jesus, "We would that thou shouldest do for us whatsoever we shall desire"(!) "Do not refuse me" is a warning bell to the wise. The Jews often came with "small petitions" to Jesus, to trap him, but he "perceived their wickedness" (Mt. 22:18). Sometimes, when their ancestors made selfish demands, God "gave them their request, but sent leanness into their soul" (Ps. 106:15). But don't bank on this – an evil and covetous attitude will bring destruction, if we don't repent of it.

**If I regard iniquity in my heart, the
Lord will not hear me.** (Ps. 66:18)

DIVIDE THE CHILD

(3:25)　Divide the living child in two, and give half to the one, and half to the other.

Although we recoil in horror at this pronouncement, one woman actually agreed! Wisdom showed she couldn't be the real mother. Anyway, what good is another dead baby to anyone? In marriage, Jesus said, "... a man will leave his father and mother and be united to his wife, and the two will become one flesh. So they are no longer two, but one. Therefore, what God has joined together, let man not separate" (Mt. 19:5,6 - NIV). So, divorce is like cutting a live baby in half, and expecting all to be fine. The law says, "If a man's bull injures the bull of another and it dies, they are to sell the live one and divide both the money and the dead animal equally" (Ex. 21:35 - NIV). To divide a dead bull is one thing, but a live baby is something else. To some, a divorce is just dividing up a dead ox and a bunch of possessions. But what do you do with a child? Divide him in half? Give him to one or the other? And what about a person who does not want a divorce? Divide his heart in two pieces? Solomon's wise judgment brought about justice, because at least the real mother had a heart. The other belongs in an insane asylum! At least, she is not a fit mother. And a society that doesn't recoil in horror at divorce is headed for destruction; it is a sign of the end of sanity. God, like Solomon, gives us over to the results of our sin if we choose to divide the baby in half. True Christians should say, "Let the other have his way instead of destroying a life". Abortion is just as selfish: destroy the innocent child instead of admitting you have sinned, and living out the consequences.

Heads I win, tails you lose.

PRIORITIES

(7:1)   But Solomon was building his own house thirteen years.

The word "but" shows the writer's feeling about this: the Lord's temple took seven years (6:38). Isn't there something wrong with this picture? It shows where Solomon's real priorities were. Shouldn't his desire to build God a house (a good desire) show his love for God to be greater than his love for himself? Now, forever in the Bible's pages, is the statement that he spent twice as much time on his own beautiful home. No doubt, he needed quite a house for 700 wives and 300 concubines, but isn't that also a little beyond his humble needs? A similar picture for me is to see at the end of a year how much I've spent for God's work, and how much on personal things. Or, how much time in a day do I spend with God, in prayer, Bible study, witnessing or other 'Kingdom pursuits'? Once again, no doubt the temple was magnificent – "exceeding magnifical" in the KJV ($3 billion in gold), but once a man decides to make himself a name in history by being the one to build God a house, the project should be his crowning achievement, as it is represents his love for God. Once I decide to serve God, nothing else should take even a "close second" to my service to God, let alone to supersede it. Building a beautiful "church" (really, only Jesus could ever do that!) is meant to honor God, but what will the world think of a "man of God" spending even more of poor people's faith offerings to then build a bigger mansion for himself? Vanity? No wonder God told David "You are not the one to build me a house to dwell in…I declare to you that the Lord will build a house for you" (1 Chron. 17:4,10b - NIV).

**Except the Lord build the house, they
labor in vain that build it.** (Ps. 127:1)

ISRAEL SHALL BE A PROVERB

(9:7) *"...and Israel shall be a proverb, and a byword among all people"*

The church, or God's people, or any nation that represents the God of the Bible, can also fit this scripture. The United States of America, for example, is known the world over as God's nation of Christians. It started out as such, for the sake of religious freedom, and still has "In God we trust" printed on its money, but because it has (*as a nation*) forsaken God and his precepts, and has turned to other gods, it is today in danger of being forsaken by God. Last week I cut out a news clipping from "USA Today": "Commandments Banned from US Courthouses". When we turn from God's Commandments, God will turn from us. Americans may say "that will never happen", but greater nations by far have seen the same – and USA will be joining that list of proverbs. "Like Sodom and Gomorrah" is a proverb we use when a city becomes wicked and is due for judgment. But soon they will say, "Like the USA" when judgment falls there (if America does not turn its face back to God in humble repentance). "Babylon the great is fallen, is fallen..." (Rev. 18:2) will be a proverb applied to any nation that falls because of its prideful turning away from God. But especially Israel, the one nation chosen by God, has seen the fulfillment of this in history: "The Wandering Jews" finally came back to Israel in 1948, after the horrors of the "Holocaust" (ironically, the name commonly applied to a wholesale slaughter, which means "Whole Burnt Offering"). They were a byword to all the people, until they were humbled by their God. Take heed!

**...Judgment must begin at the
house of God...** (1 Pet. 4:17)

WISE COUNSEL

(12:8)   *But he forsook the counsel of the old men.*

This is Rehoboam, a son of Solomon, the wisest man on earth, who wrote all the proverbs on "hear[ing] the instruction of thy father", and addressed to "my son". Solomon also said "A soft answer turneth away wrath: but grievous words stir up anger" (Pr. 15:1). Solomon labored very hard to bring the kingdom of Israel to its zenith in every way, but despaired "because I must leave them to the one who comes after me. And who knows whether he will be a wise man or a fool?" (Pr. 2:18-19 - NIV). The old men "... stood before Solomon his father while he yet lived" (12:6), and gave godly, wise counsel, but Rehoboam rejected their counsel for that of his young friends. Why? "The cause was from the Lord" (v. 15). What lessons do we learn from this? "Remove not the ancient landmark, which thy fathers have set" (Pr. 22:28); "...Fools despise wisdom and instruction" (Pr. 1:7); and "Likewise, ye younger, submit yourselves unto the elder" (1 Pet. 5:5). Notice also: Solomon himself (!) was guilty of forsaking good counsel, that of his elders, who taught him not to multiply wives and riches, thereby falling into a snare. David wrote, "Blessed is the man that walketh not in the counsel of the ungodly..." (Ps. 1:1). So, both Solomon and his son Rehoboam sadly had rejected "the counsel of the old men". "Remember the days of old, consider the years of many generations: Ask thy father and he will shew thee; thy elders, and they will tell you" (Deut. 32:7). Wisdom comes with age! As a nation, we should return to the God of our fathers, or we may become an historical object lesson for future generations of what becomes of a nation that forgets God. Let the gospel be our "smart bomb".

Education is the chief defense of nations.

SODOMITES IN THE LAND

(14:24)   And there were also Sodomites in the land...

...and they did according to all the abominations of the nations which the Lord cast out before the children of Israel. "Homosexuals" don't like the term, but this is what the Bible calls them: "Sodomites". Actually, the term denoted male temple prostitutes, devoted to the 'gods' or demons that inspire such perversions. This verse gives insight into why God commands the Israelites to go in and destroy men, women and children of all the Canaanites (Amorites, etc.). It is not that the children were also involved already with these abominations, but rather that, *as a nation*, God was showing his anger against their perversions and sins and idolatry. Truthfully, we have very little feeling of the intensity of God's hatred for sin. God was showing his nature, not the goodness and righteousness of Israel, but <u>his</u> righteousness. The vivid picture of whole people groups being wiped out shows us how much God hates <u>our</u> sin! In light of this, the question is not "How can God destroy these people?", but rather, "How can God not destroy <u>me</u> for my sins?" Maybe an alternate reading could be: "And there were also sins in <u>my life</u>, according to all the abominations that caused God to destroy Sodom and Gomorrah", (or some other judgment of God). Beware! "For if God spared not the angels that sinned... And spared not the old world... bringing in the flood upon the world of the ungodly... and turning the cities of Sodom and Gomorrah into ashes..." (2 Pet. 2:4-6), then if he finds "Sodomites" – if he finds defiant and uncontrolled sin in my life – he will also destroy me. Repent and turn to God!

Do not judge, or you too will be judged.

SHOOT THE MOON

(15:19)   There is a league between me and thee,
and between my father and thy father…

Sometimes the best way to defeat an enemy is to "pull the rug out from under him", so you can see his true colors. In a card game called "hearts", one can win a hand either by taking no points (or the least number of points), or by taking all the points; it is then counted as zero, or "shooting the moon". If I feel someone else may try for "the moon", I can call his bluff, if he is trying to appear to have a bad hand, by taking one or more points in a "trick", so that he cannot take all points. King Asa attacked back against Baasha, king of Israel, not by a frontal attack, but by testing his weak point, and by this he "won the trick". We are all fighting a clever enemy, the devil, who keeps us feeling secure, as if he were doing nothing, until it is too late. But, as soon as we take a trick, by becoming Christians, suddenly his plan is exposed and we see he is fighting against us, trying to shoot the moon and make us lose our salvation. Fortunately, although he has made a league with us through Adam's sin and our own, there is a previous league standing, which we can call upon for help. Christ made a treaty with us and our forefathers, by faith in the blood of the Messiah. Nothing else will call off his attack on us but this; and suddenly we see how cleverly he has been plotting our downfall, when we didn't even know we were in a battle! Like crossing a street and walking the other way, when we think we are being followed, this calls his bluff, so the enemy will be exposed, and will call off his attack.

When in doubt, win the trick.

A HANDFUL OF MEAL

(17:12)   *...to make a meal for myself and my son,*
         that we may eat it – and die. (NIV)

This is the point to which God must bring us, so that we can understand we need him. Not only that, but Elijah still asks of her that first she give to him, as God had directed him, to really put her in the faith realm. Like the four lepers during Elisha's time (2 Kings 7:3-10), who were ready to die, there is almost a comedy to the scene, as we the readers know how close they are to God's answer. The widow's answer is not the worldly "eat and drink, for to-morrow we die" (Isa. 22:13) attitude, but a pathetic resignation to her hopeless condition. She was probably at the point of tears, as Elijah asks her to share her last meal with him. But as the request came, along with it was a promise, which she believed. "A handful of meal", and a son to share it with, then her son died! When Jesus comes to us, through the gospel message, it is not to "take our last meal", but to give us eternal life. But, unless we are ready to forsake all we have, we cannot follow him. In fact, it will cost us our life, not just our last possessions. But as we die, we are raised again to new life, and can say, "Now by this I know that thou art a man of God, and that the word of the Lord in thy mouth is truth" (17:24). Only God can resurrect us to new life. What he asks of us is nothing compared to what he has to give. But, to us, it is our last meal, and the last of our earthly hope. It must all go, that God will be glorified. Jim Elliot's quote seems appropriate: "That man is no fool who gives what he cannot keep, to gain what he cannot lose!" He did, and he did.

Give, and it shall be given unto you... (Luke 6:38)

WHO'S HOLDING WHOM?

(19:18)   Yet I have left me 7,000 in Israel, all the
knees which have not bowed to Baal...

God's answer to "I only am left" is that it is he who is responsible if we, or anybody else, remains faithful to him. Elijah had lots of works and miracles to commend his faith to God, as did Paul the Apostle, along with much learning, family lineage, and outward obedience to God's laws. But Paul counted "all things but loss... that I may win Christ" (Phil. 3:4-8). Paul spoke of the virtues of "faith, hope and love" (1 Cor. 13:13 - NIV) being the most enduring of all virtues, but what would even these be if they were withheld at our will? God's love is constant and "never faileth", and if our faith, hope or love fails, it is not founded in God, but in our striving to attain favor and not making it. Like all of God's commandments, when we understand how perfection is the requirement, we must throw up our hands and say, "I can't do it!" Elijah was ready to give up and die, feeling he was the only faithful man of God left. But, constancy is not only a necessary part of virtues, it is their foundation. When we see Jesus, and how constant (even to death!) he was in his love for us, it becomes the strong foundation for us to continue on in hard times. Elijah had been constant, but was at the limit of human endurance. He needed to be refreshed by a new glimpse of how constant God's protection for his people is. Because God assures us in both old and new testaments (Dt. 31:6, Heb. 13:5) that he will never fail, it is a strong foundation for our faith (2 Tim 2:13), our hope that is secure in heaven (Heb. 6:19), and our love for God and his people (1 Jn. 4:19). When these are founded on God's promises, we also can never fail.

Constancy is the foundation of virtues.

UNDER COVER AGENTS

(22:30) And the king of Israel disguised himself, and went into the battle.

King Ahab was an evil man and a coward. He was dominated in his life by Jezebel, whose name is synonymous with evil. His life is devoid of any truly noble deeds, and when he did repent, it was with a show of humility before God, that people could see. His disguise in battle was no noble deed, but an act of cowardice, so he wouldn't be a target; and, he was killed, anyway. Jehoshaphat did his noble deed of helping Ahab, openly dressed in royal robes, and had to flee to escape death; a noble attempt, but a shameful retreat. About the only noble deed at all in these chapters is that of Micaiah the prophet, who dared to speak the truth in the midst of two kings and four hundred hostile prophets of Jezebel. First, he concealed the truth, believing that only "reverse psychology" could get through to King Ahab. He couldn't win anyway, as he was instructed to "tell only the truth" while the king felt "he doesn't ever prophesy good, but only evil to me". For him, it was nobler to conceal the truth to try to save Ahab! "A man that flattereth his neighbor spreadeth a net for his feet" (Pr. 29:5); that is what the other prophets did, but Micaiah is to be commended for wisely concealing the truth, so Ahab would listen. He was brave enough to go to prison, then, for speaking the truth. Jesus did the noblest deed of all time. He could have broadcast his mission and had a great earthly following, but he concealed who he was from all but his closest disciples, so that he could be the savior of the world. Let us also be brave enough to live and die for the gospel, not looking for popularity, but suffering in secret, if necessary, that others may be saved.

Noble deeds that are concealed are most esteemed.

BRAVE FAITH

(1:15) *"Go down with him: be not afraid of him."*

James 5:17 says, "Elijah was a man just like us" (NIV). Faith is a funny thing: in a sense, it is easier to call down fire from heaven to destroy those who are opposed to God's kingdom, than go down and face them. Jesus said it is easy for a man with only a mustard seed of faith to call for a tree to be thrown into the sea, and that it is from another spirit (besides God's) to just call down fire upon those who don't listen to us (Luke 17:6 & 9:51-6). We may feel it is a sign of great faith to speak and see fire from heaven, but God considers it greater faith to face our enemies when it may mean suffering or death for us. God's prophets have always been men of courage, and "wimps" need not apply. When Elijah was about to be taken to heaven, Elisha asked for a double portion of his spirit (and of his faith, no doubt!). The condition was "if thou see me when I am taken from thee" (2:10), and it may have been a fearful thing, but he followed him to the place of his fiery chariot, and got his double portion, doing twice the recorded miracles of Elijah. When Elisha asked "Where is the Lord God of Elijah?" as he stood alone with only the cloak of Elijah in his hand, what he really asked is, "How do I get God's presence into my life, as Elijah had?" Jesus told his disciples they would do "greater works" if they believed in him. His condition: to follow him to his death. Most of these disciples ran from him on the night of his betrayal, but after his resurrection, they certainly did follow him to his death. Do you want to be a man "full of faith and power" (Acts 6:8) like Stephen, who "did great wonders and miracles among the people"? Be a man or woman of courage, and follow footsteps.

A man of courage is also full of faith.

SOMEWHERE OVER THE RAINBOW

(4:2)   ...tell me, what hast thou in the house?

When faith, the essential ingredient for receiving anything from God, is present, we don't have to look far for the answer to our needs. God asked Moses, "What is that in thine hand?" (Ex. 4:2) and used his rod as the means of performing miracles. Likewise, God used this woman's oil as the answer to her financial need. By faith, Elisha called for some flour that was on hand to heal the "death in the pot". Naaman was told to dip seven times in the Jordan to be healed of his leprosy, not because it was any better than the rivers in Damascus, but because it was <u>there</u>! Elisha used a nearby stick cut from a tree to make the ax head float. When the city of Dothan was surrounded, he didn't have to call for Egyptian troops, but simply prayed for his servant's eyes to be opened, to see the great company of heavenly troops at their disposal. As the great famine developed in Samaria God didn't open the "windows of heaven" (7:19), but brought the answer out of the very troops that caused the famine, frightening them away, and having Israel spoil them without a fight! This pattern is seen throughout Jesus' miracles, as he asks "Whence shall we buy bread, that these may eat?" (Jn. 6:5) and then multiplies the boy's loaves and fish, or tells Peter to pull up a fish, to pay for their temple tax, by taking the money from its mouth. Loren Cunningham, founder and president of YWAM, says that the ability to answer any need is always present within the context of the need. Why not? God only waits for us to acknowledge him as Lord over our lives, and he will supply all we need, just like Dorothy and the ruby slippers, and a word of faith.

Ability and necessity dwell near each other.

CANNIBALISM

(6:29)   *"So we boiled my son, and did eat him".*

Much more shocking than the action is the attitude! All she is concerned about is her next meal, not that she boiled and ate her own son. If the idea of eating another human being is hard to swallow, what about when it happens to be your own son? How can people sink to this level of depravity? It fulfills the prophecies (Lev. 26:29, Deut. 28:53,57) of what will happen when people forsake the true God. It should shock the people into repentance, but instead we see Israel's king blaming Elisha, because of the results of Israel's sins. In the same way, the people today blame God for their problems, or blame preachers when their warnings come to pass. We must all be careful – we can stoop to any level of depravity if we begin to turn our backs on God's law. Sin starts by small decisions and grows rapidly if we fail to repent. But cannibalism with your own son!? Again, the shocker is the attitude – if we are not appalled at sin in small stages, we will be unconcerned when it gets absolutely disgusting. God knows we are capable of any kind of evil, as soon as he removes his grace and outward restraints. The wise Christian will walk very humbly with the knowledge that he is only kept from great transgressions by God's power and mercy (Ps. 19). Paul writes in his letter to the Corinthians (1 Cor. 10:11): "Now all these things happened unto them for ensamples: and they are written for our admonition, upon whom the ends of the world are come". Let us learn from history, and know our own wickedness.

Pride comes before a fall.

SIN APPEARS BEAUTIFUL

*(9:30) ...Jezebel... painted her eyes, arranged her
hair & looked out of a window. (NIV)*

What a picture: here is Jezebel, the epitome of sin, trying to "look good" and maybe entice away the righteous anger that is coming to destroy her. Sin is like this when, by the grace of God, we have had enough and decide to rid ourselves of it. Suddenly we will be tempted by all of its charms again and, if possible, the devil will again ensnare us with it. But, to a spiritually minded person, sin will look like a cheap and pitiable prostitute with too much gaudy eye and face makeup. When we see Christ's righteousness and get a taste of it, all of sin and its gaudy makeup will be disgusting to us. Then we can throw Jezebel down with no feeling of guilt. Sin has made its decision: it is evil and is out to destroy us, and must be thrown out and destroyed by us instead. Don't be swayed by its façade of beauty. Idols may look beautiful, but within their outward gold and silver is the power to destroy man. We must decide to love God and hate sin, no matter how beautiful it appears to our flesh. Peter tells Christian wives not to be adorned with "braided hair and the wearing of gold jewelry and fine clothes" (1 Pet. 3:3-4 - NIV), but to have a heart of submission to God, to her husband, and to all godly authority. When we know the inner beauty of a "gentle and quiet spirit" (NIV), the beauty of Jezebel will be repulsive to us, and we can throw it to the dogs where it belongs. "Charm is deceptive, and beauty is fleeting [and sin is deceitful]; but a woman who fears the Lord is to be praised. Give her the reward she has earned" (Prov. 31:30-31 - NIV) and let Jezebel be given the reward she deserves!

Beauty is only skin deep; ugly is to the bone.

ZEAL WITHOUT KNOWLEDGE

(10:16)   And he said, "Come with me, and see my zeal for the Lord."

A few verses later we read, "But Jehu took no heed to walk in the law of the Lord God of Israel with all his heart" (10:31). In Proverbs we read, "It is not good to have zeal without knowledge, nor to be hasty and miss the way" (Pr. 19:2 - NIV). If the foundation of repentance, based on conviction of personal sin and weakness, is not there, we will be failures in God's sight, no matter how zealous we are before men. We can detect a bit of pride here, too: "Come and see my zeal'" which shows an underlying problem. Any carnal man may destroy temples and idols, (as Hindu zealots did against Muslims at Ayodhya), or call down fire from heaven (Lk. 9:54). But be careful! Many boasting of works will hear Jesus say "I never knew you!" (Mt. 7:23). The story of Mary and Martha (Lk. 10:38-42) shows that it is more important to know God than to work hard. In a simple sense, "zeal without knowledge" would be an apt description of Ahimaaz (2 Sam. 18:22), who had the zeal to run, but no knowledge of what to report when he got there; but the greater problem is having no knowledge of the true God who judges the heart. Paul speaks of the Jews: "For I bear them record that they have a zeal for God, but not according to knowledge" (Rom. 10: 1-3). Is it any advantage to us to run if we don't even know the message? Jehu was zealous about destroying infidels, thinking he was doing God's work, but he didn't know God's heart. Muslim zealots succeeded in destroying the twin towers on 9/11, and hoped to win God's favor for punishing a nation of "infidels", but zeal without knowledge will lead to "Depart from me, ye that work iniquity!" (Mt. 7:23).

It is not good to have zeal without knowledge.

FOR HIS OWN SIN

(14:6)   "…but every man shall be put to death for his own sin".

This is echoed by Ezekiel: "The soul that sinneth, it shall die" (Ez. 18:4, 20). But, are we not also judged as guilty through Adam's sin? And the Ten Commandments speak about "…visiting the iniquity of the fathers upon the children unto the third and fourth generation of them that hate me" (Ex. 20:5). Yes, and if we continue in our fathers' sins, we will be judged as guilty, but if we repent, we are no longer under God's wrath. "Put to death" means both physically and spiritually (in the Judgment). "Every man" means all will be judged equally, and since "all have sinned" (Rom. 3:23), all deserve to die. When God "visits the iniquity", he sees it, condemns it and judges it. He "sees" us doing the same as our fathers, and condemns it because it is sin, and judges the unrepentant sinner. We die for our father's (or Adam's) sin because we ourselves are sinners – dead in sin and trespasses. If I don't repent, I will die for my own (many) sins, not for my father's. Amaziah killed those who murdered his father, but not their children, as they were not guilty of that sin. That would be unjust. As Abraham asked God, "Wilt thou also destroy the righteous with the wicked?" No! "Shall not the Judge of all the earth do right?" (Gen. 18:23-5). Yes, and every man who sins will die for *his own* sin. All will die – but Jesus died for no sin of his own – the just for the unjust. He is the only exception, and the only perfect sacrifice for our sin. Every man has been and will be put to death for his own sin, but for that one exception to God's rule. Thank God! "Behold therefore the goodness and severity of God!" (Rom. 11:22).

Mercy triumphs over judgment! (James 2:13)

WASTE NOT WANT NOT

(16:8)   And Ahaz took the silver and gold...and sent it for a present...

This was a bribe given to a king who didn't need any more wealth. It proved to be a waste, in several ways. First, Tiglath-Pileser didn't need it. Secondly, it was not right for Ahaz to give away what was dedicated to God, and thirdly, it didn't work anyway – they still went into captivity. Can we learn something from this? Our lives also belong to God – he is both creator and redeemer of us all, and for any of us to miss heaven is a waste. God's desire is for us to be saved. Unfortunately, many will sell out to the devil for what appears to be terms of peace, but, like the Assyrians, Satan has no intention of quitting with our silver and gold. He wants our souls. Satan will be no richer with our souls because he, too, will be burning. It is also a waste to give him what really belongs to God, and we will only find that our covenant with death has not procured any good for us when it is too late and we lie in torment. So, what shall we do? Don't waste your life, but give it to the one who cared enough to die for you. If Ahaz had turned to God and not to the king of Assyria, God would have saved him. Your life is also valuable to God, enough so that he gave his blood to buy you and me. Don't waste what you have, but give it to God, and don't hold back. Don't give your gold and silver, or your precious soul, to one who hates you. That is waste. Give your life to God for safe keeping.

Willful waste makes woeful want.

BORN (AGAIN) LOSERS

(18:36)   But the people held their peace, and answered him not a word...

Jesus did the same thing, as he was falsely accused and condemned to die, but losing that day meant that he won the whole human race a place in heaven. We don't have to answer every slanderous statement against us – God will be the final judge. This is not weakness, but meekness, or power under control, and knowing who we are in God's eyes, in Christ. "For whosoever will save his life shall lose it: and whosoever will lose his life for my sake shall find it (Mt. 16:25). The "secret" is not in losing our life, but in doing it for Christ's sake. If the Muslim way is to fight to the death for God's honor, then surely the crucifixion does not make logical sense; so, for them, it never happened. How sad! Those who never learn to lose will never win God's favor. God's terms of surrender are simple. He might say it like this: "**I own you**, and all that you possess. Surrender to me your sins and all rights to your life, and admit that you need a savior. All of you, good and bad, belongs to me, so don't try holding anything back. Confess your sins and I will forgive them. Give me the title deed to your whole life and all of your activities, and I will be Lord of you completely." God needs nobody to fight for his honor – he's quite able to do that, without our help. Martin Luther once said, "I would rather defend a lion" (than to try to defend God or his word). These Jews showed real faith in God, by not responding to the taunts of Rabshakeh. It may have seemed like weakness to him, but it was not. It showed their strength was in God, and they were the real winners.

Sometimes the best gain is to lose.

Put Your House In Order

(20:1) ...because you are going to die; you will not recover. (NIV)

Death will come, no matter if we are good or evil. It may be delayed, even after a prophet of God announces from God that I will die soon. Hezekiah, by God's mercy, lived after his own prayer for another 15 years, but three years after his prayer, Manasseh was born, who became the next king at age 12, and very evil. If Hezekiah had simply "put his house in order" by making a will, Manasseh would not have been born, and someone else would have been king. God had his way, no doubt, regardless of these possible changes of history. "Put your house in order" may mean much more than making a will, for any of us. Is my family really following God? Did Hezekiah set Manasseh in order as a child, and if so, how did he end up so bad? Why did Hezekiah cry when he was to die, and not when he heard of the fate of his descendants? It appears that he set his house in order to show it off to the king of Babylon. His physical house was beautiful, and full of treasures, and put in order, but what of the spiritual house of his posterity? Fortunately, even Manasseh repented before his death (2 Chron. 33:10-20), but what about my house? Should I be more concerned with beautiful possessions, or even a will, to make those possessions pass on to my descendants? Or should I be more concerned with the spiritual condition of my children and my wife, so that I may pass on godly seed?

**Put your outdoor work in order and get your
fields ready; after that build your house.**

BLUES BREAKERS

(22:11)   *...when the king had heard the words of the book of the law...*

Josiah was quite a contrast to his grandfather Manasseh. This chapter records that he tore his robes and wept in God's presence (v. 19) as he heard God's law read to him, instead of rebelling against it. His sorrow was not over the punishment, but over how their disregard for God's law hurt God. Paul wrote of two kinds of sorrow, saying "For godly sorrow worketh repentance to salvation not to be repented of: but the sorrow of the world worketh death" (2 Cor. 7:10). The psalmist says, "Rivers of waters run down mine eyes, because they keep not thy law" (Ps. 119:136). Sorrow drives men to act, but even this may be for good or bad reasons. Had Josiah's been the "other" kind of sorrow, he may have done all his acts of tearing down idols to impress God, or to show his sorrow outwardly. Pharisees loved the law, but never repented. Josiah did more than weep and tear at his clothes: he tore down idols, and turned his sorrow into something productive, which brought about a time of revival. Some stay busy just to forget about their sorrows, but Josiah wanted to eradicate the cause of sorrow, which was man's repeated sins against God's holy law. An old blues song said something like this: "When a man is troubled with a worried mind, he just wants to sleep <u>all</u> the time!" But sleep doesn't remove the problem. If you really are sad and want to get over it, <u>get to work</u>! It's the best therapy for "the blues". But get to work at something productive that will cut at the root of the sorrow, and real joy can then return.

Sorrow's best antidote is employment.

SERVE THE KING OF BABYLON

(25:24)   ...dwell in the land, and serve the king of Babylon...

...and it shall be well with you." This almost unbelievable pronouncement came from the prophet Gedaliah (also Jeremiah – 27:12). What else was there to do? They were overpowered, due to their rebellion against God. Some chose to escape to Egypt for rescue, but really each one was running from his own conscience. Babylon was God's answer to people who rejected his authority. To serve this king would mean to choose against his idolatry, and to remember the blessing of serving only God. For those, like Daniel and friends, who served this heathen king without submitting to idolatry, there would be blessing. It would be chastisement, but not annihilation. God had promised a messiah, and those with faith would repent and continue waiting for his coming. We are to be "in the world but not of it" (Jn. 17). "When a man's ways please the Lord, he maketh even his enemies to be at peace with him" (Pr. 16:7), but when we rebel, God uses these enemies to teach us submission to him. Paul commanded (Rom. 13:1): "Let every soul be subject unto the higher powers", and he wrote this to the Romans who were under the wicked and demented Nero. Serve him?! Yes, and "it shall be well with you". Here, in this evil world, Satan is the "king of Babylon", but God has left us here to chastise us, and to form Christ in us. "Stand fast therefore in the liberty wherewith Christ hath made us free, and be not entangled again with the yoke of bondage [to sin] (Gal. 5:1).

Heaven without God would not be heaven.

FORGOTTEN CHILDREN

(3:9)   These were all the sons of David, beside the sons of the concubines...

Not exactly true: there was another son, who is not even named because he died in infancy, the firstborn son of Bathsheba. However, in the book of Chronicles no mention is made of David's sin of adultery, because it is written as an encouragement to the Jews returning from captivity in Babylon. Solomon was God's gift to David, to show his forgiveness after David's repentance. It is an interesting irony that Solomon is known for his wisdom, while the previous unnamed son was the fruit of an idle mind, at a moment of mental weakness in David's life. "Be sober, be vigilant; because your adversary the devil, as a roaring lion, walketh about, seeking whom he may devour" (1 Pet. 5:8). No idleness or weakness in him! He doesn't sleep, or even relax, in his relentless pursuit of his goal of destroying God's work. The best defense against this "roaring lion" is to be sober, vigilant and busy with God's business. Years ago I returned to a discipline of a daily meditation on God's Word, and later on even writing down these "mini sermons", to keep my mind and spirit from growing weak. Idleness in God's Word resulted in so many problems in my life. I had forgotten some of the simplest things that would have been the remedy to the troubles I went through, and can only blame my own laziness for them. A strong mind may be a gift from God, as in Solomon's case, but even he was responsible to cultivate it to keep it sharp. Often, we forget the "sons of our past", the sins that were a result of a momentary lapse into idleness. How easily we remember our famous sons and forefathers; but we should also recall the fruits of idle minds, to remind us not to slip again.

Idleness is only the refuge of a weak mind.

GOD'S SOVEREIGN CHOICE

(5:1)   ...the genealogy is not to be reckoned after the birthright.

God is sovereign in his selection, even in the selection of the lineage of Jesus, the messiah of promise. This verse is a key to understanding God's sovereign choice in salvation. "Birthrights" – the rights that come along with being the firstborn (or often the firstborn son) – do not sway God's choices. David was the last born son, and was chosen as king over his brothers, similar to this case with Joseph. If even David was not chosen by birthright, how can the Jews presume that birthright has anything to do with their own salvation? Abraham, Isaac and Jacob all exercised this - by God's sovereign choice, giving the promise of the genealogy of Christ to other than their firstborn sons (Isaac, not Ishmael; Jacob, not Esau; Judah, not Reuben). "It does not, therefore, depend on man's desire or effort [or birthright!], but on God's mercy"... "in order that God's purpose in election might stand: not by works [or birthright!] but by him who calls..." (Rom. 9:16, 11-12 - NIV). This is a humbling thought to anyone who would presume upon God's mercy: only God decides upon whom to bestow it. Even after Reuben's "birthright was given unto the sons of Joseph" (1 Chron. 5:1), the genealogy was still reckoned as for Judah. Salvation is all of grace; nobody has a corner on it. "Do not be arrogant, but be afraid" (Rom. 11:20 - NIV) – fear God and keep his commandments. By God's sovereign choice, "though Judah was the strongest of his brothers and a ruler came from him, the rights of the firstborn belonged to Joseph" (5:2 - NIV); Ephraim and Manasseh got large portions of land, but not the messiah in their line.

It is the Lord's purpose that prevails. (Pr. 19:21 – NIV)

ZELOPHEHAD HAD HAD
ONLY DAUGHTERS

(7:15)　Another descendant was named Zelophehad, who had only daughters. (NIV)

The number of times this name is repeated in Scripture shows God's loving concern about every detail that troubles us. The story or name appears here, and also in Numbers (26:33, 27:1-11), and in the whole chapter 36:1-12, then again in Joshua (17:3-7). There were five daughters born to Zelophehad, and no sons. This may have been the case for hundreds of other families, but only these five daughters had the faith to do something about it, and it became a law along with the rest of God's commands in the desert. It was done out of honor and respect for their father, in order to keep his name alive, and to preserve for his posterity a right to have and own land. They even went so far as to limit themselves to marrying within their own clan, with their cousins, so that the land would not pass on to another clan or tribe. They could have been just as happy to marry anyone else, but chose to honor their father's name by their choice. Now, their father's name is remembered for all time by those who read Scripture and many who had sons are not remembered at all. The passage in Joshua relates how they followed up on their boldness and faith, and made sure that Joshua gave them the land they requested. If Zelophehad had had only sons, there would be no remembrance of his name at all. The fifth Commandment says "Honor thy father and thy mother: that thy days may be long upon the land which the Lord thy God giveth thee" (Ex. 20:12). These women of faith got to live long in the land given especially to them, because they chose to honor their father. Let us honor God our Father, as well.

Honor thy father and thy mother.

MIGHTY MEN

(11:10)　These also are the chief of the mighty men whom David had...

What would a "mighty man" look like today, and where would we look for him? Possibly in the army, a man of valor like John Wayne portrayed in the movies? Maybe among the men of professional wrestling, or someone like "Rocky" who won against great odds? No doubt David's men were strong, but what made them "mighty" was their great courage and dedication to David, like the three who risked their own blood to get a drink of water for David from behind enemy lines. He didn't even drink it! We used to compliment our brothers in Christ by calling them "mighty men of God", and sisters as "virtuous women" (Pr. 31:10-31), the highest honor to each. Today, "we wrestle not against flesh and blood" (Eph. 6:12); our battles are spiritual, but no less fierce. Now, a "mighty man of God" must be mighty in spirit: not casting down walls (2 Cor. 10:3-6), but imaginations; taking captive our own thoughts, not capturing prisoners, "and having in a readiness to revenge all disobedience, when your obedience is fulfilled". In the world's eyes, the "mighty men" are those who get away with adultery, murder or robbery, and boast in it! (Soap opera "heroes"). But they are slaves to their own sins – weak, not mighty. Today, "if sinners entice thee, consent thou not" (Pr. 1:10, 4:16). Be a mighty man of God! "Why boastest thou thyself in mischief, O mighty man?" (Ps. 52:1). Today, young men, be mighty in spirit, not "mighty in drink" – "their glory is in their shame" (Phil. 3:19 - NIV). Let us take the devil's weapon out of his hand and defeat him with it (11:23). By the might of God's spirit, we can be godly and still "mighty men".

Be strong in the Lord. (Eph. 6:10)

DESPISING GOD'S ANOINTING

(15:29)   ...Michal...saw king David dancing... and she despised him in her heart.

Michal was "looking out at a window", not being part of what was going on. This was a great occasion: the ark finally coming to rest in Zion! Having learned from Uzzah's death for touching the ark, they were now doing everything correctly, and God himself was not angry, but pleased with David's show of emotion and dancing for joy. I myself used to watch as people danced with joyful abandon when the Spirit of God moved upon a gathering of his saints, but I could either watch and despise, or let God's Spirit fill my own heart, and despise the "shame" of my own show of worship. Michal despised David in her heart: not just a chuckle at a childish display of joy but she put herself above him as judge and despised his pure act of worship before God. We must be very careful how we judge in our hearts – God sees it all, and it will surely manifest in an outward act or word of disrespect, and God will judge us for it. How much better to discern correctly what is truly from the Spirit of God. Jesus said to the scribes, "But he that shall blaspheme against the Holy Ghost hath never forgiveness, but is in danger of eternal damnation": Because they said, He hath an unclean spirit. (Mk. 3:29-30). Michal had judged a godly act of worship as something base and unclean, seeing only with her own eyes and sinful heart. We are to be warned here – don't speak evil of God's anointed, and be careful how you judge spiritual things.

Judge not, that ye be not judged. (Mt. 7:1)

HAPPY HOUR

(16:27)   ...strength and gladness are in his place.

It was once explained to me that there is a difference in pleasure, happiness and joy. The first has to do with bodily feelings, like warm sun on the skin. The second is the feeling experienced in the soul when things are going well, but it goes away when things turn against us. Only joy, which belongs to the realm of "fruit of the Spirit", can remain when things are going absolutely wrong for us. So, true joy is probably only possible for those born of God's Holy Spirit. Anyone can be happy or feel pleasure, but joy in the Spirit is reserved for the truly great, those who have hope in God in the midst of trials, and joy in the face of death. Jesus had it: "who for the joy that was set before him, endured the cross" (Heb. 12:2). The "Hebrew" Christians had it and "took joyfully the spoiling of [their] goods" (Heb. 10:34), just as Jesus had instructed his followers (Mt. 5:11-12). Daniel and his three friends didn't lose their joy as they faced lions and a fiery furnace, and were delivered unharmed. Paul and Silas sang songs in jail at midnight, with their backs laid open with cruel whips, and their feet in the stocks. And, Christ's faithful martyrs continue until today, being joyful in their persecutions and executions, at the hands of communists and religious extremists of various other persuasions. Their joy cannot be taken away (Jn. 16:22) because it wells up from deep within their spirits, not subject to bodily pleasure, or "soulish" happiness. They find "strength and gladness are in his place" and can "rejoice and be exceeding glad" (Mt. 5:12) even while being persecuted and killed. They are truly great.

The happy only are the truly great.

FORESHADOW

(22:10)   ...I will establish the throne of his kingdom over Israel forever.

This is a pretty heady promise for Solomon, who was a mortal man, but like many prophecies, it was meant as a fore-shadow of the real fulfillment in Christ. In a sense, a man could begin a dynasty that goes on for generations, but no dynasty on earth has been established forever. People are so prone to sin and corruption that God must intervene and stop their rule at such times. Solomon's kingdom was great, and went on for some generations, according to God's promise, but a "kingdom forever" seemed to be lost during the Babylonian captivity. Still, believing in God's promise, the Jews kept the genealogy of the kingdom throughout their generations, until the coming of Christ. When Jesus came, he spoke of the destruction of the temple, and in the same terms he said "Destroy this temple (his body), and in three days I will raise it up" (Jn. 2:19). According to his word, the temple was destroyed in A.D. 70 by the Roman army under a commander named Titus, and all records were destroyed with it. Had God's promise to Solomon failed? No, it was only a shadow of the real promise. Christ died and rose again, never to die again, and he is the "son", the "man of rest", who built the real house of God, not with stones or gold, but with eternal human souls, bought not with silver and gold, but with his precious, incorruptible blood. He became the true "Solomon" ("Prince of Peace") whose kingdom will never end. Solomon had a kingdom that outshined all other kingdoms, and built a temple worth more than 5 billion dollars of gold and silver, but it was only a shadow of God's kingdom to come.

Coming events cast their shadows before.

FOR TOMORROW WE DIE

(23:1)　So when David was old and full of days...

At that point in my life, what will I do, and how will I feel about my life? David "made Solomon his son king over Israel", to hopefully carry on whatever he could not accomplish in his lifetime. At the end of life, it will be too late to think "I should have spent more time doing this instead of wasting my time on that". Whatever Solomon was by this time, there was no more time for David to spend preparing him to be king, and fortunately he was a very good one, except for his idolatry later on. Jesus, Stephen, John the Baptist and many others in the Bible never lived to be "old and full of days", but they lived lives that counted for God's Kingdom. We must try also to live daily as though today may be our last, and we won't have to be anxious at the end of life. Procrastinators say "Never put off for tomorrow what you can do the day after", but wise people will succeed in life by their planning each day, getting priorities fixed, and having goals set. "Only one life, it will soon be past; only what's done for Christ will last". Can I say, like Paul at the end of his life, "I have fought a good fight, I have finished my course, I have kept the faith" (2 Tim. 4:7)? I have already wasted much of my life in things that were not important, and I've done wrong to people who have died, so I'll never be able to ask their forgiveness. While others still live, I will make every attempt to go to them and make things right. While I am still relatively "young and full of days", I will try my best to not put off for tomorrow what I can do today. Life is too short to waste!

Lost time is never gained again.

MAN O' WAR

(28:3) ...thou hast been a man of war, and hast shed blood.

David, for all his greatness, even called a "man after God's own heart", was still a man of war. He had served God in his generation, but he would not be the one to build God's house. His son Solomon ("peaceable") would have that honor. As "there was war in heaven" (Rev. 12:7), so there had to be here on earth. "The kingdom of heaven suffereth violence, and the violent take it by force" (Mt. 11:12). John the Baptist prepared the way for Christ by his violent preaching, but only the Prince of Peace could build the church. We are all men of war; my own track record is very bloody and filled with violence, but I hope to pass on what I can win, through patient struggle, to my posterity. God has chosen me, like David, to fight his battles here on earth, to prepare the way like John the Baptist, so that his peaceable kingdom may come "in earth as it is in heaven" (Mt. 6:10). Like Moses, John could show the way, but could not lead the people into the land of promise. I have been zealous for the Kingdom of God, but I'm a man of war, and have shed blood. My shameful sins, before I was saved by God's grace and anointed for his service, are still my sins. John Newton always remembered he was a slave trader and a man of war, so he would never be lifted up in his own mind, to think he was anything great on his own merits. He wrote "Amazing Grace" to show God could love and use a man of war like he was, who had shed blood. God has been able to use my sinful life, even my anger (now turned against sin), but "the wrath of man" can't build a house for God.

Except the Lord build the house, they labour in vain that build it. (Ps. 127:1)

HEART OF GOLD

(1:11) *"Since this is your heart's desire and you have not asked for wealth…" (NIV)*

What would you ask of God or a "genie" who said, "Ask for whatever you want me to give you" (1:7 – NIV)? Riches, honor, the death of your enemies or long life? Hard choices! Can I trust my own judgment in a case like this? Jesus said "But seek ye first the kingdom of God, and his righteousness; and all these things shall be added unto you" (Mt. 6:33), and he may have been thinking about Solomon's request for wisdom. A person may seek after many things, but God wants us to seek after him. Solomon had "gold coming out of his ears"; it was so plentiful because he first had a heart of gold. If God can find such a heart in you and me, it will be worth much more than gold, and gold will be easy for God to pour out upon such a faithful hearted soul. In heaven we will walk on streets paved with gold because it is that which is most precious here on earth. A heart of gold is one that is set upon doing God's will, regardless of what the circumstances may be, and such a heart comes only from God himself, and is given to whomever he wills. Solomon asked for the godly wisdom to lead God's people, and not for riches, but in so doing he showed he already had wisdom to choose rightly. God rewarded him with more gold than he could possibly manage to use. Will we also seek God's kingdom, or will we seek after gold and become spiritually bankrupt? The "golden rule" of the world: He who has the gold makes the rules!" Seeking gold is idolatry, but those who seek the one who makes the gold show that they have already received a new heart, a heart from God – a heart of gold. To covet gold is sin, but to covet God is gold!

A good heart is worth gold.

DELIGHT SAVING TIME

(5:14) ...the priests could not stand to minister by reason of the cloud...

...for the glory of the Lord had filled the house of God. This gives a little hint about heaven. When we are in the presence of God, all other activities cease. The main event has come for which all other activities are only a prelude. It will be the final "Sabbath rest", as all work will stop and we will simply bask in the awesome presence of God. The people of all nations will be a "sea of glass" (Rev. 4:6), still before their maker, in worship of his holiness. Nobody will be able to stand in his presence, but all will be prostrate before him. Here on earth we learn to "enter into his gates with thanksgiving, and into his courts with praise" (Ps. 100:4), but before his presence will be worship, as all work will cease. After sacrifices, which were the preliminaries to God's presence manifesting, thanks and loud praises were the ministry here. In God's presence, Martha will have to stop her work and sit silently at God's feet as Mary did. Here, we are all preoccupied with evangelism and all the priestly duties, to bring in worshippers to God, but there all this activity will be past. "For anyone who enters God's rest also rests from his own work, just as God did from his" (Heb. 4:10 - NIV). The priests could not stand to minister, because there was no longer any need to minister; we can turn off the lights (of man's works) when the sun is up to bring us light. In the meantime, however, let us not be wasting time, but "redeeming the time, because the days are evil" (Eph. 5:16), and do not waste God's time praying if your heart is not right. Confess your sins and ask for God's forgiveness, that your prayers may be heard, then *delight* spending *time* with God who *saves* us.

Turn Off The Lights (The Sun Is Up!)

NARCOLEPSY

(7:11)   …all that came into Solomon's heart to make…he prosperously effected.

A pretty energetic statement! I wish I could say that about my work, and I do try to do everything that comes into my heart, to completion. But even the most energetic of men and women have their "off days" sooner or later. Solomon had a little more to say on the subject of work: "I undertook great projects…yet when I surveyed all that my hands had done and what I had toiled to achieve, everything was meaningless, a chasing after the wind; nothing was gained under the sun" (Eccl. 2:4,11 - NIV). Solomon could hardly be called "lazy", and was probably closer to being a "work-a-holic". Truth be told, being busy in work may actually be a disguise for indolence in another more important area; God wants our whole "heart, soul, mind and strength" to be directed to him. It seems that Solomon also "prosperously effected" to marry every desirable woman who came down the pike, both Jew and Gentile, and "his wives turned away his heart after other gods" (1 Ki. 11:4). Solomon, through too much work and too many "strange women", was lulled to sleep in his brilliant mind. Who could match his intellect? But, I suppose even Albert Einstein could "fall asleep at the wheel" if he let his prodigious, prolific perception processes produce prolonged prayerlessness. Then, where does that leave you and me? After seeing "Forrest Gump", I see how productive men can be with an I.Q. of only 75, and how easily the minds of the world have slipped back into spiritual unconsciousness. Maybe we should return to simpler things and keep the collective conscience of the country on track, instead of majoring on the mind.

Indolence is the sleep of mind.

THE CAUSE WAS OF GOD...

(10:15)　...that the Lord might perform his word...

How could it be God's plan to have Israel and Judah split? We might well ask the same about the split between the Jews and Christians, the Catholics and Protestants, or the denominations that have split from each other. In some cases, separation and divorce are "of God", although God hates divorce (Mal. 2:16). How could it be? If the division results in purifying God's people, then "the cause was of God" when it happened. The people on either side of any split can see more clearly their own sins, and repent and turn to God. God split man into many language groups (Gen. 11:7-9), but will bring to himself some of each in his heavenly kingdom. As Joseph said, "You intended to harm me, but God intended it for good to accomplish what is now being done, the saving of many lives" (Gen. 50:20 - NIV). The Jews also rejected Jesus, but God used it for good, to save us all! "All things work together for good..." (Rom. 8:28) in God's purposes. God will be honored through good or evil. In this case, God performed what was spoken through Ahijah the prophet (1 Ki. 11:29) that Solomon's sins would not go unpunished, but that he would still preserve a godly lineage for the Messiah. And the effect of splits in God's people was always a purifying of those who would seek after God. Jesus did this (Jn. 6:66) and didn't feel bad: thinning out the ranks was purifying his followers. Paul and Barnabas had such a dispute that they split, thereby doubling their ministry. But... a word of caution: don't use this as a pretext for divorce or splits; unity is still God's plan.

Divide... and conquer!

But You Have Forsaken Him

(13:11)   *...we keep the charge of the Lord our God, but ye have forsaken him.*

This sounds like a very proud statement, to any who have forsaken God. A bumper sticker years ago stated "Christians are not perfect, just forgiven", which also sounds proud, though a bit more humble, to those outside of God's family. It is an escape, however, for many who call themselves Christians, although they continue in hidden or even open sins daily, and lead lives of total defeat. It is one thing to be forgiven, but quite another to presume upon God's forgiveness and go on in bondage to the same sin, and hope daily for God's forgiveness. Our attitude must be that any sin is a slap in God's face, and grow in our hatred for even the appearance of sin. Abijah's statement is not one of pride but simply the truth. If, by God's grace, you have escaped from slavery to sin in most areas of your life, only God can be thanked for it. We may never reach "sinless perfection" in this life, but if we do, only God can be thanked for it. However, there are two attitudes towards sin that determine if we are really "in" or "out". To be resigned to sin as something "I just can't give up" is defeat, when the truth is that Christ died for our sins; but to hate sin with all that is within me, and to say daily "by God's grace I will not sin today", that is pleasing to God, and gives the honor to him. The law is perfect, and it is there to drive us to Christ. And, if someone says to you "You have forsaken God", it will either drive you to repentance, or harden you. By the grace of God, choose to repent, and then be gracious in how you view your own standing with God, and reach out to call others back.

'Tis only noble to be good.

SHEEP WITHOUT A SHEPHERD

*(18:16) ...I did see all Israel scattered upon the
mountains, as sheep that have no shepherd...*

"Smite the shepherd, and the sheep shall be scattered" was how Zechariah (13:7) said it. Whether a leader is killed, removed, runs away, or simply doesn't do his job, the people left without proper authority will scatter and lose their direction. I have seen it when my father left home, leaving his eight children without leadership, and in a church, when a pastor quits and turns his authority over to another who has no relationship to the sheep. Israel, when the king turned from serving God, was as sheep without a shepherd, and when Jesus was crucified, his disciples scattered. Sheep need a shepherd, and wives need husbands, and children need a father and mother or they are lost, with no sure direction. The devil knows this well, and continues to strike shepherds, as he knows a whole flock will be affected. When we reject authority, we do so to our own destruction. Here, in this passage, why should people go to war when their own leader is not submitted to God? And how can we go for evangelism if we have no church and authority structure to put new believers into? The church, or the family, must be founded on solid relationships between shepherd and sheep, or it will scatter and become nothing at all, or at least ineffective in its function. Jesus said to "make disciples", not simply to make lots of sheep. We all become shepherds when we lead others to Christ and disciple them into the kingdom of God, because they look to us to guide them until they can do the same for others. Be a shepherd and stand your ground.

The Lord is my shepherd; I shall not want. (Ps. 23:1)

AN ATTITUDE OF GRATITUDE

(20:7)   Art not thou our God, who didst drive out the inhabitants of this land...?

An attitude of gratitude is kept alive in our memory of the good things done for us, and our memory is kept alive through telling the stories over and over again. Jesus told his disciples, the night he was betrayed, "this do in remembrance of me" (Lk. 22:19), so our memory of his death on the cross for our sins would be periodically brought to our minds. Here, when Jehoshaphat saw the Moabites and Ammonites gathering for war against him, he remembered two important things: first, how Israel had been kept by God from invading them (V. 10), for which the Moabites should have been grateful, and second, he remembered so many times when God had shown himself faithful to the nation of Israel, and had been their savior. Gratitude, however, is more than memory, which is in our minds. It is something which touches the heart. It is a heart attitude, like love, which grows by our exercise of it. Jehoshaphat didn't have to search deeply in his memory banks to remember all the times and ways God had helped the Jews; it was all very close to his heart, and he spoke out of his heartfelt thanks to God, which gave him a quiet confidence. God's mercy had also been extended to Moab and Ammon, but they had never let the memory of it enter into their hearts, but probably counted that grace as a victory of their own strength. We should learn to cultivate an attitude of gratitude towards God and men, by remembering their favors to us, and recounting them to others, or back to God as in Jehoshaphat's prayer. Contrast this with the ingratitude that led to murder only four chapters later (24:22)!

Gratitude is the memory of the heart.

LOWER THE RIVER

*(25:2)   And he did that which was right in the sight
of the Lord, but not with a perfect heart.*

Well, who has ever done right with a perfect heart? This all seems pretty relative when we see even David and Abraham sinning. Still, we are told by the Lord Jesus Christ to "be ye therefore perfect, even as your Father which is in heaven is perfect" (Mt. 5:48). Can anyone ever reach such an ideal? Jesus also said, in the same chapter, "I am not come to destroy [the Law, or the Prophets] but to fulfil" (Mt. 5:17). The Law is meant to be an ideal, kept perfectly, not just the best we can do every day. That is why we need a Savior, because we can never reach perfection alone. People speak of "sinless perfection" in this life but, although that is a great ideal, nobody but Jesus has ever really attained to it. Thomas More wrote of "Utopia", and Communists have tried to bring it about, and have miserably failed. Still, we don't throw out the ideal when we find we can't reach it, but try hard each day to do better. Failure at least teaches us that we need to be saved by someone greater and, although we can never reach our ideal ourselves, Jesus did make it possible. Instead of reaching up to perfection from this "real" world, we see Jesus, the ideal, coming down to touch us here in our "real" world. God commands perfection, although he knows it is not within our grasp to reach it; nevertheless, he doesn't lower the standard, or "grade on a curve" as other religions would believe is the answer. A wise and inventive thinker once said, "If you can't raise the bridge (to allow a ship to go through), then lower the river!"

An ideal is that which never touches the real.

HELP WANTED

(28:21)   ...and presented them to the king of
Assyria, but that did not help him. (NIV)

Bribery doesn't always work, usually because there is no relationship connected to it. In India, nearly everything is tainted with the bribery system, and it makes the whole nation struggle under the guilt of dishonesty. How much better is the help of one who does so out of a cheerful heart, giving not out of constraint, but willingly (1 Pet. 5:2, 2 Cor. 9:7). Bribery didn't work for Ahaz, so a few verses later we find him trying something even more stupid: he thought "Because the gods of the kings of Syria help them, therefore will I sacrifice to them, that they may help me. But they were the ruin of him, and of all Israel" (28:23). His relationship to God had not been right, or surely God would have been there to help him, but he turned to idolatry. One of Aesop's fables tells of a lion and a mouse, and how the little mouse was able to pull a thorn out of the lion's paw, as an act of gratitude for saving his life. Maybe the lion thought that the mouse was too small to ever be of any help to him, but how reassuring to find he had a helper when he had a need. Hezekiah, the son of Ahaz, was a more godly king, and in his reign we see that when "...the priests... were too few... their brethren the Levites did help them, till the work was ended..." (29:34). Help based upon relationship beats all of these human manipulations. God wants us to help in his work of salvation, not to gain his favor, but as those who give freely, because of his grace to us.

Sweet the help of one we have helped.

SETTLE DOWN!

(30:8) ...serve the Lord your God, that the fierceness of his wrath may turn away from you.

We understand hatred in human terms. When we become angry, too often it is for a selfish reason and, if we don't forgive, soon it grows into hatred. If we are made in God's image, though, then what can we say about God's anger? His is always righteous anger, but does it also turn into hatred? Yes, God had a perfect hatred for sin, and he expects us to develop that, too. God is too pure to look upon evil, and as we live with him, we become like him more each day. We must learn to think of sin as completely evil so we will stop flirting with it. God is not only angry with sin, but he abhors it, and our supposed "smallest mistakes" are enough to turn his stomach. "God demonstrates his own love for us in this: while we were still sinners, Christ died for us" (Rom. 5:8 - NIV), but God also demonstrated the depth of his hatred for sin when he allowed Jesus to die on the cross for our sins. Our problem of getting rid of sin has a root cause: we can't wholeheartedly reject sin if we still love it. We must settle in our hearts that "whatever God hates, I also will hate". Don't hate people, but hate the sin that destroys them. God's law is settled in heaven, and we must settle it in our hearts, and love it, and hate when it is broken, "that the fierceness of his wrath may turn away from you". We must stop trying to explain away the final judgment, and realize God's utter hatred for our sin, and stop hating God's Law, and start hating sin. Our God-given ability to hate must be rightly used, and directed against the right things.

Hatred is a settled anger.

GOD LEFT HIM

(32:31) ...God left him, to try him, that he might know all that was in his heart.

Does God not already know our hearts? The truth is that we need to be reminded of our capacity and tendency to sin. When God backs off from granting us grace, we naturally fall back into sin. Hezekiah and his son Manasseh show us a good contrast: Hezekiah was a good man, but pride was in his heart whenever God removed his grace. Manasseh was a very evil man, but repented when God carried him off to Babylon with hooks and fetters. Thus, it was God's grace to him to put him in bondage, and God's grace to Hezekiah to leave him alone, to show him the pride of his heart. Both of these men show the grace of God, but in opposite ways. Sometimes I need to be reminded of "all that is in my (wicked) heart"! When I question "Where has God's presence gone?" it may likely be God's way of showing me how great his grace has been to keep me from sin. Deuteronomy 8:2&3 are good parallel verses: we need to remember how <u>consistently</u> it has been only God's grace that makes us a Hezekiah, instead of like Manasseh. God "tested" Job to show him the same, and to have him remain humble. When God leaves us, it shows us our complete dependence on him. Prosperity makes us get lax and easy going, but the "dry" times are God's grace in another way to us, and we need both. We must learn "both how to be abased, and... how to abound: everywhere and in all things I am instructed both to be full and to be hungry, both to abound and to suffer need" (Phil. 4:12). There's a little of Hezekiah and Manasseh in all of us!

**The heart is deceitful above all things...
who can know it?** (Jer. 17:9)

BESIDE STILL WATERS

(36:21) …for as long as she lay desolate she kept sabbath…

Israel and Judah have had a long and rocky history, but this small nation has outlasted most of the great empires of the world. What is the secret of the Jews' survival? Here we find one hint. Whenever they got too far from their roots in God, he restored what they had lost of their depth. Like a river that looks most calm on the surface when it runs the deepest, so the Jews needed to return to their real strength of resting in God. If you are working seven days a week to try to get more out of life, you are missing it. Try taking six days to complete your work and give the seventh to God, so you can renew your strength in him. God is serious about keeping the Sabbath of rest, not because he has such a great need of our worship, but because we so desperately need his deep and abiding strength. Babylon, which seemed like such a great kingdom, was used by God to give some depth to Judah again, so that Judah could again become a mighty nation. Babylon never had the quiet trust in Almighty God that Judah had, so Judah continued to grow in strength during her captivity in Egypt and Babylon, and later under Rome and even Germany in the last century. Persecution will make us stronger if we have our faith running in deep and time tested channels. The most desolate times in Jewish history are when the Jews returned to their Sabbath rest in God. Jesus is our real Sabbath, and our depth in him will determine whether or not we will last until the end. God alone is the source of all power.

The mightiest powers by deepest calms are fed.

HOMING INSTINCT

(1:5)   ...everyone whose heart God had moved – prepared to go up... (NIV)

This was in response to King Cyrus' proclamation to rebuild the Jerusalem temple. First, "the Lord moved the heart of Cyrus" (NIV), but Cyrus gave the Jews the honor of returning to build it, and something arose in their hearts to respond. Much like the homing instinct of pigeons, or of geese migrating thousands of miles and, by instinct alone, returning to the same place each year, so there is a "homing instinct" in man that draws him back to a fellowship with God that Adam once lost for us all. The "wandering Jews" are again, in these last days, going back to Israel, a place where many of them have not been, nor their ancestors, for generations. Yet, there is a "homing instinct" in them to return to the Promised Land. As Noah prepared the ark for the coming flood, God caused the animals to come, apparently by instinct, to escape danger. Jesus also died on a cross, and some may ask, "How did he know anybody would respond to the call of salvation?" But, like the animals on the ark, God has put a homing instinct in the heart of each of his "prodigal sons" to return to God, as they hear the good news of the cross. The Holy Spirit will awaken the homing instinct in the hearts of God's children as they hear the message. A salmon will fight his way against the current of miles of stream, up waterfalls, through white water rapids, to spawn in a place where he was born, and all by instinct; and there he will die. We also must fight against a stream of life, flowing to destruction, to return home to God, and many will die as martyrs to give this life to others.

There is no instinct like that of the heart.

SUCCESSFUL SERVANTS

(5:11)   *"We are the servants of the God of heaven and earth…"*

Humility is defined well as "knowing ourselves for who (or whose) we are" or as "knowing that every good thing that we are or have comes from God". Pride tends to fight back when accused, but humility allows us to see who we really are. God can make anyone succeed, but waits generally until they acknowledge that success comes from him. Our desire should always be to bring glory to God, not to ourselves. When the enemies of God try to stop God's people from doing a work he has given them to do, it is pride to try to fight against their accusations. We all have past sins that can be called into question. A clever T-shirt message once proclaimed: "The next time the devil reminds you of your past, remind him of his future!" Meekness, however, is turning to God, saying "This is your problem, not mine, so please, God, stop their mouths". Anyone can "name drop" God's name, but to be truly submitted in heart, as his willing servants, that is what brings a swift answer from God. These accusers, Tattenai and his friends, were not submitted to God, nor even to Darius the king, but were motivated only by a desire for personal gain. The Jews, by contrast, were submitted to God, and were willing to submit to Darius and his decisions, so God heard their cries for help. When you find yourself in trouble, don't attempt to be a big "hero", but humbly tell God you are his servant, and tell him your needs, and God won't let you fail. "When a man's ways please the Lord, he maketh even his enemies to be at peace with him" (Pr. 16:7), even if the "enemy" is a king, or and evil governor.

Humility is the key to quick success.

HOME SWEET HOME

(7:13)   ...any of the Israelites...who wish to go to Jerusalem...may go. (NIV)

Wouldn't <u>everybody</u> go?!? These Jews were away from home, in captivity in Babylon, and were now being given a chance to go home. But many, because they had not lived in Israel for as long as they had lived in Babylon, were quite comfortable ("thank you very much!") to stay in Babylon. Incredible! And yet, this is the state of people today in the world. We are away from God because of our sin and are in captivity to our own sin in this world. When given a chance to choose life, to go back again to God's kingdom, our "free" will naturally chooses the comfort of staying where we are: truly, "home is where the heart is". To the child of God, "This world is not my home, I'm just a-passing through", but sadly that is not the case for the rest of humanity. In fact, if left to our own "free will" decisions alone, we all would choose this earthly life, with all its problems, over a future life we cannot see. It took Jesus, as God in the flesh, to come and bring back a love for heaven to our hearts. Many Jews today still desire to return to Israel, though they have never been there. Such a love for a home we've never seen must be instilled in our hearts by the word of God, and we are to plant that seed in the hearts of people who are blinded by the love of this world. Our real home is not here, but in heaven with God who made us. However, people will never be "at home" there until the love of this world has been replaced by a greater love. It is hard to wrestle a bone out of a dog's mouth, but drop a juicy steak in front of him and he will drop the bone to get the steak. Heaven is our true home, and so much better than the dry bone of this dying world.

Home is where the heart is.

ADULTEROUS MARRIAGE

(10:11)   Separate yourselves from the people of the land, and from the strange wives.

Like the Nazirite vow (Num. 6:1-21), God's people are to be separated *from* the world, separated *unto* God. From dietary laws to other customs and moral laws, the Jews (and Christians) are separate from "sinners". God gave strong warnings against inter-marriage with unbelievers, as this would encourage the Israelites in other sins, particularly in idolatry. One notable time was when "...Israel joined in worshiping the Baal of Peor" (Num. 25:3 - NIV) and was judged, and then Phinehas used a javelin to thrust through a man with a Midianite woman, He was considered "zealous for God" and blessed for clearing Israel of the sin. Now, Ezra is astonished once again at Israel's brash sin in the face of their condition of being judged for idolatry by being in captivity. We are all slow learners, but responsible to learn from history. This seems like an extreme decision: to divorce women taken as wives, since even God says "I hate divorce" (Mal. 2:16 - NIV). But it shows also that God is serious about sin – it will destroy us, and should be removed like cancer. People today will divorce their own wives to marry others, with the thought that as soon as they are married, it is sanctified by God. But this passage shows it is sin, and that they are "living in adultery": strong words for a time when half of U.S. marriages are the result of previous infidelity. We need this kind of holiness today, to tremble at sin, and be willing as a nation to acknowledge our sin of adultery. Imagine every adulterous marriage ending in divorce and people in America living holy lives: it would be revival! It will take this kind of shaking to awaken us to the gravity of our rebellion.

"...Be ye separate" saith the Lord... (2 Cor. 6:17)

SO I PRAYED

(2:4)   So I prayed to the God of heaven.

This was a quick prayer, made during a conversation with the king. God is honored when, in great or small things and at any time, we take the time to acknowledge our dependence on him. Nehemiah was a man of both prayer and action. We must be men of action, but no action will prosper without prayer, because God must be honored. A "quick" prayer like this will be effective only because of a man being habitually in prayer. Nehemiah, even as he writes, continues to pray; notice how often it happens: (1:4, 2:4, 4:4-5, 4:9, 5:19, 6:9, 6:14, 9:5-38, 13:14, 22, 29, 31), showing how ready he is, moment by moment, to share his burdens with God. Those who are in the habit of praying are those who will remember to pray in a moment of crisis. Like Solomon, who asked for wisdom when God said "Ask for whatever you want me to give you" (2 Chr. 1:7 - NIV), Nehemiah also looks to God for wisdom when the king asks him "What is it you want?" (2:4 - NIV) We, likewise, should pray in the Spirit, because "We do not know what we ought to pray for" (Rom. 8:26 - NIV). Prayer is an attitude of the heart, one of submission to God's will. "So I prayed to the God of heaven" means that was his natural response out of habit, and out of true faith, based upon previous answers. We also are in God's service, and can expect God to answer in times of instant prayer, if we know him and are sure we pray according to his will. May we be as Nehemiah, and look to God at all times for the things we need. Hudson Taylor once said, "God's work done in God's way will never lack God's supply". Put God to the test, and trust in his providence.

Prayer Changes Things.

SAVE THE WHALE!

(5:8)   ...and will ye even sell your brethren?

Nehemiah was shocked, just as we are when we read of Joseph's brothers selling him into slavery. Here it is most amazing to Nehemiah because they had also been in the same position of slaves in Egypt, and just now in captivity in Babylon, and still dared to treat their own brothers as slaves and property. But slavery, in any society, is just as wrong and inhuman. We are all brothers and sisters, and can trace our ancestors back only as far as Noah, no matter what "race" we belong to. The Bible has no reference to any "race" at all, except the human race, as distinct from the animals. It sounds so good and righteous for people to care about "animal rights", but the result is always a lack of concern for humans. Christian songwriter Randy Stonehill once sang, "Well it's okay to murder babies, but we really ought to save the whale." Abortion and euthanasia are the results of teaching evolution to children, as are the selfish decisions of suicide and divorce. Man who rejects God as his Lord and Creator will always degenerate into worse and worse degrees of inhumanity towards his fellow man. Jesus came to reverse the process, not by more hard judgments, but by being sold by his own brothers! Once again, man stooped to his lowest level, this time by the selling of his own Creator and Lord, to be crucified. God's greatest gift of love shows us our true nature in the shame of our inhumanity. We should be kind to animals, but we should be even more kind to our brethren who are created in God's image.

No greater shame to man than inhumanity.

WATERGATE

(8:8)   *"They read from the Book of the Law of God, making it clear...*

...and giving the meaning so that the people could understand what was being read." (NIV) [See 8:1 – "before the Water Gate"] The people's reaction was that "all the people wept" (v. 9). In Lancaster, Pennsylvania years ago, Pastor Morris preached on this chapter just after the infamous "Watergate" wiretapping incident that brought down President Nixon. "The unfolding of your words gives light; it gives understanding to the simple" (Ps. 119:130 - NIV). But Ezra not only read the word, he made it "clear" so all would hear and not miss it. Then, he gave "the meaning", or explained it, so they could understand what was read. If we do this, people will also tremble and weep at their own sinfulness compared to the holiness of God's Law. "Watergate" happened because people were blindly trusting leaders, and were shocked when they saw that the President could also lie and "cover up" truth for his own ambitions. It shook the whole country, and people wept over their own sins. I was saved at that time, seeing my sinfulness, as God's Spirit was at work throughout America [Romans 3:19-20 & Galatians 3:24]. We need revival today before social reforms can come. Let us read aloud, preach and explain God's Word to men and women, beginning with Christians as Paul did, "first for the Jew, then for the Gentile" (Rom. 1:16 - NIV). Let us not just weep, but put away sin, and hate it! Then we can preach the gospel, and in so doing will "go and enjoy choice food and sweet drinks, and send some to those who have nothing" (v. 10).

Judgment must begin at the house of God. (1 Pet. 4:17)

A CURSE AND AN OATH

(10:29)   ...all these now... bind themselves with a curse and an oath... (NIV)

A covenant is a sacred and very serious decision, not to be entered lightly. God is witness to our decision. It involves an oath with blessing for continuance, and a curse for failure to continue. When you enter a binding agreement, you had better "read the fine print". We tend to think only of the blessing, and when that seems to go we feel we can just walk away. But there is also a curse attached for breaking the oath. In oaths of brotherhood for the Mafia, and other secret organizations, often a card is burned on the hand, or a blood covenant is "cut" and blood is somehow exchanged. To break the confidence of the brotherhood oath will mean death, as that is the curse attached. God has entered into a blood covenant with us, through the one time sacrifice of Christ on the cross. If it meant death for him to make it, "how shall we escape" (Heb. 2:3) if we neglect the binding oath and curse attached to it? God is serious, and the curse is not only death, but eternal punishment. "Cursed is everyone who does not continue to do everything written in the Book of the Law" (Gal. 3:10 - NIV). It is better not to make a vow or an oath, than to make it and then break it. Marriage is "til death us do part". Blood covenants are to be taken more seriously than physical kinship, because they are entered into by a willful choice, and God is the witness of our commitment, whereas physical kinship is something we can do nothing about. The blessings of a covenant are there, but so are the curses. Do not enter lightly into an oath and a curse!

Say what you mean and mean what you say.

HAVE NONE WILL TRAVEL

(13:27)   …being unfaithful to our God by marrying foreign women… (NIV)

Marriage is such a serious step in a man's life that it must be considered well. Arranged marriages, which are common in India and other Eastern countries, allow the parents to thoroughly "check out" a prospective bride for their sons. While in the west we may think this strange, it was common also among the men of the Bible times. Young people know little of what to look for in a spouse and are led strongly by physical beauty and outward qualities that have nothing to do with building a lasting home. Paul said, "I wish that all men were as I am" (1 Cor. 7:7 - NIV), [unmarried is implied], because "an unmarried man is concerned about the Lord's affairs – how he can please the Lord. But a married man is concerned about the affairs of this world – how he can please his wife…" (1 Cor. 7:32-3 - NIV). If we understand the seriousness of this statement, we will not quickly jump into a sudden decision to marry, without any thought beyond our own desire to "possess" a beautiful wife. How much worse, though, for Christians to be "unequally yoked together with unbelievers" (2 Cor. 6:14). If we don't keep to God's standards, we can go beyond choosing a spouse for physical beauty's sake [who is at least a believer], to making an even more serious error of judgment, and being drawn into a marriage with an unbeliever. It would be better by far to trust the decision of wise parents, or even to put off marriage altogether, than to be led into sin by someone whose charms may lead us away from Christ. Better to travel alone.

He travels fastest who travels alone.

A PARABLE

(1:4) ...he displayed... the splendor and glory of his majesty. (NIV)

Today, in Chitradurga (India), the pastor expounded this: Esther is a book showing a microcosm of God's kingdom and his dealings with man. God is not mentioned, just as in Jesus' parables, because his dealings are seen clearly enough, and by allegory, in the actions of King Ahasuerus. Vashti is his queen who typifies Israel, and who refused to be shown off by God to the world, so Esther ("Star"), led by Mordecai ("Small"), became God's bride, as the Christians, led by the Holy Spirit, are espoused to Christ. Haman (as Satan, the adversary) tries to kill off all of God's people [Note that he is an Agagite, descended from the people King Saul was to have destroyed]. Haman gets worship from all, until Mordecai refuses, and he plans to hang him on a tall gallows pole (the cross). The "cross" becomes the means of his own destruction. Esther must decide to suffer with her own people to be their deliverer, and is prepared to die, but God delivers her because he has a greater plan (the king's scepter is like God's mercy extended). God "shows the riches of his glorious kingdom" forever, not only for 180 days. Jesus, like Mordecai, pleased God and was promoted to his own right hand, and the church follows him obediently and becomes his queen (4:14 is a key verse). Those who hate and persecute God's people will be destroyed by God's righteous decree, sent through all the earth, "far as the curse is found" [from "Joy to the World"]. The final verse (10:3) is another summary statement regarding Jesus. A rich allegory!

A picture is worth a thousand words.

HAMAN HANGED FOR HATRED

(7:6) *The adversary and enemy is this wicked Haman".* **[Jesus Hung for Love!]**

Some of the most wicked people that exist are those who never personally kill or harm anyone. Haman was hanged, not for any crime he had done, but for his own wicked designs against Mordecai and the Jews. We consider some people like Charles Manson and Adolph Hitler to be the most violent of criminals, and yet they did not personally kill anyone! However, we are all aware that their hatred was the motivation behind the murders that they compelled and convinced others to do. Even Satan has not really killed anyone; he gets others to do his violence for him. Jezebel, through lies and deceit, had people like Naboth killed, although she didn't personally raise a finger against them. Jesus rightly said that "thou shalt not kill" (Mt. 5:21-2) extends beyond the act of murder to the heart of hatred, and John says plainly, "Anyone who hates his brother is a murderer" (1 Jn. 3:15 - NIV). Had Haman been able to do all that was in his heart, the Jews would have been exterminated, just as Hitler tried to do in Europe. Hate is the fuel for all the wars that have ever been fought, including all the crusades and "holy wars" of history. If you hold bitter hatred or unforgiveness in your heart for anyone, don't fool yourself! You are as heinous and horrible as Haman and Hitler! Haman never got around to having even one of his plans accomplished, but was executed for conspiracy. God's righteous judgment will burn up all of his adversaries someday, as he judges the "thoughts and intents of the heart" (Heb. 4:12), and the lowest places in Hades will not necessarily be for those who actually commit crimes of violence. Repent now, if you have hatred in your heart!

Hate is the subtlest form of violence.

SO, HOW DID YOU GET SAVED?

(8:17)   And many… became Jews; for the fear of the Jews fell upon them.

Actually, the fear of God seized them, as it was God's power that brought about the change of affairs. Whenever God's people begin to seek his face in their problems, God answers and people take notice [see Gen. 35:5, Ex. 15:16, Ex. 12:33, Deut. 2:25]. "If you can't beat them, join them!" That is how the enemies of the Jews suddenly came to be Jews, too. Historically, many people have changed allegiance from one country or religion to another through fear of death. As a humorous cartoon showed it years ago, a zealous Christian has his foot on a man's neck and holds a Bible in his face, while the man says "Tell me more about this Jesus, I'm fascinated". Of course, if they became "Christian" for this reason, it doesn't mean they are truly "saved". There must be a conversion of the heart, from allegiance to self to allegiance to Christ. But the deepest reason why people would believe in or sacrifice to any "god" is out of fear, which later may be simply reverence, or "custom" handed down through generations of instilled fear of the god's wrath. No doubt, when people see the real power of the true God, even shown through his people, it is time to fear the real God. Fear came upon the people in the New Testament times [Acts 2:43, 5:5, 19:17] not through fear of the sword of man, but a fear of God himself, when the Holy Spirit worked in various ways. Ultimately, all will bow in fear and reverence to God [Ps. 66:3, Phil. 2:10-11], "through the greatness of thy power". But our job is to establish God's kingdom in their hearts here on earth, and to see them saved.

So great is your power that your enemies
cringe before you. (Ps. 66:3 – NIV)

CURSE GOD AND DIE!

(2:9) "Are you still holding on to your integrity? Curse God and die!" (NIV)

Job is a book about spiritual warfare, and Job is a soldier in it. It is easy for a person to speak about forgiveness when he has never been hurt, but Job was tested to an extreme limit to see how far his faithfulness to God would stretch. In the world's opinion, the way for a tough soldier to die with honor would be to curse God and die, like a real self-made "macho". Many soldiers may be decorated for feats of bravery, but curse God and hate the enemy that has maimed them. One who has been in the heat of battle is qualified to speak about forgiveness, because warfare tends to harden people's hearts. The real hero of a soldier is one who has been deeply wounded, but does not hold any bitterness against those who wounded him. Ultimately, our bitterness will be directed against God if we are not ready to forgive people. Our integrity is not touched by the wounds of others, and a soldier does not need to be "integrated" with all his arms and legs intact to retain his integrity. Job was wounded in his body, and had his family and property destroyed and finally he had his "friends" and wife tell him to "curse God and die", or to confess some guilt he had done. Satan's plan was to unveil Job's lack of integrity, but the testing of Job has rather made him a model for all time of patience in suffering. Finally, God calls on him to pray for his friends who have wounded him, an in the end he is rewarded with a double portion of God's blessing for it. May we be like Stephen, who prayed for those who stoned him to death saying, "Lord, do not hold this sin against them" (Acts 7:60 - NIV).

Forgiveness adorns a soldier.

JUST BEFORE GOD

(9:2)   ...but how can a mortal be righteous before God? (NIV)

Paul says, "no one will be declared righteous in his sight by observing the law" (Rom. 3:20 - NIV). If we hope to be justified by the law, we will surely fail. So, how should man be just with God? The only answer is by faith in Christ. Even Job knew this, saying "I know that my Redeemer liveth" (19:25). Man will forever try to justify himself, and Job was no exception. The problem is that we are born in sin, and it comes naturally to us. Even if we could stop, we cannot undo our past, or our heritage of being sons and daughters of Adam. Our only hope is in the risen Christ, who "was delivered for our offences, and was raised again for our justification" (Rom. 4:25). We are not left dead with Christ on the cross, but raised with him to stand justified and sinless before God. Our hope is the resurrection: "and whoever lives and believes in me will never die. Do you believe this?" (Jn. 11:26 - NIV). No religious exercise, prayer, fasting, repentance, giving alms or anything else can wash away my sins, "nothing but the blood of Jesus!" Job was a just man by all human standards, as were the Scribes and the Pharisees, but "except your righteousness shall exceed the righteousness of the scribes and Pharisees, ye shall in no case enter the kingdom of heaven" (Mt. 5:20). So, "how can a mortal be righteous before God?" (NIV) Only by God's way: faith in Christ, who is the just one. In ourselves it is impossible, "but with God all things are possible" (Mt. 19:26). Man continues to try to be just before God, but we cannot attain it: it is imputed, not imitated. The humbling fact is that we must come to Christ to be made just before God.

**Justified: "Just-as-if-I'd" never
sinned, but done only good**

CAN A TREE SPROUT AGAIN?

(14:7)   For there is hope of a tree, if it be cut down, it will sprout again.

Job wasn't sure of any hope of future life, but in a few passages he does say that he will see God [13:15, 19:25-7]. Here he compares man's hope to that of a tree. When it is cut down, the tree itself may sprout, if water comes, but it will never live again as a tree unless grafted back somehow onto the root. The root, on the other hand, can grow another tree under some conditions. At least there is hope for something like that. Paul uses this same thought in Romans 11:15-24, but if the whole root system is destroyed, can anything be grafted in? Our faith is in the gospel of God's salvation through Christ, and it came by revelation through prophets, one being added to another until the whole picture of God's redemption was revealed. But, if we now say "The root is destroyed; let us build a new religion out of the fallen tree", it may sprout for a short while, but will not live. If, however, the whole tree be cut down (as the Jews in dispersion), as long as the root remains (the Scripture), anyone can be grafted in, and will live. But destroy the root, and there is no hope of its sprouting again. If someone tells me "The Bible has been corrupted", I have no hope at all, even if another comes to build on the leftover ideas. The root is there, and if it is not we all perish. The root is the history of the Jews, and God's dealings with them. Destroy that and any "new" religion cannot live. We must have the root for the tree to grow, not the tree for the root to grow. Nature itself will be our teacher in this.

I am the vine, ye are the branches... (Jn. 15:5)

HALITOSIS

(17:1)   "My breath is corrupt, my days are extinct..."

We have many proverbs about the importance of inner character over outward appearance. "Don't judge a book by its cover"; "Beauty is only skin deep"; "Pretty is as pretty does", etc. Although we know that is true when things are going well, still when things go wrong we become more concerned with outward appearances. Job is talking here about his bad breath, because it betrays the death he feels inside of him. It is hard to think of spiritual things when we are in extended periods of pain in our bodies, but Job's friends made it even harder for him by judging his character by his appearance. Even Job's wife was repulsed by his breath (19:17) and she, who should have known about his good character more than anyone else, told him to "curse God and die" instead of standing with him in his time of need. What she and his friends were busy saying to Job was also repulsive, and it revealed the death that was in them. Like Saul of Tarsus, "still breathing out murderous threats against the Lord's disciples" (Acts 9:1 - NIV), so these revealed their true character and lack of spiritual insight. We should be more concerned with the words that come out of our mouths, and how they influence others for good or evil, than with covering our bad breath with some mouthwash. Jesus said, "...what comes out of [a man's] mouth, that is what makes him 'unclean'" (Mt. 15:11 - NIV), and he wasn't talking about bad breath. Let your speech influence others for good, not for evil.

Influence is the exhalation of character.

NURSERY SCHOOL

(28:12)   *But where shall wisdom be found?*

Solomon says, "The fear of the Lord is the beginning of knowledge: but fools despise wisdom and instruction" (Pr. 1:7). It is generally conceded that instruction teaches knowledge, which gives understanding when we begin to think for ourselves, and wisdom when we learn to apply it. But teaching alone cannot build character, nor lead always to wisdom, because the fear of the Lord must be there to give form and boundaries to all of man's learning. Everyone in the story of Job seems to overflow with wisdom, freely given to anyone who will be impressed, and forced upon any who are not. To God, the fear of the Lord is of primary importance, and without it, "professing themselves to be wise, they became fools" (Rom. 1:22). If "education begins with life" then what happens when we ask "Where does life begin?" If life to us begins with a "big bang", then there is no fear of the Lord, and no real understanding of life will be possible, when we deny the Creator who made us for himself. So, the truly wise are those who love and fear God, and submit to his will and kingdom. And where does life begin? "This is eternal life: that they may know you, the only true God, and Jesus Christ, whom you have sent" (Jn. 17:3 - NIV). When life begins, so does education; but when real life, the life of God's eternal Spirit, enters our hearts, we will begin to think God's thoughts. The real education for Job began when God revealed himself to him, and he listened in silence.

Education begins with life.

Covenant With My Eyes

(31:1)   I made a covenant with my eyes not to look lustfully at a girl. (NIV)

Jesus said "anyone who looks at a woman lustfully has already committed adultery with her in his heart" (Mt. 5:28 - NIV). Job considered this to be so serious that he actually made a covenant with his own eyes not to look with lust upon another woman who was not his wife. A covenant involves curses for failure to keep it, and Job even calls these curses upon himself, should he be caught offending this covenant. In verse 7, first the eye sins, then the heart follows, then our feet walk into the trap, and our hands take hold of what we have lusted after. So, "making a covenant with my eyes" means stopping lust at its first stage, before it becomes even a conscious thought. This progression is exposed in James 1:13-16 and in Psalm 19:12-13, and the wise man will discipline himself not to even look. Proverbs 23:31-5 shows the same solution for an alcoholic, who may also be led as a result into adultery. Paul says to "take captive every thought to make it obedient to Christ" (2 Cor. 10:5). Job went a step further, and decided it was a sin even to look, so the thought would not follow. I have made the same "covenant" with my eyes, by saying "it may not be a sin for someone else, but for me it is", so I don't have to wonder each time. A covenant, like marriage, simply says "all others but my own wife are out for me". Job was innocent of even sin in his mind. Let us take seriously the warnings of Scripture, and take a stand against the lust of the eyes that the world calls good. Man up and call it sin.

Be careful little eyes what you see.

EVERYBODY'S A COMEDIAN

(36:4) *For truly my words shall not be false: he*
that is perfect in knowledge is with thee.

Elihu's words are either the height of pride, or he refers to God's wisdom, and is speaking for him; hopefully the latter! Why were these men so quick to condemn Job? If we understand this it may help us to not judge others. When we do wrong and are caught in it, we want to somehow redeem the situation so we won't look so bad, so we judge others because "misery loves company". We do, hopefully, learn from our mistakes, but we shouldn't use our new-found wisdom to condemn others. Job's friends must have made plenty of mistakes in their lives, much more than Job, but they seem to jump at the chance to "teach" this godly man, and to assume they were now godlier than he. Comedians get most of their material from past mistakes, and can use it to poke fun at themselves. But, when we become self-righteous about our experience, learned from the many mistakes of our past, it is not funny, but rather hurts people. Shouldn't our "mistakes" be called "sin" so we will be humbled by them and learn not to judge others? Experience is good if it leads us on to godly humility. Job's exclamation "no doubt but ye are the people, and wisdom shall die with you!" (12:1) is poking fun at their self-righteousness, as these men have more of the making of comedians than teachers of righteousness. Jesus made fun of the men who would say "God, I thank thee, that I am not as other men are..." (Lk. 18:11), while really we are all equally wicked. If you learn something valuable through your mistakes, keep it to yourself, unless someone asks you for it. Silence is considered wisdom.

**Experience is the name everyone
gives to their mistakes.**

LAURA POWELL

*(42:10)   After Job... prayed for his friends, the
          Lord made him prosperous again (NIV)*

Last month was Laura Powell's funeral. She was loved by everyone as a model of a "virtuous woman" (Pr. 31:10), one who loved and cared for people. Everyone wept at the funeral service, not for her death (as she is now with Jesus) but because we miss her being with us. Everyone's life was brightened by her example. The saddest thought when one like she has died is that we wish we had appreciated her more when she was here. Job's godly example was allowed to shine again, as God healed him. He could have been bitter through the hardness of his friends in his time of weakness and greatest need of encouragement, but instead "he prayed for his friends", and probably changed their lives in the process. Why must we wait until people like Laura Powell die before we say something nice about them?! It is always a reminder to us that we, too, are an example to others every day of our lives, either for good or for bad: "Redeeming the time, because the days are evil" (Eph. 5:16). If you are caught up in bitterness, or anger or other bad attitudes, you are destroying not only yourself, but others by your example. God will do for you as he did for Job, if you will release forgiveness for friends who hurt you, and rather pray for God's blessing on their lives. Laura Powell had few, if any enemies, because she prayed and took time for everybody. Huey, her husband, cried and said "I've lost my best friend". Be the best friend of everyone you meet. Job prayed, like Jesus and Stephen at the moment of their deaths, for his persecutors (Mt. 5:44). Don't look for a role model, be one!

Nothing is as infectious as example.

THE CHICKEN OR THE EGG

(8:2) From the lips of children and infants you have ordained praise. (NIV)

"Which came first: the chicken or the egg?" So goes the eternal riddle –
the answer depends upon your perspective. The Bible scholar says the
chicken, because God created Adam whole, and creatures "after their
kind" (Gen. 1:21), but it could be argued: was it the "seed-bearing plant"
(Gen. 1:29) or the "seed, bearing plants" that came first? I suppose that
depends on which you see as the finished, mature product. Chickens
lay eggs which are produced for eating; but eggs also produce mature
chickens, to be eaten as well. But, isn't man different, because mature man
is the obvious end product of God's creation of babies? Man matures in
physical strength, in his size, his mental aptitude and even in his spiritual
perception. Then, why did Jesus speak about children, and even babies,
as being the inhabitants of heaven? It may be that man and woman were
created to bring forth babies, the real purpose of God's creation! Jesus said,
"…Except ye be converted, and become as little children, ye shall not enter
into the kingdom of heaven" (Mt. 18:3). And Peter added, "As newborn
babes, desire the sincere milk of the word, that ye may grow thereby" (1
Pet. 2:2). Growing spiritually is simply becoming more like children in our
faith in God. Perfect praise arises from the lips of children who haven't
thought about having doctrinal battles in words, which progress into
"holy wars". They simply love to praise God, and love others without any
personal gain required. Jesus said, "Let the little children come to me, and
do not hinder them, for the kingdom of God belongs to such as these."
(Mt. 19:14 – NIV)

A hen is only an egg's way of making another egg.

PURIFIED SEVEN TIMES

(12:6)   The words of the Lord are pure words, as silver tried in a furnace of earth...

How is God's Word <u>tried</u>? When applied to my life, it works! It will try me (with persecution), but I also will come out of the trial as gold. Trials (as by fire on silver) purify. Pure silver has no dross, and neither does God's Word. We try God's Word when we put it to the test, and it works. Also, it is precious, like silver. Truth must stand up to <u>every</u> test. Then it is tried and tested, and found to be true and precious! Why should heaven's silver be tried in earth's furnace? Because the world is in rebellion against the Word of God, but God's Word will endure forever (Isa. 40:8). Jesus said, "In the world ye shall have tribulation: but be of good cheer; I have overcome the world." (Jn. 16:33) We are tested, as is God's Word, not to fail, but to come forth as silver and gold, tried by fire and purified seven times. Seven is the number that signifies perfection, and although we are not perfect, Jesus commands "Be ye therefore perfect, even as your Father which is in heaven is perfect" (Mt. 5:48). How? "...For a little while you may have had to suffer grief in all kinds of trials. These have come so that your faith – of greater worth than gold, which perishes even though refined by fire – may be proved genuine..." (1 Pet. 1:6-7 - NIV). By faith, we can come to Christ and be made perfect in him, "because by one sacrifice he has made perfect forever those who are being made holy" (Heb. 10:14 - NIV). Only God and his Word are perfect, "But we know that when he appears, we shall be like him, for we shall see him as he is. Everyone who has this hope in him purifies himself, just as he is pure" (1 Jn. 3:2-3 - NIV).

The crucible for silver, but the Lord tests the heart.

THE LITTLE RED HEN

(18:25-6)   *To the faithful you show yourself faithful...but to the crooked...*

...you show yourself shrewd (NIV). Talk is cheap, but a man's actions show his real character. We choose our friends, not by what they say when things are going well, but by their behavior to us when things are also going wrong. God judges his friends in the same way, so if you want to be God's friend, you must be his friend at all times, not just when it pleases you. The "little red hen" had lots of friends when it came time to eat; but none of them came forward when she asked for help to prepare the food, so she didn't count them worthy to eat with her. As Paul said, "...if any would not work, neither should he eat" (2 Thes. 3:10). The story of Noah is much the same: all the people who mocked him while he was building the ark probably tried to remind him of their friendship, as they beat on the outside of the ark when the rain began to fall. Neither God, Noah nor the little red hen forced any person to help with their work, but there is a day of judgment and rewards coming when it will be too late to change our minds. The miser of "A Christmas Story", Ebenezer Scrooge, had very few (if any) friends, but he was fortunate enough to have a vision that changed his behavior. We must live lives that will win friends into God's kingdom. Our behavior, not our words, can change their behavior. Jesus came not just to preach how we should behave, but to give his life on the cross, and to create new creatures. It is true that we are saved by grace and not by our deeds, but James (2:14-26) explains that it is by our deeds that we prove our faith in God. Let us thank God for his grace that has even given us faith to believe in him, and then behave like those who belong to him.

Behavior alone creates friends and foes.

JUDGE RIGHTEOUS JUDGMENT

(25:9)   The meek will he guide in judgment: and the meek will he teach his way.

Paul applies this to the church (1 Cor. 6). For God's kingdom to be established on earth, his people must begin to do the judging, and do it fairly. "Meek" means not proud: those who know they are sinners, but forgiven by God's grace. Today, when judges don't give fair judgments, it may be because they themselves are also guilty, remembering Jesus' words, "Judge not, that ye be not judged" (Mt. 7:1). But courts of law must judge fairly, as though sitting in God's place, because Jesus also said, "Stop judging by mere appearances, and make a right judgment" (Jn. 7:24 - NIV). There seem to be two equally dangerous extremes: one is to become a "lawman" and go about as a Pharisee, judging as though I am perfect; the other is to not judge at all, or to be very lenient in dispensing punishments that we know should be harsh, for the sake of justice. That is being a "laxman", being loose in our own conduct and therefore also in discipline, and failing to be strict and exact in our duties (Eccl. 8:11). Those in authority may become so afraid of being accused of being lawmen that they become laxmen, equally evil. Judging righteous judgment means to "discern", not to condemn – always to have the ultimate good of the person in mind, cutting out the bad so the good will win out. "For the time is come that judgment must begin at the house of God: and if it first begin at us, what shall be the end of them that obey not the gospel of God?" (1 Pet. 4:17) If capital punishment is wrong, then God would be wrong to send people to eternal punishment. But if it is just punishment for the good of society, against unrepentant sinners, then we should not be lax in dispensing just judgment.

**Those who show favoritism in
judgment are not good.**

CRUEL HATRED

(35:19)   ...neither let them wink with the eye that hate me without a cause.

David elsewhere refers to this as "cruel hatred" (25:19). Hatred is always cruel, unless it is hatred of sin, which is probably the only reason God gave this capacity to us. Hatred that is directed against people, which begins with unforgiveness, soon turns to bitterness, and it is not possible to hold bitterness without being affected by it. I wondered for years as my mother held bitterness in her heart against her mother. It continued long after her mother died, when she could not even feel my mother's hatred. The funny thing is that she probably never even felt it for the time she was alive, because it remained only in my mother's heart. The only one who ever felt the results of my mother's hatred was my mother! When I reasoned with her from the Bible about God's perspective, and that she was only judging another fallible human who also needed God's grace, she finally released her from her hatred and was able to begin her own inner healing. Jesus died on the cross to receive our punishment for us, but we must also forgive others to receive the benefits of his forgiveness (Mt. 6:12-15). If we refuse to forgive others, we will not need to wait until death to be punished. That will come, but we will suffer here on earth as we continue to hold our hatred inside. Hatred is cruel, not only for the one we may hate and even persecute with our hatred, but it is cruel to ourselves. If you are holding in cruel hatred against one who may have done wrong against you, do yourself a favor and forgive him. Forgiveness may lead that person to repentance. Don't be deceived: you cannot hate (except to hate sin) and stay in God's family.

Hatred is self-punishment.

LET THERE BE LIGHT

(36:9) ...in thy light shall we see light.

God called us "...out of darkness into his marvellous light" (1 Pet. 2:9). The sad thing about blindness is not just that we don't see, but if born blind, we don't even know what we are missing. Jesus spoke in parables so "that seeing they might not see" (Lk. 8:10). He said, "If therefore the light that is in thee be darkness, how great is that darkness!" (Mt. 6:23). And when the Pharisees asked, "Are we blind also?" Jesus said, "If ye were blind, ye should have no sin: but now ye say, We see; therefore your sin remaineth" (Jn. 9:40-41). Someone has said, "There is nobody quite as blind as he that is willfully blind!" Not until God's light comes to illuminate our dull senses do we even know we are blind. Outside of God's light, we don't know how to discern between good and bad, light and dark, black and white. We can only compare sin with sin and have no perfect standard of comparison, but "in thy light shall we see light". When God's Spirit comes upon us, we can distinguish between good and evil. The first recorded words of God in the Bible are "Let there be light" because "the earth was formless and empty" (Gen. 1:2 – NIV) – in chaos. Jesus, the true light, gives light to all, that none need to walk in darkness. When the light comes, for the first time we see that we were not seeing before. That in itself is revelation. But soon, we can also "see light", or recognize what is light and what is not. God gives us his light, to understand and choose what is good over what is not. We can then decide to do what is good for us, and willfully follow the light and truth. We can then be lights to lead others to see.

Ye are the light of the world. (Mt. 5:14)

MOPPING UP STREET CLEANERS

(41:4)   I said, "Lord, be merciful unto me: heal my soul..."

Why mercy? Because "I have sinned against thee". God is the author of forgiveness: it is what he does best for sinners. But, listen again to David, just six verses later: "But thou, O Lord, be merciful unto me, and raise me up..." Now why mercy? "That I may requite [or 'repay'] them"(!) Does something here sound funny to you? When sinners do what sinners do best (sin), they are quick to excuse it with "I'm only human", and quick to look for forgiveness from God. After all, it is what God does best! But how does David then call out to God for judgment on his enemies? God loves to forgive and he commands us to do the same, when people do evil to us. God will not excuse "I'm only human" on Judgment Day. He says, "Be ye therefore perfect, even as your Father which is in heaven is perfect" (Mt. 5:48). "To err is human, to forgive divine" doesn't mean we leave all the responsibility of forgiveness to God alone. If truly it is humanly impossible to forgive, then we need the divine nature inside of us, so that we may also forgive. That only comes when we are born again with God's Spirit in our hearts, by faith in Christ. David's cry for mercy, that he may judge sin in others, shows how much we all need a Savior. A newly saved motorcycle gang leader once was taunted by his unbelieving second-in-command to see if he would really turn his other cheek if he hit him. His response was, "If God gives me the grace, I'll turn the other cheek. If not, I'll wipe up the sidewalk with you!" If you want God to do what he does best, you had better do the same.

To err is human, to forgive divine.

LICK RAZOR

(52:2)   Your tongue plots destruction; it is like a sharpened razor...

Spoken to whom? "...you who practice deceit." (NIV) I'll always remember a pastor named Rick Lazer – he said a young boy once called him 'Lick Razor' by mistake; that sent chills down my spine! A razor is good when it is used for shaving, but used 'deceitfully' it is a lethal weapon. A scalpel may be used by a physician to save a life through surgery, or by a murderer to slit someone's throat. So the tongue can be used to praise God or to curse men (Jas. 3:9); it can speak words of comfort and it can be used to cut, hurt and kill people. Doeg, referred to in this psalm, spoke and caused an innocent priest to be killed. It is even worse when it is done by a friend in betrayal of friendship and covenant. Ahithophel, called "David's counsellor", betrayed him and sided with Absalom, and David refers to it like this: "It was not an enemy that reproached me; then I could have borne it...it was thou, my guide and mine acquaintance. We took sweet counsel together, and walked unto the house of God in company" (Ps. 55:9:14). Be careful how you speak, especially to your friends when anger overtakes you, or if you suddenly feel you have to correct them. Make sure that the motivation is love. We cringe at the thought of licking a razor as our tongue is a very sensitive part of us. But when the tongue becomes a razor, we should be careful not to cut someone's sensitive spirit. "A brother offended is harder to be won than a strong city" (Pr. 18:19). Guard your tongue and don't use it as a razor. Jesus will come to judge even the idle words of our mouths, and he will have "a sharp two-edged sword" coming out of his mouth to strike down the nations (Rev. 1:16).

An injury is much sooner forgotten than an insult.

ANSWERS TO PRAYER

(57:2)   I will cry unto God Most High; unto God that performeth all things for me.

This was from the portion of my Bible reading for today, which was Rufi's wedding day at her home in Srinagar, Kashmir. She is the sister of my Muslim friend Showket, whose family invited me to participate in the celebration. In their home, I join them at their five times of prayer each day, as well as during their fasting for Ramadan, although I pray for them to God the Father, and am observed in all that I do. Today, on Rufi's wedding day, ominous clouds and wind came up in the morning, so the mother asked me to pray for no rain. I read James 5:16-18 to Showket, Zaffar and the father of Naim before I prayed, and soon it was sunny. I also prayed for two days for my flight ticket, worth $77, to be returned, having small faith, and praying "help thou mine unbelief!" I had left it in a newspaper, just like the man did in the movie "It's A Wonderful Life". Today, I called the airport, and it was found! Hallelujah! God answers prayer! They said "you're very lucky it was found", but I know that God did this for my faith to grow. Showket asked for prayer for peace today: gunshots were being fired nearby (common in Kashmir). The military came in the doors at 2:00 pm and there was lots of tension, but we prayed and all returned to normal. Thank you, Jesus! This was an abnormally good day of answers to prayer, though I must say there have been many other prayers answered during our visits here. Once we prayed for a longer ladder so the cross atop St. Luke's Church could be repaired. By God's favor, the local fire company brought their biggest hook-and-ladder truck, and a hundred local Muslims clapped as a barefoot carpenter was hoisted to fix it. God is great!

Listen to my prayer, O God, do not
ignore my plea (55:1 - NIV)

CUSTOMS: ANYTHING TO DECLARE?

(65:4)   Blessed are those you choose and bring near to live in your courts! (NIV)

Anything to declare? Yes: Jesus is Lord! How are we to be reconciled to God? It is by his choice and through the blood of Christ. "Custom reconciles us to everything"; well, almost, that is. Custom cannot reconcile us to God. If we perform all of our forefathers' customs, we will not be excommunicated from their religion. If we can take on the customs of another people, we can be reconciled to them. But, reconciling all of the people, religions and all of creation has no meaning if Christ is not Lord of it all. Man will try to reconcile all things by making a common religion, a custom for all to adhere to, but God will be left out of that plan. Paul has said this of Christ alone: "For God was pleased…through him to reconcile to himself all things…by making peace through his blood shed on the cross" (Col. 1:19-20 - NIV). Jesus said there is nothing wrong with custom or tradition, but it can never supersede God's Commandments. If custom could reconcile us to everything, it would reconcile us to all sinful things also. God's plan is to reconcile *all things to himself,* not *us to everything.* An intelligent "antichrist" may someday succeed in a plan to reconcile man to everything, through custom, but such a person can never reconcile us to God. Only Christ's blood can do that. Let all customs first be subject to the lordship of Christ. For those outside of Christ, the following Psalm speaks of God's awesome deeds: "So great is your power that your enemies cringe before you" (Ps. 66:3 - NIV). That is something short of reconciliation, and a disappointment to everyone. Let true reconciliation be from God.

Custom reconciles us to everything.

BE YE FOLLOWERS OF ME

(72:1)   Give the king thy judgments, O God, and
thy righteousness unto the king's son.

Psalm 72 is subtitled "A Psalm for Solomon", and ends with "The prayers of David the son of Jesse are ended". Although this is an excellent prayer by David, Solomon needed the example of a good father more than a prayer alone. Fortunately, David's worst sins were done before Solomon was born (2 Sam. 11:1-12:25), so this was a sincere prayer that Solomon could have God's righteousness in spite of David's failures. A good foundation for faith in God must begin with "precept upon precept" (Isa. 28:10), as the Jews had in the Law of Moses, and surely David and Solomon had that. But, when precepts are demonstrated with living examples, they are more effective. Israel, in the Old Testament, learned by living and making mistakes, and became living examples for us (1 Cor. 10:11). Jesus came finally as the ultimate example for us all, living a holy life, and suffering and dying for sin. God has even used examples of evil to teach Israel to follow him and "sent the ark of his might into captivity" (Ps. 78:61 - NIV). If we won't listen to the law and won't be coaxed by good example, God will use bad circumstances to get our attention. If we listen to the law and receive God's judgments, we can pray effectively for God's righteousness to be given to our children. But, don't bother to pray this prayer, as David did, if your life is not submitted to God's precepts. It is doubtful that God will hear you. "Practice what you preach". Do not say "Do as I say, not as I do". That is hypocrisy. As Paul said, "Be ye followers of me, even as I also am of Christ" (1 Cor. 11:1). Let that model spur us on to also be examples of good to others, and especially to our children.

Example is always more efficacious than precept.

TURN US AGAIN

(80:3)   Turn us again, O God, and cause thy face to shine; and we shall be saved.

Two things, both attributed to God, cause us to be saved. First, God must "turn us again". God must do it, yet he commands us to do it. Both Jesus and John the Baptist began their preaching with "Repent, for the kingdom of heaven is at hand" (Mt. 3:2, 4:17). Peter and Paul continued preaching repentance and faith towards God. But, just as we pray "Lord, save my friend, and grant him repentance", we find it is only God himself who can turn us and <u>cause</u> us "to will and to do of his good pleasure" (Php. 2:13). Here, Asaph is asking God to cause us to repent: "Turn us again towards you". As Christians, we need God to daily turn us again, by filling us again and again with his Holy Spirit. "Cause thy face to shine" means to show kindness to us, or to look with favor and not anger towards us. Like the sun shining upon us after days of storms and rain, so we desire God's mercy and love, not his wrath. We deserve none of this, but it is all of God's grace. Even the prayer itself, asking God to turn us again and look with favor, comes from God moving upon us by his Spirit. Truly, "Salvation is of the Lord" (Jonah 2:9). Revival begins with prayers like this (Ps. 85:6,7), acknowledging God as the author and finisher of our faith. It excludes our boasting, and attributes all to God, as we will surely do in heaven. Even as Asaph is praying to be turned, he realizes his prayer itself is sin, until it is God who motivates us to turn from sin. As a nation we must ask for God's mercy and favor, and that he would turn us in our hearts to him and be saved.

Every good gift and every perfect
gift is from above... (Jas. 1:17)

YE ARE GODS

(82:6,7)   I have said, Ye are gods... but ye shall die like men..."

If there were any doubt about what this statement means, Jesus quoted it when people were ready to stone him for saying he was God (Jn. 10:34-6). We went again yesterday to see "Sai Baba", a "god-man" with supposedly 50 million followers around the world. Jesus said, "For many shall come in my name, saying, I am Christ; and shall deceive many" (Mt. 24:5), and this man is one of many. People followed Jim Jones to their death, using poison, and will be responsible for committing suicide. They can't blame him, because they gave their minds to him. Multitudes followed Adolph Hitler and killed 6 million Jews. He was wrong, and deceived many. These and many more came, and they will continue to come, and will die because they are mere men. Jesus proved he was true by rising from the dead! God has given the title "gods" to men, beginning with Adam, who had dominion over the whole earthly creation. But Satan deceived him with something "more", saying "...ye shall be as gods, knowing good and evil" (Gen. 3:5). The truth is that God had already made Adam to be as much of a "god" as he would ever be, but he lost it through disobedience against God. Ever since, we all "die like men". Still, God continues to make us to be "gods", or judges in the affairs of men. If we dispense our duties correctly, there will be rewards, but if we use our power to become lords over men, even if we never become "god-men" like Sai Baba, we will die and be punished. Jesus was punished, but it was for our sins and not his, because he really was and is God. [See 1 Cor. 8:6]

...though there be that are called gods...
but to us there is but one God...

TAMING OF THE SHREWD

(91:13)   Thou shalt tread upon the lion and adder...

Humanly impossible? No. Daniel walked in a lion's den and Paul threw a poisonous snake into the fire, and there have been "lion tamers" and "snake charmers" all throughout history. If man has walked on the moon, then is there anything that man cannot do (Gen. 11:6)? Yes, sin has made it impossible for man to get to heaven. But, "The things which are impossible with men are possible with God" (Lk. 18:27). If even one man could make it to heaven, then others could do it also. That is why Jesus, as God, became a man. If he lived without sin, *as a man*, then another man could do it, and if he rose from the dead, and went up boldly and bodily into heaven, then other men and women also could follow him. If he remained as God, we would still be lost from heaven, with no hope. When Sir Edmund Hillary climbed to the top of Mount Everest, a new human record was set, and others followed. World records of human achievement are recorded in the Guinness Book of World Records, but that book and all human achievements in this world will lose meaning and someday burn up, unless we can get off this planet and get up to heaven. Solomon, who topped many of man's success stories, said it is all "vanity" unless we "Fear God, and keep his commandments" (Eccl. 12:8, 13). Jesus ran the race and won it, treading upon the lion, the adder and the dragon on the way, which are all names for the devil, and we can do the same by "looking unto Jesus" as our example and Lord. If man, by wisdom, hopes to get into heaven, God will "destroy the wisdom of the wise" (1 Cor. 1:19), and tame the shrewd.

All may do what by man has been done.

GOD'S SHEEP

(100:3)   We are his people, and the sheep of his pasture.

David said "The Lord is my shepherd", which implies that we are his sheep, and shows a certain relationship between us and God. A shepherd cares for his sheep, and is willing to lay down his life for them. The sheep have only to grow wool, which happens quite automatically as they eat and drink, and as weather changes from hot to cold. But "all we like sheep have gone astray; we have turned every one to his own way" (Isa. 53:6), so Jesus became not only the shepherd, but a lamb without spot or blemish, to die in our place. We are, by God's choice (not ours), "his people", which excludes those who are not his. God will separate the sheep from the goats at the last day, while here on earth "wolves" will come in sheep's clothing, trying to carry off and destroy unsuspecting sheep. But sheep don't think of all these dangers – they just grow wool. Saving them is shepherds' work. We just graze in his pasture, where he leads and keeps us. If we stray away, he will come and look for us until he finds us, because we are his sheep and people. Our wool, when it is harvested, becomes clothing for others who cannot grow it. But, we cannot withhold it; it belongs to our shepherd. Likewise, all that we are and own belongs to Jesus. We are an extension of his heart to the world, that others may be saved. We are helpless without the shepherd, and become prey to every evil thing. To the world, we are sheep for the slaughter, but to God, we are his own beloved people for whom he died. Take heart and rejoice in the goodness of God, who chose us and will keep us to the end. "For ye were as sheep going astray; but are now...

**... returned to the Shepherd and
Bishop of your souls.** (1 Pet. 2:25)

APPOINTED TO DEATH

(102:20) *...To hear the groaning of the prisoner;*
to loose those that are appointed to death.

Here is a pathetic picture of our lost state, being prisoners in chains and shackles, groaning for deliverance, and in pain and suffering. We are appointed to death, prisoners on death row, with no plea of pardon to ask. That we are guilty, and in prison for our own sins, there is no doubt. But, Like Barabbas, with no right to be released because he was guilty of sedition and murder, we suddenly find we are released, free to go. A prisoner has no ability to release himself. He may be on his best behavior, but his "good works" cannot free him; they are simply acts he should have done all along, or else he wouldn't be in prison. Only he who has the authority can release the prisoner. God does not look for repentant hearts – he creates them, by releasing us from the just punishment for our sins, as Paul says, "...the goodness of God leadeth thee to repentance" (Rom. 2:4). We are in a prison of our own sins. We groan, wishing we had not been so stupid, to disobey God's just laws. If we don't see this, we will continue until death, and then be thrown into the final prison of Hades. But, except for the grace of God, we will not see this. Most of us prisoners, like Barabbas, continue to groan and to curse the one who alone can set us free. God first sets us free from the prison of our own bitterness, as he shows us it is our own fault: we are condemned for our own sins, and God is only just. When a broken, groaning heart is given a merciful pardon, he won't go back to sin, but will be released to live a life of grateful thanks and service to the one who has freely forgiven him.

To serve God is to be set free.

I AM THE DOOR

(106:19)   They made a calf in Horeb, and worshiped the molten image.

If God goes before us, doors will always open. Israel had seen this graphically in Egypt and at the Red Sea, yet they built a golden calf and worshiped it. How can this happen? Idolatry is the first and worst way to break God's Ten Commandments. We in America have followed in the sin of Israel. God made America great, because our forefathers honored him as the one who opens doors. Then, slowly and imperceptibly, our affection turned from God to idolatry, in the form of money, and various other kinds of idolatry followed. Now, military strength and education, freedom and democracy, medicine and hordes of other false hopes have blinded us to the true source of blessings. God doesn't care what brand of idolatry we fall into, as it all leads away from him. The "Beatles", who sang so innocently that "money can't buy me love" changed their tune to "give me money" and "love can't pay my bills", and a whole generation that idolized the love of sex and money was led away from God. "Doors of perception" were opened through drugs, and these became the great "doors of deception". God began his Commandments with "I am the Lord thy God, which have brought thee out of the land of Egypt, out of the house of bondage. Thou shalt have no other gods before me." (Ex. 20:2,3) If we turn back to Egypt, we return to bondage. If we break God's first command in our heart, we soon break the second with our hands, and make some "graven image" idol that we can see and bow down before. Jesus alone is the door that leads to eternal life.

If money goes before, it always opens the door.

PRECIOUS IS OUR DEATH

(116:15)   Precious in the sight of the Lord is the death of his saints.

'Precious' in the Hebrew language means valuable, prized, not lightly esteemed, costly, with dignity, honorable, or bringing glory to God (from Strong's Concordance). All of these describe the worth of our life, and especially of our death, before God. He jealously guards what is most precious to him, and we can trust that nobody can easily snatch it from God's hand. Death comes to all, but the death of God's saints has significance. Jesus' death meant life for each of us. All the martyrs of history have died with honor, and have brought even more glory to God in death than in their whole lives. From "righteous Abel" (Mt. 23:35) whose blood cried out from the ground, to John the Baptist, who cried out against sin, the Old Testament saints waited to see God's salvation. But martyrdom only increased from that time, and "the blood of the martyrs is the seed of the church". Stephen's death was precious to God, as Jesus stood up and received him into heaven. Our sufferings are precious, but much more is our death. I read this scripture to Ric Carlson as he was dying from cancer. Hearing a clap of thunder, he said "Speak, Lord", needing encouragement, as he was only thirty years old, and was leaving behind a wife and three children. When death seems meaningless and senseless, like Jim Elliot's, who was killed with spears by the Auca Indians he tried to reach with the gospel, it is good to remember that it is precious to God, and won't be for nothing. We must be faithful, as we may one day be called to die for our faith in Christ. Let us be faithful unto death.

O death, where is thy sting? (1 Cor. 15:55)

GOD'S FAITHFUL AFFLICTIONS

(119:75) *...that thy judgments are right, and that*
thou in faithfulness hast afflicted me.

When afflictions come, ultimately they are from God. We can blame ourselves, or the devil, or others, but God allows it for his own purposes. When God afflicts me, it is in faithfulness, and for my own good (Rom. 8:28). Although the blood of Jesus has fully paid for my sins, God is working in me to change me into Christ's image, and that takes affliction. Hardships keep me humble when I want to judge others, and they teach me dependence upon God. They lead me to search my heart to see if I need to make some restitution for past sins, so others are not hindered from God's grace by my sin. They lead me into prayer. "...the goodness of God leadeth thee to repentance" (Rom. 2:4), but sometimes God must first get our attention, and that requires afflictions. Afflictions seem to be different from suffering, at least in one respect: afflictions are put upon us without any reason, and may exclude our choice. Suffering includes the option of getting out of it. In my early days as a Christian, I did a word study on suffering, and in the King James Version I found "suffer" can mean "to allow", as in Jesus' words: "Suffer little children, and forbid them not, to come unto me" (Mt. 19:14). If this is true, then it explains how suffering is more honorable than affliction: when suffering torture for our faith, we may opt out of it by simply denying Christ, but God's true saints will persevere until the end, staying faithful to God. It is God who shows his faithfulness to us in our afflictions. Job was afflicted, Paul and Moses rejoiced in suffering (Php. 3:10, Heb. 11:25), and we may thank God for his faithful afflictions to us!

**Be joyful in hope, patient in affliction,
faithful in prayer.** (Rom. 12:12 - NIV)

CHILDREN, CHICKENS & KITCHENS

(128:6)   Yea, thou shalt see thy children's children...

This is a beautiful blessing for all those who fear the Lord, but it is an empty, painful dream to many who set their hearts upon it without fear of God. Doubtless, many who don't even know God have had grandchildren, but it is sad when people who do know God set their affections on his promises more than on him. There are no grandchildren without children, no children without a wife, and no wife without the fear of God, as "whoso findeth a wife findeth a good thing, and obtaineth favor of the Lord" (Pr. 18:22). It's OK to have and to hold a hen, and to set your affections upon chicken's chicken's chickens, but don't count them before they are hatched. "Children like olive plants round about thy table" (128:3) will be a "favor of the Lord" when they arrive, but don't flaunt your kitchen before you are hitched. Fear the Lord, and if he adds a wife and a kitchen table, thank him and fear him, and continue to set your affection upon him. Don't count your olive plants until they sprout. But, neither should you set your affections on what you do have, because "the Lord gave, and the Lord hath taken away" (Job 1:21). Fear God, and love and enjoy your wife and children and grandkids while you have them. Counting unhatched chickens leads to disappointment if they don't hatch, because "hope deferred maketh the heart sick: but when the desire cometh, it is a tree of life" (Pr. 13:12). I would rather have children than olive plants around my kitchen table, and it is no sin to desire what God has promised his children. But even earthly parents expect their children to appreciate them more than Christmas presents.

Don't count your chickens before they are hatched.

HIS LOVE ENDURES FOREVER

(136:10)   *... to him who struck down the firstborn*
             of Egypt; his love endures forever. (NIV)

How can these two statements appear in the same sentence? Can God kill all firstborn children and still have us say, "His mercy endureth forever (KJV)"? Yet, the Psalmist boldly and plainly says it. The reason is that he is a God of covenant love and mercy. He made promises to Abraham, Isaac and Jacob of blessing their generations, and Israel remembers these promises when they are having hard times. "Mercy" is undeserved rescue from just punishment. All the world stands guilty before the holy God, and none can deserve mercy, or it would not be mercy. But God keeps his promise of mercy to the people of his covenant. If he kills firstborn sons, it is to punish the evil oppression of Egypt, or another nation who opposes God's rule. But, if he mercifully brings Israel out of captivity and slavery, it is because of covenant love. But, one may ask, doesn't God love everybody? We are ignorant of who God is outside of his revelation of himself in Holy Scripture. "For the Lord hath chosen Jacob unto himself, and Israel for his peculiar treasure...Whatsoever the Lord pleased, that did he in heaven, and in earth..." (Ps. 135:4,6). God says, "I will have mercy on whom I will have mercy (Rom. 9:15). If God loves every person, why will some be punished forever? Rather, God has chosen to shower unconditional love and mercy upon us, whom he has chosen, and others will be passed over, and will go to the place that <u>we</u> <u>all</u> deserve! That is mercy, plain and simple, for us who are saved, but he owes it to nobody, not even us. "Or are you envious because I am generous?" (Mt. 20:15 - NIV).

God is love (1 John 4:8)

192

DOES MIGHT MAKE RIGHT?

(142:6)   *...deliver me from my persecutors; for they are stronger than I.*

The sad fact of history is that truth is always persecuted by those who hate it. This has continued throughout time, since the origin of all rebellions, when Satan challenged God. But God, who is himself the truth, is all powerful, and so truth will always win out. However, in this life, we who follow the truth will come up against persecutions as long as falsehood exists. One falsehood is that "might makes right" and, although in the end almighty God will judge all falsehood to prove absolute might makes right, still in this age there are many who are very strong and very wrong! For example, if Nazism or Communism were to somehow gain world dominion, they would not suddenly change from false to true. If all the world became adulterers, God would not change his seventh Commandment. But, as long as the world exists, and until Christ returns, those who hate the truth will continue to persecute those who choose to live the truth. Communists tried for years to overpower the truth by persecuting Christians, but true believers called out to God who is stronger than all of the persecutors. Likewise, no religion that denies the blood of Christ as the atonement for sin will ever graduate to being the truth. They may persecute and kill, but they will never become true. As a funny fantasy, what if Satan could somehow overcome God. Would he then become all powerful and would evil become good? No, he would cease to exist, because he only continues to exist in the imagination of God, so if it were possible, he would only destroy himself by destroying God. Only God is eternal and right.

**The false can never grow into
truth by growing in power.**

THE LITTLE BANG THEORY

(3:19)   The Lord by wisdom hath founded the earth...

That God is a God of order is observable in all of nature. That a "Big Bang" could be the foundation of the universe is contrary to all common sense. There is order, like a Swiss watch, in every level of life, from the atomic to the astronomic. The very arrangement and beauty of all the parts of flowers and fruits, the human body, the ecology of earth and of every observable thing screams out against the thought of chaos as our beginning. Study the thoughts of Scripture and consider the following verses: "Let all things be done decently and in order" (1 Cor. 14:40); "The steps of a good man are ordered by the Lord" (Ps. 37:23); "And the Lord God took the man, and put him into the garden of Eden to dress it and to keep it" (Gen. 2:15); "And look that thou make them after the pattern, which was shewed thee in the mount" (Ex. 25:40). These verses show that in every age, man has recognized two things: God is a God of order, and he has delegated the responsibility of order to man. Order comes from orderly minds. Governments that work are the result of order, and when they fail, it is because man has gone against the prescribed order. The Ten Commandments and all of Scripture are the orderly blueprint for the government of this world. Every infraction against God's design for order will result in disorder in that part of the universe. The kingdom of God is established in men's hearts, that we may take an active part in re-establishing order in our world. "The board of education applied to the seat of wisdom" has been out of schools for too long. Maybe a "little bang" on the bottom will restore sense, before a "Big Atomic Bang" disorders us all.

Good order is the foundation of all things.

SIN IN THE SYNAGOGUE

(5:14) I was almost in all evil in the midst of the congregation and assembly.

As the author talks about the "strange woman" (v. 3), he instructs the young man to stay far away from her, and save himself for one who will be faithful. This is probably <u>not</u> written by Solomon, who "loved many strange women" (1 Ki. 11:1), and was greatly ruined by it. This is a strong temptation to young men, and will lead to destruction. Self-control is the virtue that is both needed and cultivated as we resist temptation. Sin begins with a simple neglect of obedience to teachers, or disobedience to God's laws. Soon, we are "almost in all evil" before all men, and even right in the church! It leads to rebellion and rejection of our own conscience and all authority. This is what happened with Zimri and Cozbi (a Midianite woman) after Balaam led Israel into this sin of mixing with "strange women", and Zimri brought her right into "the sight of all the congregation", and was killed for it. Adultery and fornication will lead a man, and soon a whole nation, to ruin if the sin is not considered as lethal. America is near to ruin now, with a divorce rate of 68%, and much of that among nominal Christians. Often we are at the edge of destruction before we discover how a little sin has brought us so far from God. "The lust of the flesh, and the lust of the eyes" (1 Jn. 2:16) will blind young men and women, and later will ruin any chance for a good and faithful love to develop in marriage. Luke 4:33 shows a man with an unclean spirit sitting right in the synagogue! Why was he there? Because the devil wants to ruin lives of young people, and flaunt sin right in the holy place. Let us recognize unclean spirits and rid the church of them.

**Catch...the little foxes that ruin the
vineyards...** (Song 2:15 - NIV)

WORDS WITHOUT WISDOM

(10:19)   *When words are many, sin is not absent...*

...but he who holds his tongue is wise (NIV). Probably my worst sin, closely followed by (or flamed by) anger, is my failure to control my lips from speaking caustic words. James 3:2 says "If any man offend not in word, the same is a perfect man, and able also to bridle the whole body". As a young Christian years ago, I used to meditate on this and to try to be a "perfect man". It is still a good and lofty goal for me as a Christian. Wanting to "have the last word" causes us all to keep up our arguments forever! Job's friends came to comfort him, but their long winded speeches were only words without wisdom. They should have listened in silence and let Job vent his emotions. It is better to stop and think before speaking, and much sin and hurt will be done away. "Chauncy", the gardener in the movie <u>Being There</u>, was considered a wise man because he simply spoke so little. How much better to speak little out of a true wisdom gleaned from our experience of the bad effects of saying too much. "Great swelling words of vanity" come from the mouths of those who are "servants of corruption" (2 Pet. 2:18,19). Any fool can speak volumes, but a truly wise and perfect man will learn to hold his tongue until it is truly needed. Monks often take vows of silence, to learn to control their whole bodies. Sometimes cellophane tape wouldn't be a bad idea. But the real answer is to be broken by the spirit of God, and hate the sin that results too often by opening my big mouth! Wisdom comes through experience, from many failures that lead to repentance. "Lord, break my stubborn will. Amen."

**...be swift to hear, slow to speak,
slow to wrath...** (Jas. 1:19)

Fair And Lovely

(14:24)   The crown of the wise is their riches, but the foolishness of fools is folly.

Generally speaking, we get what we deserve, and we tend to show on the outside what is really on the inside. "The glory of young men is their strength, and the beauty of old men is the grey head" (Pr. 20:29), so "if you've got it, flaunt it". But, if you've got it and don't deserve it, something's wrong. "As a jewel of gold in a swine's snout, so is a fair woman which is without discretion" (Pr. 11:22). When the "mirror, mirror on the wall" tells "who's the fairest one of all", all the beauty in the world won't make up for an ounce of fairness in good judgment. Jesus had "no form nor comeliness... no beauty that we should desire him" (Isa. 53:2). Yet he is "the chiefest among ten thousand" (Song 5:10). America has become famous because of the heroic deeds of our forefathers, but today we are living on the glory of our past. It is a gold ring that doesn't fit us. Jacob told Simeon and Levi, "Ye have troubled me to make me to stink among the inhabitants of the land" (Gen. 34:30), because he saw that their killing of the Canaanites was not an act of bravery, but was done through deceit. Cowardice stinks, but heroism has its own smell of sweetness. It is fitting that Jesus was anointed with a sweet ointment before his death, not just for burial, but as a statement of the greatness of his selfless act. Young men do nothing to get strong (it is naturally given, though it may be exercised), and old men don't need to color their hair gray. But, brave deeds should be rewarded with fame. Perfume may hide a bad odor, but there is a natural perfume that arises from one who suffers or dies for truth. Let someone praise your deeds, not your choice of deodorants.

Fame is the perfume of heroic deeds.

COWARDLY LIONS

(20:2)   A king's wrath is like the roar of a lion. (NIV)

The lion has long been known as the "king of the forest", and there are few that can challenge him. In <u>The Wizard of Oz</u>, we laugh at the cowardly lion, who is afraid of even his own tail, because everyone knows a lion's greatest characteristics are his strength and fearlessness. King Richard was called "Richard the Lionhearted" to display his fearlessness, and nobody would ever want a king or president who was a "milk toast", afraid of his own shadow. God has promised a crown to those who are "faithful unto death" (Rev. 2:10) for his kingdom, a crown of life that is not corruptible (1 Cor. 9:25). "But the fearful, and unbelieving…" will only inherit death and "…the lake which burneth with fire and brimstone" (Rev. 21:8), and there will be no crowns for them. Men who are fearless may reign on earth, but until they learn to fear God, they will never be able to reign in eternity. Satan feared nothing, not even God himself, and although he was thrown out of heaven, he soon climbed up to the exalted position of "the god of this world" (2 Cor. 4:4). He goes about "as a roaring lion" (1 Pet. 5:8), to instill fear and awe in those who will bow to him, and he offers crowns and riches to those who will join in his rebellion. He even offered Jesus the crowns of all this world's kingdoms, if he would only fearlessly forsake the fear of God, and bow before him. But Jesus rejected the quick and easy way, and set his face towards the cross. That took true fearlessness, and proved him to be the "Lion of Judah", crowned with many crowns. Satan will prove finally to be the "cowardly lion", ruling nothing.

Fearless minds climb soonest upon crowns.

LYNCHING MOBS

(24:29)   Say not, I will do so to him as he hath done to me...

"For every action there is an equal and opposite reaction". Even science acknowledges this but when it comes to justice, who can make a blameless judgment before first judging himself? Why does God say, "It is mine to avenge; I will repay" (Deut. 32:35 - NIV)? It is because he alone "is without sin...", and able to "...first cast a stone..." (Jn. 8:7) at those who have sinned. Anyone else would only bring judgment and revenge upon himself, as we ourselves are not without sin (Mt. 7:1; Rom. 2:1). "Lynching mobs" and "vigilante" groups in the Wild West days sought to bring justice when crimes were committed, but the trouble with revenge is that we do it in anger and don't know when to stop, and others are led to avenge themselves for our bitter revenge. Samson continued to avenge himself for his enemies' wrongs, and he lost his eyes and finally even his life because of it. The famous Hatfield and McCoy feud led to years of bitterness and many deaths. When we hold bitter resentment for a person who has done wrong to us, we hurt ourselves and others, and justice is never reached. "An eye for an eye, and a tooth for a tooth" (Mt. 5:38) was meant to put the fear of God in us, to keep us from sin, and not to become a platform for getting our revenge. If I see sin in others, it should lead me to search my own wicked heart, not to attempt to be their judge. Vigilant prayer, and not vigilante groups, will restore justice, and "hot lynching mobs of vengeance" should be replaced instead by "heart wrenching sobs of repentance" and hot tears.

Revenge is a kind of wild justice.

RATIONS AND FASHIONS

(25:27)   *"It is not good to eat much honey:*

...so for men to search their own glory is not glory". One of the privileges of growing up is that we get to choose our own bedtime and what we want to eat, after mom and dad have tried for years to lead us in a good way. Too many sweets are not good for the teeth or for the stomach, but that has to be made plain by tooth-aches and stomach-aches. We become the final judges of what is really good to eat, and we pay the consequences if we choose wrongly. When we dress, though, others judge whether or not we look good in the clothes we wear. The same is true of spiritual things. We choose right or wrong, and will ourselves live with the consequences if we continue to choose wrong things, (or even excesses of right things!) "Holier than thou" people have had too much honey, and probably need to be granted a trial or two to understand God's grace. But, like wearing clothes, we are judged by others as we ourselves tend to do the same. Our good works should be done to lead others to Christ, not as things to make us feel good about ourselves. God has graciously given us food and other necessities and pleasures in this life that we may enjoy him and his love for us, but he expects us to be clothed with good works, too, and to beautify his creation so that others may enjoy it. Our "robes of righteousness" (Isa. 61:10) are not to be self-righteousness, but actions and attitudes that show Christ to others. Eat the Word of God daily, and let the resulting good works show others how to be clothed also with Christ.

Eat to please yourself, but dress to please others.

Donate Your Mouth

(31:8) Speak up for those who cannot speak for themselves… (NIV)

Never mind giving your eyes or other bodily organs after you are dead, when it costs you nothing. Do something with your life, for someone who can then benefit spiritually by seeing your true Christian spirit. This verse does not mean speaking for a dumb person, like translation, but rather that we should speak out for those who are wasting away illegally in prison because of a corrupt system of law, or because they have nobody to plead their cause. Multitudes of young men and women in India have been put in jail illegally, and kept there for years without trial, and then sent out and declared innocent (oops, sorry!) Who will cry out against such evil in the legal system, if Christians don't? We are told, "I was… sick, and in prison, and ye visited me not" (Mt. 25:43), spoken by Jesus. We feel very noble, to give our eyes for a blind man after we die, or to make someone the beneficiary of our will, but how about doing something now, when it costs us something (we can't spend it, then). Jesus was quite practical in loving people in this present life, not just preaching about the hereafter. Of course, this verse means also that we should cry out to God for those who are spiritually dumb, who don't even know how to cry out for salvation, and are "appointed for destruction", as the second half of this verse states. But both are necessary, as we are to bring God's kingdom "in earth, as it is in heaven" (Mt. 6:10). Donate your mouth to God, and "Cry aloud, spare not, lift thy voice like a trumpet, and shew my people their transgression…" (Isa. 58:1).

The mouth of a righteous man is
a well of life… (Pr. 10:11)

TURN OFF THE DARK

(2:13)   …wisdom is better than folly, just as light is better than darkness. (NIV)

"Be not overcome of evil, but overcome evil with good" (Rom. 12:21). The movie "Star Wars" showed an interesting and important principle: If Luke had given in to hatred towards the very evil Darth Vader, he would have become as evil himself. God has put us all in an evil world, and when others do wicked things to us, the temptation is to "fight fire with fire" and to be as angry and belligerent in return. But Jesus came to die on a cross, and to overcome evil with good. If we retaliate with evil, the world becomes a little more evil, but when we respond in an opposite spirit, the kingdom of heaven is established on earth. Light is always better than darkness because darkness is only the absence of light. "And the light shineth in darkness; and the darkness comprehended it not" [or, 'has not over powered it'] (Jn. 1:5). Let the light in you be a blessing to those in darkness. They have nothing to give, but those with light do. Can darkness extinguish a candle? No. Maybe a breeze can, but not darkness. Light will rather extinguish the darkness. Kind acts done towards those who know only how to be angry will be the eventual means for them to change. As Jesus said, "Father, forgive them; for they know not what they do" (Lk. 23:34). Those in darkness don't even have the light to see what they are doing, so we can't expect something out of nothing. Let the light of Christ, which has been graciously given to you, be passed on to others in darkness that they may see. When the true light comes, we can say, "turn off the lights, the sun is up!"

Let a man overcome anger by kindness, evil by good.

No Discharge In War

(8:8)   *"As no one is discharged in time of war,*

...so wickedness will not release those who practice it" (NIV). In wartime, soldiers are not given discharges while the army is in the heat of battle. We are in a spiritual war that started in heaven (Rev. 12:7), and continues while life remains on earth. The battle rages on, day and night, and the enemy will not let up on his attacks. There is no discharge for us, no laying down of weapons to take leave or vacation. "So wickedness will not release those who practice it." Whoever is not on the Lord's side in this war is one who practices wickedness. Everyone is on one side or the other; we can only defect from one side to the other. Wickedness holds tightly to those who give themselves over to it, and the only escape is to join the Lord's army, through faith in his blood. Then we become sworn enemies to Satan. In God's army, "no one is discharged in time of war", and this war never stops. Until our dying breath, we are conscripted into the fighting army, and we will all die in battle. The only question is "which side are you on?" Jesus said, "He that is not with me is against me" (Mt. 12:30), an all-inclusive statement. Like it or not, we are in the war, and all we can do is to choose sides. Will we fight valiantly for righteousness and die a martyr's death, and receive a crown of glory? Or, will we choose to "enjoy the pleasures of sin for a season" (Heb. 11:25) in the devil's army, and still die in the battle, and receive God's wrath? A "pacifist" will die in the battle, just as we all will, and a "deserter" will become a member of Satan's army. With "no discharge", which side are you on?

You've got to serve somebody.

FIRE IN MY BONES

(12:9)   ...because the preacher was wise, he still taught the people knowledge...

Some things cannot simply be taught, but are born in us. It is true that Solomon asked for wisdom, but he was born with the wisdom that prompted him to ask for more. After writing the depressing book of Ecclesiastes, calling everything "vanity", "he still taught the people knowledge" because it was inherent in him. Yet, he realized that he could only teach knowledge or facts, as wisdom must come from God. When a person is "born again" it is not that he has decided to make a wise decision, but rather that he is born of God (Jn. 1:13). As Christians, we can teach others knowledge, but only God can turn it into conversion. Solomon's wisdom was not accumulated from schools, but created in him from birth. Poets have always been prophets of their generations, putting in words the highest hopes of mankind. When true prophets of God are born, they cannot help but speak the truth to whoever "hath ears to hear" (Mt. 13:9). Solomon's wisdom made him painfully aware of the vanity of sin in the world, but "still he taught the people knowledge" in the hopes of others learning wisdom. When Jeremiah grew weary of hard people's rejection and persecution and decided not to speak at all, he found he could not hold it in; it was "a fire shut up in my bones" (Jer. 20:9). If you are wise and have God's truth that leads to eternal life in your heart, thank God for it. It was born in you by his Spirit, not by your doing. And, if you are wise, then even when you are subject to vanity and persecution, "still, teach the people knowledge" so that they may be saved.

A poet is born, not made.

UNDIVIDED ATTENTION

(2:16)   My beloved is mine, and I am his.

Here is a good study of how a marriage relationship will progress, and it is how my relationship to Jesus grows as I spend more time with him. Jesus Christ is Lord, but he lets me discover it on my own. I began by "asking Jesus into my heart", the evening of September 7, 1972. I loved Jesus immediately, but trust had to grow. At first, I felt it was an equal contract: "you are mine and I am yours", but I reserved the "right" to leave, as I assumed Jesus did, too. But, God is "a jealous God" (Ex. 20:5), and will not consider any other master sharing his place, and his love won my heart. Soon I could say, "I am my beloved's, and my beloved is mine" (6:3), which put the ownership first upon Jesus, not me. Before, he was my possession first, and so I could trust him to be equal in owning me. But, as Jesus said, "Ye have not chosen me, but I have chosen you…" (Jn. 15:16). Finally, I could rest in his love and say, "I am my beloved's and his desire is toward me" (7:10), and felt no need to be an equal partner, as he is the Lord. The responsibility for keeping the relationship rests not in how tightly I can hold his hand, but in knowing he will not let go of mine. This is also how marriage should grow, with the wife forsaking all others as she grows to trust her husband as "lord", as Sarah did with Abraham. A marriage cannot work when one has divided affection. When the wife knows "I am my beloved's, and his desire is toward me", she can feel safe to give up her "right" to leave, and will never need to look for security and love elsewhere. That is the kind of love Jesus has shown me, and it teaches me how I should love my wife as a blessing from God.

No man can serve two masters. (Mt. 6:24)

RETURN TO REASON

(1:18)   *"Come now, and let us reason together", saith the Lord.*

Faith in God, resulting in obedience to his commands, is the only reasonable way to live. When we sin, it is going against reason. No reasonable person would ever kill, steal, commit adultery with another's spouse, worship idols, tell lies, divorce, or have an abortion. But, even after having done these sins, reason would have us turn back to God in repentance, make restitution, and go on in the way of reason again. Sadly, people who sin try to cover or excuse their sin, and that leads to more and worse sins. Nazi war criminals went insane with guilt, not willing to return to reason. We are all guilty before a holy God who demands that we return to reason, or die. A few chapters later, God says, "Take counsel together, and it shall come to nought..." (8:10). This is also reasoning together, but it is not by faith when God's counsel is left out. The "Age of Reason" resulted in masses of people losing faith in God, as human reasoning became supreme. When "The kings of the earth set themselves, and the rulers take counsel together, against the Lord, and against his anointed", God laughs (Ps. 2:2, 4). Reason that results in disobedience to God's commands is the opposite of faith; it is unbelief, and it will come to nothing. Eve reasoned with the serpent, and left out God's counsel and command. The result was that "death passed upon all men" (Rom. 5:12). Faith would have continued to do the reasonable thing and obey God, regardless of what human reasoning said. The greatness of God's mercy and grace is shown in that "while we were yet sinners, Christ died for us" (Rom. 5:8), and in that God continues to say, even after our sins, "Come now, and let us reason together".

Faith is the continuation of reason.

DULL OF HEARING

(6:10) Make the heart of this people fat, and make their ears heavy...

When God asks "Whom shall I send?" Isaiah responds with "Here am I. Send Me" (v. 8). This is during Isaiah's vision of the glory of God which results in his commission as God's prophet to the Jews. God's message for Isaiah to bring is chilling, and it is designed to wake up the people who are dull of hearing and blind to the truth. The fact that these verses are repeated in the New Testament at least five times is ample proof that God meant it to be taken literally and seriously, but does God really harden hearts? We read of this when Pharaoh continued to harden his heart against the word of God that he should "let my people go!" (Ex. 5:1). It was after he continued many times to harden his heart (Ex. 7:13,22, 8:15,19,32, 9:7) that God gave him over to his evil desire, and we read that God hardened his heart (9:12). Elsewhere in Scripture we read statements like this: "My Spirit shall not always strive with man" (Gen. 6:3) and "He, that being often reproved hardeneth his neck, shall suddenly be destroyed..." (Pr. 29:1). Isaiah does not argue with God's assignment to him, but says simply, "Lord, how long?" Will he have to continue to preach to a people who are hardened in their unbelief and unwilling to hear the plain truth of God's word? Judgment Day will be the final cut-off time for all who are unrepentant. There will be no question about the justice of a holy God, and those who don't make the cut will have only themselves to blame for their stubborn rebellion against God's preaching. We must not boast in our own belief, but thank God for his grace that has allowed us to believe, and pray that others may turn to God.

None is as blind as the one who chooses not to see.

PINOCCHIO'S PROBLEM

(10:15) Does ... a club brandish him who is not wood? (NIV)

Pinocchio really had no problem; he was just a piece of wood carved by Gepetto, with moving arms and legs – a wooden puppet. The real problem was with Gepetto, who thought "I wish this could be a real son to me". People dream up stories like that of "Frankenstein", or make big computers or robots, and scare themselves with the idea that these could somehow come back and overcome their maker. We are all as dead and lifeless as Pinocchio without God's Spirit making us alive, and an evil nation like Assyria is foolish before God to think they can rule the earth, or conquer anything on their own. They were simply a wooden tool in God's hand to perform a task, and will be thrown away when they are no longer of any use to him. Satan is the best example of this, if it is true that he exalted himself against the Lord who made him. God still uses him, like Assyria, to bring his judgment (10:6-7), but he will also be destroyed when he ceases to be useful to God. And you and I? Who are we but puppets like Pinocchio, unless God grants us eternal life by his divine grace? Like him, we don't even know we have a problem until we are awakened to our sin, and until God sovereignly makes us alive. The grace of God is shown in God's love, who became a man like us, so we "might be partakers of the divine nature" (2 Pet. 1:4). Only God can give life. Pinocchio's problems can only come when he is alive, and begins to think he can do anything by himself. Let God be God, and thank him for life, and there will be no problem.

You are the potter, I am the clay.

BABYLONIANS

(14:14) ...I will be like the Most High.

"Babylon, the glory of kingdoms" stands for all time as the city that is opposed to God's Kingdom, whose city is Zion. Nobody escapes the choice of which city he lives for, and nobody can live for both. Godliness and worldliness will not mix, although many will try to have the best of both worlds. And many will say "I live for myself", but they automatically become "Babylonians" by not serving God alone. God will not share his glory with any other "master" or "guru", or any selfish and self-centered rebel who challenges his authority. Some self-acclaimed gurus may seem to be humble, some very proud, but all who refuse total surrender to the Lord Jesus Christ ultimately are saying "I will be like the Most High". That is the spirit of Babylon, which can never live in Zion, the heavenly city of God. Whenever we hear the grace of God preached, and the message of the cross, we choose either Zion or Babylon. Some will receive it "not as the word of men, but as it is in truth, the word of God" (1 Thes. 2:13), and will submit joyfully to Christ, and become "Zionions". Others say "Bah! Baloney!" and they join the ranks of the "Bah-baloney-uns". But, there is a way to "be like the Most High", and that is to repent of selfishness and let the Spirit of Christ and his word "dwell in you richly in all wisdom; teaching and admonishing one another..." (Col.3:16). Then, "when he shall appear, we shall be like him, for we shall see him as he is" (1 Jn. 3:2). Make your choice: "no choice" is already a choice. If you want to be "like the Most High", leave Babylon behind and follow Christ.

No man can serve two masters. (Mt. 6:24)

FOOL'S GOLD

(19:3)   ...and they shall seek to the idols, and to the charmers...

What are idols, anyway? The word means "nothing" or "worthless". So, why do so many millions of people worship some worthless thing? Because, as long as things are going well, idols are beautiful to look at, but when someone really needs his "god" to do something, when the real God of heaven comes to judge sin, they are worthless. Lots of flash, but with no power to save. Charmers are just as useless, dazzling the eyes for personal gain, but out of charm when it is really needed. All the idols, gurus and false hope peddlers of the world, religious or not, have some kind of flash, good looks, money or power, or some beauty to beguile those who look to them for hope. But God came with no flash at all, "no form nor comeliness; and when we shall see him, there is no beauty that we should desire him" (Isa. 53:2). All that Jesus came with was his own inner virtue and power, to overcome the effects of sin on mankind. Simply by his own true Godly nature he overcame sin and death, and he offers himself to us, if we repent of sin, and receive him as the Lord of all. Still, people "seek to the idols and to the charmers", hoping to get something out of nothing, because they don't want to give up their hold on worldly riches or beauty. It is like the man escaping with heavy bags of gold, who will not let go of them when he falls into quicksand. What use will there be for riches when he drowns? Jesus came with no flash, but with all power to save the lost souls from sin. What will you choose? Gold not only cannot save from quicksand, but it will be the very cause of destruction, just as idols will lead to destruction. Jesus alone can save us from the flash of fool's gold.

Charms strike the sight, but merit wins the soul.

TURN THE WORLD UPSIDE DOWN

(24:1)   See, the Lord is going to lay waste the earth and devastate it. (NIV)

God destroyed the whole world once before, saving only Noah and his family, and he will again visit the earth with destruction when the time is right. Life goes on day after day, and evil men seem to "get away with murder", but a day of reckoning will be coming! As in Noah's day, God said, "I will destroy man whom I have created from the face of the earth" (Gen. 6:7), and so there will be a final judgment, and an end of the earth as we now know it. How that will be we do not know, but the point is that God is the sovereign Lord of all the earth, and he will judge correctly. "Waste" and "devastate" are terms of desolation, and the King James Version says he "turneth it upside down", calling to mind Jesus' words "the last shall be first" (Mt. 20:16). Evolution teaches "survival of the fittest", but Jesus said "the meek...shall inherit the earth" (Mt. 5:5), not the strong or smart. It appears that "all things continue as they were from the beginning of the creation...but the day of the Lord will come..." and "seeing then that all these things shall be dissolved, what manner of persons ought ye to be...?" (2 Pet. 3:4, 10-11). When we see that a day of final reckoning is coming, it will make us to no longer think "How can a loving God send anyone to destruction?" but rather, "How can I be saved?" If God will turn the world upside down, how can we stop him? But, if we yield ourselves to his purposes, we also will "turn the world upside down" (Acts 17:6), as workers together with him, and not against him.

...he hath appointed a day, in the which he will judge the world in righteousness... (Acts 17:31)

WHO REDEEMED ABRAHAM

(29:22)   ...The Lord, who redeemed Abraham...

This means God "severed" Abraham, or "took him away by force" from the land and culture of his fathers. Abraham, called "the father of faith", seems to be such a pillar of faith that we can hardly remember that he was one of the idolaters, along with his father and ancestors. To the Jews, especially, this is a shameful reminder that there is nothing in Judaism to boast in. Salvation, from beginning to end, is of God. When the Jews said to Jesus, "Abraham is our father", Jesus reminded them that "If ye were Abraham's children, ye would do the works of Abraham" (Jn. 8:39). Isaiah proclaims, "The Lord, who redeemed Abraham", showing that the Lord is the real "father of faith". Our works, and even our will to do them, are a result of God's work in us, showing us to be his children. We need reminders, now and then, that we are only Christian because of God's redemption. This statement of Isaiah is one that strikes at the root of our pride: if it is true that Abraham had to be redeemed, then what can I offer to God? Mary, the mother of Jesus, said "My soul doth magnify the Lord, and my spirit hath rejoiced in God my Saviour" (Lk. 1:46-7), showing that she also had to be redeemed by the blood of her own son for her sins. If anybody is great, it is only due to God's gracious redemption. The hero of the Bible is not Abraham who believed God, but "the Lord, who redeemed Abraham". Unredeemed Abraham is just another sinner, and the same is true for me. If I do anything worthy to be remembered, it will be because of "the Lord, who redeemed me". May the Lord forcefully sever us from our spiritual pride!

Praise undeserved is scandal in disguise.

BEAUTY AND THE BEAST

(33:17)   Thine eyes shall see the king in his beauty...

"Beauty is only skin deep" if beauty is only what we can see with our eyes. "Miss America" and "Miss Universe" are titles given in beauty pageants, to women whose winning attribute is a natural, God-given beauty. "Beauty and the Beast" strikes a chord in all of our hearts, because we know there are more important and enduring attributes of beauty than a perfect face or body. To "see the king in his beauty" surely does not mean that he has a handsome face, and even if it is speaking of his magnificent robes, or splendid surroundings, nobody would really call it "beauty" unless he were also a good king. Ezekiel's prophecy against the king of Tyre says "Thine heart was lifted up because of thy beauty" (Ezek. 28:17), and when that kind of pride comes in, beauty becomes a beast. So, beauty is deeper than the skin if it is real beauty. "Worship the Lord in the beauty of holiness" (Ps. 29:2) has beauty being something that involves holiness. Some years ago I heard someone say "you can get rid of fat, but you can't get rid of ugly". I don't believe it. I've seen people who were considered "ugly" to look at (physically speaking) who became strikingly more beautiful as they responded to the love of God. From the inside, they were changed so much that people soon overlooked their outward "ugliness" and soon even their faces began to change. In heaven, many who were never close to becoming "Miss Universe" or "Mr. World" will be stunning to look at, as they worship God in the beauty of holiness.

Real beauty is the beauty of soul.

Flattery And Mockery

(36:21)   But they held their peace, and answered him not a word...

This was a fitting response (or refusal of response) to the mockery of Rabshakeh. To answer anything at all would only have been flattering to Rabshakeh's vanity, and would be playing into his hand. Mockery and flattery appear to be closely related. Mockery is designed to offend an opponent through ridicule and derision, and usually the receiver and the mocker know it is not all necessarily true. Rabshakeh's speech is a masterpiece of mockery designed to devastate but so is the response an effective invective (or lack of it). "Answer not a fool according to his folly, lest thou also be like unto him" (Pr. 26:4). Flattery is designed to be used when mockery won't work and is, in fact, an appeal to the vanity of the one who is to be manipulated. Again, like mockery, flattery is known to be untrue by both parties. "Answer a fool according to his folly, lest he be wise in his own conceit" (Pr. 26:5). The Jews used neither mockery nor flattery, but lifted up a prayer to the God who answered them. "Be not deceived; God is not mocked: for whatsoever a man soweth, that shall he also reap" (Gal. 6:7), and it is evidently just as impossible for God to be flattered. Manipulation is bad in any form, and we will reap whatever we sow, but flattery is worse than mockery because flattery is not only evil, it is deceitful. The effect of mockery is only to corrupt the mocker. It may devastate to hearer, but it won't corrupt him. The use of flattery may seem more "positive", but ultimately it is far worse. Hold your peace, remain silent, and don't engage in either of these corruptions, or you will become as bad as your adversary.

Flattery corrupts both the receiver and the giver.

AMNESTY OR AMNESIA?

(38:17)   In your love...you have put all my sins behind your back. (NIV)

This chapter is about Hezekiah's illness and recovery, and it is a reminder of how tenuous our lives are in God's hands. We cannot control the timing of our death, and death becomes a time when we are most aware of God's judgment. We remember our sins and wish that God did not, but like Hezekiah, we hope God will also "remember...how I have walked before thee in truth..." (v. 3). This verse is a refreshing reminder of God's love, but does God really forget our sins? After the flood, "...God remembered Noah, and every living thing...with him in the ark" (Gen. 8:1). But verses like this speak of God's concern and love, not just remembrance. Compare some of these verses: "I, even I, am he that blotteth out thy transgressions for mine own sake, and will not remember thy sins... But Zion said, The Lord hath forsaken me, and my Lord hath forgotten me. Can a woman forget her sucking child, that she should not have compassion on the son of her womb? Yea, they may forget, yet will I not forget thee. Behold, I have graven thee upon the palms of my hands" (Isa. 43:25; 49:14-16). When we return to God, he will forgive and forget our sins, but he will not forget us! Like tying a string on my finger to remember something, God has done much more, engraving us on his hands. It reminds me of the scars on his hands from the nails on the cross. "You will tread our sins underfoot and hurl all our iniquities into the depths of the sea" (Mic. 7:19 - NIV). As Jerry Russell used to say, "Into the sea of forgetfulness, with a NO FISHING sign." God has no problem of amnesia, but we have a problem with amnesty.

**When the devil reminds you of your
past, remind him of his future.**

MY SERVANT

(42:1)   *"Behold my servant, whom I uphold; mine*
             elect, in whom my soul delighteth...

...I have put my spirit upon him: he shall bring forth judgment to the Gentiles." This is a prophecy attributed to Jesus, the suffering servant who, "being in very nature God...made himself nothing, taking the very nature of a servant, being made in human likeness" (Php. 2:6-7 - NIV). It was enough of a shock to the disciples that Jesus their master washed their feet as a servant, but God himself took on the form of his creature (man), and even of the lowest of servants. Muslims have no problem with Jesus being "the slave of Allah", but have a big problem with his being God. Jesus was "in very nature God", meaning he was and is God. He never ceased being God, but clothed himself with another form or nature, that of a suffering servant to man. All that Jesus did, he did as a man, but empowered by the Holy Spirit, while he remained in perfect submission to the Father, his beloved Son in whom God delighted. But, why was this necessary? To bring justice to the nations. Jesus, by his willing submission, filled all space from Heaven to Hades to be a faithful priest for every kind of person, even the Gentiles. A lesson for us is that if we want to reach anybody with the gospel, we must come as a servant to them, and be ready to even be killed by them, and still forgive them, that the Gentiles might be saved. What Jesus came and did was all done as a man, filled with the Holy Spirit of God. If Jesus did this, we also can and must do so for the Gentiles to be saved. Then God will delight in us as he does in Christ, his servant.

**If anyone wants to be first, he must be
the very last.** (Mark 9:35 - NIV)

NO PEACE FOR THE WICKED

(48:22)   There is no peace, saith the Lord, unto the wicked.

The moment after my conversion, I was filled with "the peace of God, which passeth all understanding" (Php. 4:7), a peace that was evident to me mainly through the lack of peace beforehand. Now, I was at peace with God and with people, and moments before, I was at war. "When a man's ways please the Lord, he maketh even his enemies to be at peace with him" (Pr. 16:7). Whenever that peace would leave after that moment, I became acutely aware of it, and prayed for forgiveness for any sin that may have caused me to lose it. Jesus is the Prince of Peace, and to lose his fellowship is to be bankrupt of any real peace. All the world seeks for peace, but it is an "elusive butterfly" if they seek it outside of Christ or without true repentance. "The wicked" referred to here are the people of Israel, the rebellious and idol-seeking nation of God's covenant, not just some 'heathen' nation. When we as Christians disobey God, there is no peace for us, "but a certain fearful looking for of judgment..." (Heb. 10:27) because we have willfully disobeyed one of God's precepts. The only way back is to repent because God promises no peace to the wicked. Peace is one of the gifts of the Spirit, and God's desire is to fill us with it: "If only you had paid attention to my commands, your peace would have been like a river" (48:18 – NIV). But, if we resist the Spirit's promptings to forgive, or to obey his just laws, we will find no peace. Lack of peace is God's way of driving us to repentance, to break the hardness of our hearts, but man will sometimes kill himself through suicide, ulcers from not forgiving, or drinking rather than to repent and receive God's peace.

Know God, know peace; no God, no peace.

THE ROCK

(51:1)   Look to the rock from which you were cut, and to the quarry... (NIV)

God is speaking here to the Israelites who were in exile, and wondering again if God even remembered them. To answer, God has Isaiah remind them about their humble beginnings, back to his promises to Abraham and Sarah, when they were living in Ur of the Chaldeans. The point is that if he cared for them when they were still in their sins and living in an idolatrous nation, he is now even more concerned for their welfare when they are his own treasured people. The rock from which I was cut was a hard place, and my own granite heart was hardened by the years of bitterness against those who had offended me, whether directly or otherwise. Sometimes we are tempted to return to "the good old days", when things are not going well now. It is worth taking a good look to remember how bad those days were without God's loving care for us. A quarry is just a big pit, but what is taken out of it is used for something of value. Nobody wants to return to a quarry and to be once again part of the huge wasteland of rock in which he is a "nobody". God cuts us out of the rock to give us purpose in life, to use us for his purpose. We would like to forget the wasteland of our past, but God calls us to remember, that we may know the greatness of his salvation. His purpose is not just to cut us from the rock, but to use us to reach others: "my salvation is on the way, and my arm will bring justice to the nations" (51:5 - NIV). Now, we call the Lord "the rock of our salvation" (Ps. 95:1). The wise will build their house on the Rock, and hide in the cleft of the Rock when troubles come, but we remember the rock from which we have been cut.

For their rock is not as our Rock (Deut. 32:31)

THE STING

(53:10)   Yet it pleased the Lord to bruise him; he hath put him to grief...

It was not the devil, but the Lord God who designed and brought about Jesus' suffering and crucifixion. It was prophesied from the time of Adam and Eve that Jesus would crush Satan's head, and Satan would "strike his heel" (Gen. 3:15 - NIV). Isaiah's language is in the past tense, long before it came to pass, because it is sure to be. Why did it please God to have him suffer and die? He had no sin, yet he willingly took our suffering for us. God watched as his beloved Son suffered and he never called it off, but he took no sadistic "pleasure" in Jesus' suffering, either; it grieved him to do it. But also, he was "pleased" because it was the necessary means to his purpose being fulfilled. No doubt, it pleased Satan to "bruise his heel", but it was his own head that was crushed in the process. God used Satan, and the Romans and the Jews as his instruments to bruise Jesus, but it was all the Lord's doing, and he knew what he was doing. Like a master chess player who sets a trap while pretending to be trapped, this was the ultimate "sting operation". God's pleasure was in seeing his perfect plan come to pass, right under Satan's nose, while Satan unwittingly hanged himself! And "the sting" is still being played out as we, the members of Christ's body, continue to suffer and die to see God's kingdom triumph. For us, who have died to ourselves, even "the sting of death" is gone (1 Cor. 15:55-6). We are more than conquerors through Christ who loves us, and we can join with Jesus in saying, "O death, where is thy sting? O grave, where is thy victory?"

The sting of death is sin. (1 Cor. 15:56)

GRASP THE GRAVITY OF THE SITUATION

(58:1)   Shew my people their transgression…

It is not popular today to speak about "sin", and especially not "in church". We hardly think of how important it is to "show God's people their transgression" during our worship assemblies, because we assume all who come "to church" are already saved. Few of our gatherings would stay so filled to capacity if we ever began to preach heavily about the Law of God. We want to "feel the Spirit" in our times of worship, but many who are present are hiding gross sins in their hearts, and expecting God to make them feel good for attending the worship. God's Law has not changed for us because we have "received Christ as our personal Savior". Even though Christ's blood has paid the price for my sins, I am now responsible to search my heart daily to put away sin from me. The problem is that before or after 'conversion' no preaching of God's Ten Commandments ever seems to make it into our preaching, because we want to jump right into the preaching of grace before the hearts are prepared to understand it, and that preparation of the heart is the whole purpose of the Law. Until the Law breaks our hearts and our stubborn pride, we can never understand the depth of God's grace. Just as gravity doesn't cease to function after we learn something of how it works, so we can never say the Law is now behind me. Forever we must preach the Law and its punishment, to bring about the fear of God in man. But first, we need to meditate on God's Law before we preach to others, and ask for God's grace to live in it.

The Law is eternal and of inherent value.

HOLIER RAGS

(65:5)   Stand by thyself, come not near to me: for I am holier than thou.

In India, the caste system has pronounced a certain class of men to be holier than others. It was the same sin of spiritual pride that affected the Jews [see Luke 18:9-14]. God made a difference between clean and unclean, but never meant for there to be pride in it. Pride heads the list of sins, being that which brings about all others. How much better to say "But we are all as an unclean thing, and all our righteousnesses are as filthy rags" (Isa. 64:6) "Woe is me! for I am undone; because I am a man of unclean lips" (6:5). When we see God's holiness, it shows us how unclean we are, with nothing to boast in. We may as well say "My filthy rags are holier than thine". As I am fasting, I am acutely aware of this "holier than thou" attitude in my own heart. I have judged my father for sins that are negligible compared to mine. The sins I have committed over the years are my fault, not his, and my pride kept me from sharing the gospel with him for years. "Holier than thou" people are always judgmental people. I have no reason for any pride, as I've done every possible sin myself and can say with Paul, "Christ Jesus came into the world to save sinners; of whom I am chief" (1 Tim. 1:15). Fasting and missions work make nobody holier than anybody, but it has taken these activities to show me the sin in my heart, and all the spiritual pride and blindness in me. Thankfully, in spite of my proud attitude, the Lord has allowed me to share the gospel with my parents, and lead each of them to him before they died. "Lord, please make my heart pure, and redeem all the lost years I've wasted".

Moral indignation is jealousy with a halo – H.G. Wells

Witty Wittle Witnesses

(1:6)   Ah, Lord God! behold I cannot speak: for I am a child.

I remember the panic in fifth grade of being told to stand before the class and give a speech. My cold sweat was not from fear of not being witty enough, as I had trouble enough with just the content of what to say, and I'm sure it was the same for Jeremiah. But how different it is when God says "I have put my words in thy mouth" (Isa. 1:9). A genuine transformation occurred in me when at the age of twenty-two I was born again and Christ came to live in me. For the first time I felt confident when I spoke in front of people, because I knew what I said was true, being God's Word. The Bible became "food for thought" and I ate it daily with real hunger for more. Jesus said "ye are the salt of the earth" (Mt. 5:13). It is not enough for us to merely hunger and thirst for righteousness, but we must create hunger and thirst for truth in others. The Gospel is food for life, and "you can lead a horse to water but you can't make him drink". That is where salt comes in. Salt melts ice, so icy cold hearts may warm up to the gospel. We are "as sheep in the midst of wolves: be ye therefore wise as serpents, and harmless as doves" (Mt. 10:16). The gospel of Christ is the food, but we need wit and wisdom to awaken people's hunger for it. Still, all the wit in the world can never lead a person to decide to follow Christ. It is the gospel itself that is the power to save (Rom. 1:16). No amount of "wittiness" can make "witness". Like Jeremiah, we are only witnesses of the bread of life to those who are starving.

Wit is the salt of conversation, not the food.

TO SERVE MAN

(5:12)   He will do nothing! No harm will come to us… (NIV)

It is easy to say "…we will never see sword or famine" as we watch violence on TV or in the movies, but life is not a spectator sport. We are so used to having the option of standing up and saying "It's just a movie!" that we forget God's judgment is coming. Attitudes change when it is "us" and not "them" being thrown into the arena with hungry lions. In an old "Twilight Zone" episode, aliens from outer space came and showed people a book called "To Serve Man". One man's face changed from delight to horror when he discovered it was not a servant's manual, but a cook book! Thanksgiving Day means feasting for us, but it is bad news for the poor turkey. It's exciting to watch an approaching tornado funnel with binoculars as it gets bigger and bigger, but when I drop the lenses from my eyes to see the storm now upon me, I become part of the spectacle, and no longer a spectator. Jesus also came to the earth from far away "to serve man", and "to give his life a ransom for many" (Mk. 10:45). But, to those who say "He will do nothing! No harm will come to us", they will see a delight turn into horror. They will miss the marriage feast, and will themselves be screaming in torment as they shout out "but I don't believe in this!" Sorry, too late to switch the channel. The rich man just turned off the sad spectacle of Lazarus lying on his doorstep, with dogs licking his open sores, while he feasted inside. But Lazarus was a real man, suffering real pain. If we turn our eyes from the sufferings of hurting people, and turn a deaf ear to their cries for help, their place will soon be ours. "Serve man while you can, get out of the fire and into the pan."

Life is not a spectacle or a feast; it is a predicament.

BAND-AID DOCTORS

(6:14)   *"They dress the wound of my people as though it were not serious...*

...'Peace, peace,' they say, when there is no peace" (NIV). Like putting a 'bandaid' on a gunshot wound, so it is ridiculous to say "peace" to one who is ready to die or to be punished for eternity. If we, as God's messengers, are not ready to do what is necessary to meet people's needs, it is hypocrisy to say "peace" or "be warmed and filled". When God's prophets and priests resort to only saying "nice" words that don't offend, even when strong rebukes are needed, judgment will come soon, and unannounced. A doctor is expected to tell the truth to a patient, and when he has a serious disease like cancer, the doctor's duty is to tell him, so he can make some important decisions. To "slightly" heal him is a false comfort, and is worse than doing nothing. In preaching the gospel, we must use God's Law to show the true nature of sin to men's hearts, so they will repent. To help somebody's feelings of guilt by saying "peace, Jesus loves you" instead of dealing with his sin is to encourage him in his delusion of safety, and he will still be destroyed if he doesn't repent. Jeremiah and most prophets were not liked for telling the truth, and people won't love us anymore, but we cannot put bandaid on fatal wounds. People will love us in heaven someday for telling them of their lost condition, instead of encouraging them to continue in sin. Those who are lost will hate the preachers of false peace. I thank God some faithful Christians took the time to tell me the truth about my sin, even though I hated them for it and had murderous thoughts about them. Now I can praise God and thank them for their loving witness to me.

Open rebuke is better than secret love. (Pr. 27:5)

THE CITY OF ANGELS?

(11:13)   You have as many gods as you have towns, O Judah. (NIV)

Idolatry like India, but in Israel! Today it could be spoken of America, which the world sees as the bastion of Christianity; we have gone far downhill from our Christian beginnings. In India, Calcutta is named after the goddess Kali, and Mysore's pride is Chamundi hill, but the same thing is happening in the U.S. Homosexuality is becoming the god of San Francisco, second only to Amsterdam in "gay" population, and other cities boast in some other "shameful" thing to which they build monuments. Gilroy, California, has annual festivals for garlic, and "Rough and Ready" has a drunken festival yearly to celebrate their "day of secession" from the rest of the U.S. San Francisco also boasts of its "First Church of Satan". Where is the worship of God? Even Christian TV programs worship the god of prosperity, while they continue to tolerate every kind of perversion imaginable on the other networks. God is openly blasphemed, and people laugh themselves silly, instead of crying, while disgusting perversions are daily paraded before their eyes. Movie and TV "stars" and idols are worshiped and their pride is in their alcoholism and the number of marriages they can joke about having had. Our incense to them is the hours of time and the money we invest in supporting them, as we watch their sins on the screen. Las Vegas, the gambling city, is famous for "lost wages", and Dallas, Texas is famous for "dollars and taxes"; Miami for "Vice", and Philadelphia is not known for brotherly love. "New York, New York, so nice they had to name it twice" is crime ridden, and…

**What city is named for worshiping
the true God? "Los Angeles"?**

MY NAME IS MUD

(14:9)   You are among us, O Lord, and we bear your name; do not forsake us! (NIV)

What's in a name? It is more than a word to call someone, chosen at birth because the parents like the sound of it. It is the reputation that goes with it that matters. People say "I'd better not do that, or my name is mud!" which refers back to Dr. Mudd, who treated Abraham Lincoln's assassin, and as a result his name became marred. "For when God made promise to Abraham, because he could swear by no greater, he sware by himself" (Heb. 6:13). If he broke his promise, his own name would be marred, so Abraham knew he could trust the promise. When we pray, to ask for something "in Jesus' name" it means "because of who Jesus is", or according to Christ's righteousness, and because of that we can be assured God will hear and answer. Sweet perfume will never be as sweet as honesty and integrity when we find it in a good person. When God's people say "we bear your name, do not forsake us" they are giving public declaration that they belong to him, and have taken his name to be their own, as a wife takes her husband's name. Jesus has been given "a name which is above every name" (Php. 2:9), to which every knee should bow, and he calls us to be his bride and to take on his name as "Christians". Even if we have been born with a bad name due to our parents' sin, God offers us a new name (Rev. 3:12). We can say, "Thy name is as ointment poured forth" (Song 1:3) because of the love shown to us in Christ's name. We should strive to spread the ointment of Christ's good name over those who know only the "mud-slinging" of self-seeking. That's not a good name.

**A good name is better than
precious ointment.** (Eccl. 7:1)

VIRTUE IS ITS OWN REWARD

(16:13)   ...and there shall ye serve other gods day and night...

Eventually, the good or evil we live for will determine the course of our lives: "You've made your bed, now sleep in it!" Men who are caught up in an addiction to adultery and lust of the flesh will joke, saying "Chastity is its own punishment!" But it is this same crowd that later toys with thoughts of suicide, because they cannot live with their dirty consciences, having ruined not only their own lives, but those of many others as well. The opposite is the real truth: "Virtue is its own reward", as those who live honest and upright lives reap the joy of having virtue, and not sin, ruling their lives. Habits, good or bad, are hard to break. Heartbreak is what follows after sin, and those who are captives of sin will soon be overcome with the mastery of sin and its heartbreaking toll on their consciences. I read from <u>The Book of Virtues</u> this morning, and was struck by all the areas it covers. Many stories of courage, work, loyalty, honesty and many other facets of virtue have been compiled, which strike a yearning chord in our hearts, and all of these virtues contain their own rewards for those who practice them. God will not drag anyone into heaven, but the pathway of virtue is shown by his Commandments. The worst punishment of those who perish may be the "persistence of memory" (Salvador Dali's painting of the melting watches was named this), where memories of past sins will never be erased, time will melt away, and "How have I hated instruction" (Pr. 5:12) will be heard everywhere. How much better to live the life that Christ lived and offers to those who follow him, and to serve the True God day and night.

Virtue is its own reward.

THREE MUSKETEERS

(21:10) *I have determined to do this city harm*
and not good, declares the Lord. (NIV)

God had joined himself by covenant with Israel, for good and not evil. But a covenant has two sides, and each party must do his part. God has revealed himself as trinity, or "tri-unity", in which the Father, Son and Holy Spirit are in perfect harmony and unity. Jesus prayed, "...that all of them may be one, Father, just as you are in me and I am in you. May they also be one in us so that the world may believe that you have sent me" (Jn. 17:21 - NIV). The story of the "Three Musketeers" probably takes its idea of "all for one and one for all" from the unity of the three "persons" of the Godhead (Col. 2:9) and God desires that unity be extended to those he bought with his own blood on the cross. Unfortunately, Israel (and later the church) has forgotten her side of the bargain. It was easy for Caiaphas to say "it is better for you that one man die for the people than that the whole nation perish" (Jn. 11:50 - NIV). And, it was easy for Pashur, chief governor while Jeremiah prophesied, to put Jeremiah in jail, thinking to save Judah from the captivity in Babylon that he predicted. But these men had forgotten that "all for one and one for all" works both ways. If we are truly sold out to God, so that we are ready to face persecution and death for his kingdom, then his death is the payment for our sins, but for those who will not keep their faith in Christ, God will "determine to do them harm and not good". Consider the extent of God's love for us, that he chose to bring us into his eternal relationship of union, for good and not for harm, and cherish the bond of love he has created among us that we may live to serve him and one another.

All for one and one for all.

228

CHAFF ON HARD GROUND

(23:28)   *"For what has straw to do with grain?" declares the Lord. (NIV)*

This is the analogy or comparison God gives for the lies of false prophets to the true Word of God given by his prophets. The false ones know they can become popular if they can play on the emotions of their listeners. Even those people who have become hardened in gross sins still like to have a sympathetic ear that will listen to their side. False prophets tend to make the true prophet look like a hard-hearted, unloving person. In preaching the gospel there is no offense in saying "Jesus loves you and has a wonderful plan for your life", but tell a person he has broken God's holy Law and will perish if he doesn't repent, and he will very likely be offended because it is the truth. It is not "chaff" to speak of God's love to the sinner, but if he is not also told he must stop his sin, it will be like throwing "pearls before swine" (Mt. 7:6); he is simply not equipped to see the value of the gift. There is a time for sympathy, and a time for straight talk about sin. The true man of God will use God's Law to uphold righteousness, and may not be very popular for it. When the Law has done its work of awakening the conscience and breaking up the hard ground of the heart, then there will be real rejoicing in the heart of the repentant sinner, and he will now understand that is was not sympathy at all that made others skirt the issue of sin, but a desire for being popular. When the Law has truly broken the hard heart, only then will real sympathy work. It was Ray Comfort who opened this truth to my heart. "Or do you show contempt for the riches of his kindness, tolerance and patience, not realizing that God's kindness leads you toward repentance?" (Rom. 2:4 - NIV).

Sympathy is the key that fits the lock of any heart.

ESCAPE ARTISTS

(25:28)   *if they refuse to take the cup from your hand*
          and drink, tell them, You must drink it (NIV)

This morning, in my prayer time, I realized this is a pattern in my life. I've continued to refuse the cross in my life, always finding a way to escape responsibility for things that would be hard to bear. I have been "pampered" in this by my parents and others, or have simply made decisions myself, to escape responsibilities. I don't know when it began, or how, but I have gotten out of writing papers and practicing piano, lied my way out of punishment, dropped out of an Ivy League college, and left a string of broken hearts and people. I have hitchhiked several times across the United States to avoid conflict, and refused responsibility for my own sins that caused so many broken relationships, and it is only now becoming obvious to me that it is a pattern. But, through sickness and lack of peace, I now see my own wicked life, and I hate it. I'm tired of hurting people and shirking responsibilities. I want God's rest in my life, and I'm ready to go back, regardless of the consequences, and to come to terms with my "cup" from God's hands. Like Jacob escaping from Esau and Jonah trying to escape his call from God, I see that God's blessings in my life are in spite of my rebellion, and not due to any goodness in my life. I can't deny that God has used all of it for good, and that my time of missions in India has been productive, but I am aware that it could have been even better in God's time. I'm thankful to God for opening my eyes to my sin, and I want to, if possible, make restitution to anyone I've hurt in my selfishness. May God grant us all the grace to drink the cup from his hand, and to refuse the temptation of trying to escape from his will for us!

Escape quickly from the company of fools.

BREAK EVERY YOKE

(28:10)   …took the yoke from off the prophet Jeremiah's neck, and brake it.

Jesus said, "Take my yoke upon you, and learn of me" (Mt. 11:29), and in this passage God had called Jeremiah to make and wear a yoke as a sign to Judah that they would soon be under Babylon's yoke of bondage. Paul says "stand firm, then, and do not let yourselves be burdened again by a yoke of slavery" (Gal. 5:1 - NIV) and that yoke is to be broken, but unfortunately too many times a well-meaning "prophet" like Hananiah presumes to take the yoke off the necks of people when God has put it there. Jesus' yoke is easy, and it involves breaking the old yoke of slavery to sin, but if we remove the yoke of Christ we will soon be hopelessly enslaved again to sin. Jeremiah's yoke was from God, and a good thing for Judah to get under. Jesus' yoke was the cross, and he told his disciples that "anyone who does not carry his cross and follow me cannot be my disciple" (Lk. 14:27 - NIV). Peter was of the same spirit as Hananiah when he tried to "remove the cross" or yoke from Jesus (Mt. 16:21-4), and Jesus rebuked this as a spirit of Satan himself. In the "Jesus" movie we see Jesus strapped to the upper 'crosspiece' of the cross, looking just like a yoke. Maybe that is why he spoke of his "yoke". God wants his people to be free from the yoke of bondage to sin, but we must be careful to check first which yoke people are under. Hananiah died for his action, because he "taught rebellion against the Lord" (28:16), but how could Babylon be called God's yoke? We could as easily ask how a death on a cross, looking like he himself was a criminal, could be Jesus' "easy and light" yoke. God will use anything to kill us and get sin out of us, and we must not take the yoke off that he puts on.

**…set the oppressed free and break
every yoke…** (Isa. 58:6 – NIV)

SOUR GRAPES

(31:29)   The fathers have eaten a sour grape, and the children's teeth are set on edge"

There is another "sour grapes' story, one of Aesop's fables, in which a fox who is unable to reach high enough to get some grapes goes away and rationalizes that "they were probably sour anyway!" "Sour grapes" has become a proverbial way of making an excuse for covering up our inabilities. Likewise, we may try to excuse ourselves of guilt by saying "I sin because of my father's faults". For years, I used my unforgiveness toward my father for his sin of divorcing my mother as the excuse for my sins. Don't be deceived! Take responsibility for your own sins. God says in a parallel passage in Ezekiel that uses the same proverb of "sour grapes": "The soul that sinneth, it shall die" (Ezek. 18:1-4). So why should the grapes get the bad rap? The clusters of grapes brought back from the Valley of Eschol (Num. 13:24) were the biggest and best to be found anywhere, yet they became "sour grapes" when the people made excuses for their refusal to enter the Promised Land. No problem with the grapes, but it is "the little foxes, that spoil the vines: for our vines have tender grapes" (Song 2:15). Sly foxes that we are! We would not disdain the luscious grapes of God's promise of heaven if we could see our inability to attain it as the problem. He will give us the grapes and the ability to reach them if we will look to him. God is good, but I am sold under sin. It is my sin that is evil, not God's mercy. If I can admit it is my sin, then God can provide the Savior. Don't let the lie of "sour grapes" turn God's mercy into "Grapes of Wrath".

Any fool can despise what he cannot get.

WAIT IN THE SITTING ROOM

(32:5) "…and there shall he be until I visit him, saith the Lord."

Or is it "Sit in the Waiting Room"? You may say what you like, even when you are king of God's own nation, but God alone can save you, and that only when he is ready. Joseph, too, was put in prison, and had to stay "until I visit him", God said. Whatever your plan may be, whether for marriage, promotion, or being paroled from jail, you may be going nowhere until God decides to visit you. If Joseph thought he had the situation under control, as he asked the butler to remember him when he saw the Pharaoh, he was mistaken. It was two years later, when God visited Pharaoh in a dream, that Joseph was remembered and set free. "But God, you would never do that to me!" Well, you, too, may be there until God decides to visit you, when you can say, "I could do nothing until God visited me." God gave us all the ability to formulate plans, and to pray and petition God to bring them about, but not until you give your situation to God will you ever appreciate how completely it is in God's hand. Fortunately, "God remembered Noah" (Gen. 8:1) and visited him on the ark, or he would have died on the ark. And, thanks be to God, "he hath visited and redeemed his people" (Lk. 1:68). You may do all your "religious duties", building an ark, or a temple or a kingdom, but until God descends in fire and visits you with his Spirit, "there shall you be", waiting for his visit. God decides when to visit us in revival. Make big plans for God's kingdom, but learn also to wait for his visit.

Man proposes, but God disposes.

MAKE MY JOY COMPLETE

(36:6)　...read to the people from the scroll the words of the Lord... (NIV)

God's word, when obeyed from the heart, will always bring peace and joy, although outwardly it may look like only pain and problems. Jeremiah wept often because of the results of his preaching of God's word to people who refused to listen. This time, as the king read the words, he even cut off pieces of the scroll until it all burned in a fire, but again Jeremiah wrote the words on a new scroll to share with all the people. We may not enjoy speaking of God's judgment to those who are lost, but it will result in some who will also fear God, turn from sin back to God and be saved. My joy on the day I repented of sin and turned to Jesus as my Lord and Savior was something I had to share with others. Although it had caused me grief to remember and repent of all my sins, the result of it was a deep and lasting joy that could not be taken away. It is said that you can never really appreciate the beauty of a sunset, or any other joy, until you can speak of it and share it with someone else. Also, a possession is never truly mine until I give it away to someone who needs it more, and from that time on the person will always say, "This was a gift from my friend", or "This is his shirt", and my name will always be attached to it. Paul said to the Philippians, "Make my joy complete" (Ph. 2:2 - NIV) by having the same giving attitude that was in Christ and in Paul. If you have found joy in salvation, share it with others.

Happiness is not perfected until it is shared.

WORRY WARTS

(37:17)   ...The King asked him secretly, "Is there any word from the Lord?"

King Zedekiah was a pathetic puppet in a bad situation. He was worried, first of all, because the Babylonian army could come and conquer Jerusalem at any time. Secondly, he was afraid to openly seek any counsel from Jeremiah, because the unbelieving princes had put Jeremiah in prison for reporting God's word that Babylon would surely come and conquer. The antidote for worry is faith, and especially faith in God's word, which cannot fail. The problem for Zedekiah was that, even when he heard the word of God, he didn't act upon it. True faith must act upon the word of God. Troubles will come, and prophets are sent to warn people, but why listen to a prophet if you don't want to do what he says?! Job said, "For the thing which I greatly feared is come unto me" (Job 3:25), and he was a righteous man. How much more, "The fear of the wicked, it shall come upon him" (Proverbs 10:24). Jesus said, "Therefore do not worry about tomorrow, for tomorrow will worry about itself. Each day has enough trouble of its own" (Matt. 6:34 - NIV). Don't worry! It won't keep evil from happening – it will only add ulcers to your other problems. Faith in God's word causes peace, even when we know that problems are coming. Maybe Zedekiah secretly hoped for a word that Babylon was now going to leave, and not come back. If you keep a secret hope that maybe God will change his mind about the Day of Judgment, then it's time to worry – it is a reality. Better to put your faith in God's word, so you don't have to worry about eternity.

Worry is interest paid on trouble before it is due.

SATURDAY MORNING CARTOONS

(43:9) ...take some great stones in thine hand, and hide them in the clay...

Why did prophets speak in parables, or use "skits" to get their message to the people? The idea is much like our Saturday morning cartoons: you must speak in a language your hearers can understand, if you want to reach them. When grown men say, "We will certainly do everything we said we would: We will burn incense to the Queen of Heaven and will pour out drink offerings to her just as we and our fathers, our kings and our officials did... At that time we had plenty of food and were well off and suffered no harm" (44:17 - NIV) – I might be tempted to give up on them! But Jeremiah didn't and God didn't. "Calvin and Hobbes" is a cartoon that shows us a child's imagination has a whole different reality from what is real. How do you reach a child like Calvin with the gospel? If "Looney Tunes" will get his attention, then let Daffy Duck tell him the truth. The Muslims, Hindus, Buddhists and Communists, cultists and occultists, humanists and evolutionists of this world all truly believe in a different reality from that of the Bible. In fact, sin has blinded all of our eyes to the truth. If God went so far as to send Jesus in a human body, to act out his nature in a body so we could understand and be saved, shouldn't we also use any means possible to reach into the hearts of those lost in darkness? If you grow weary of hearing some "New Agers" talking nonsense, or feel like giving up on a Jehovah's Witness with a one-track mind, don't despair. "At one time we too were foolish, disobedient, deceived and enslaved..." (Titus 3:3 - NIV). Ask God for more love, and an appropriate parable, or a cartoon that may bridge the gap and open blind eyes to the truth.

**Never seem wiser or more learned
than your company.**

SECRET SERVICE AGENTS

(46:28)   Fear thou not, O Jacob my servant, saith the Lord: for I am with thee...

This is how God speaks to Israel, even when they have been sent into captivity for their sins. The name "Jacob" would always remind "Israel" of their humble beginnings, before Jacob's name was changed as he wrestled with God (Gen. 32:24-32). Jacob had told his name and God made him "Israel", but when he asked God's name, it was God's secret, and a name he would not reveal. Jacob knew that his grandfather Abraham had put his servant in charge of all his possessions, to find his father Isaac a wife. Also, his son Joseph, a servant to Potiphar, was given all of Potiphar's house to oversee, and later became the second ruler in Egypt, when Pharaoh made known his secret dream. But pride had lifted up King Hezekiah of Judah, and as he showed the secrets of his kingdom to the servants from Babylon, Judah was again put into captivity. It appears to be true that "when I am weak, then am I strong" (2 Cor. 12:10): Israel always became stronger in captivity, as when they were in Egyptian bondage. As God's servants, they could cry out to God, who would "hear them in secret, and reward them openly" (Mt. 6:18 - NIV). God only waits for his servants to come in humility, and he will act on their behalf. Even Joshua, who was tricked into taking the Gibeonites as servants instead of killing them, would not refuse Gibeon's plea for help when they came under attack. How much more will God do for his own servants, who cry out to him for help in times of trouble. Even so, he who trusts his secrets to a master makes him servant!

**He who trusts his secrets to a
servant makes him master.**

DECEITFUL WORK

(48:10)   A curse on him who is lax in doing the Lord's work! (NIV)

The King James Version is translated "Cursed be he that doeth the work of the Lord deceitfully", or treacherously as a traitor, one who cannot be trusted. We are to do all the Lord commands us, not like Saul, who was cursed for keeping Agag alive, as well as all the goods he wanted. God wants obedience and trustworthiness, otherwise we will receive God's curse and not blessing. Why try to do the "work of the Lord" and then try to deceive God? Utter futility! Judas was cursed, as was Saul. Be diligent to complete whatever God gives you to do. God rewards those who "diligently seek him" (Heb. 11:6) so be thorough in any job you do. In the next chapter, Jeremiah speaks to Edom and says, "The terror you inspire and the pride of your heart have deceived you" (49:16 - NIV). This self-deception is almost expected in those who serve themselves, but when one is "doing the Lord's work", it deserves God's curse. Consider the prophet who was lax in following God's message, and was killed by a lion for his mistake (1 Ki. 13:18), because another "prophet" said God told him something different. Jeremiah suffered because King Zedekiah was lax in doing his God-appointed job as king, and said, "He is in your hands. The king can do nothing to oppose you" (Jer. 38:5 - NIV). He let a mob take over when God had put his authority in him, and Pontius Pilate failed as miserably in his duty for fear of another mob. Aaron pretended the same inability to control the mob, and tried to excuse his guilt in making the golden calf (Ex. 32:21-4). But, before we rise in judgment against these weak-willed workers, let us remember: God will hold us responsible for laxity in his work.

How much better to be diligent and trusting God!

LOST SHEEP

(50:6)   *"My people have been lost sheep; their shepherds have led them astray*

...and caused them to roam on the mountains. They wandered over mountain and hill and forgot their own resting place." (NIV) Lost sheep! Helpless and simple, trusting in leaders who led them astray. That is a picture of us. We get lost, and soon we forget where our resting place is. God blames the shepherds [see Ezekiel 34], but he says that he himself will seek and find them, as he is the true shepherd. "Over mountain and hill" refers to the places where pagan gods were typically worshiped, on the "high places". Like Israel, America has bought into these false comforts and forgotten God, the place of rest that had made her great in the beginning. God warned Israel that prosperity and blessings in the land of promise would become a snare, and soon would become a false god (Deut. 6:10-14). Like sheep, we are followers who assume that our leaders know the way to go; and as long as they are following the true shepherd, they will lead us in the right way. But, we must always seek after the true shepherd ourselves, and be sure that it is according to God's word that we are making decisions. This is the same tendency that happens to mission organizations, or to any other group that starts with a mission statement and drifts away as temptations of greater power and wealth come with compromise. The leaders must carefully keep to their commitment to God, or they will stray like sheep without a shepherd, and they will be judged by God for being shepherds themselves, who lead their sheep astray.

All we like sheep have gone astray. (Isa. 53:6)

THE LAST THING I SAW

(52:10,11) *"…the king of Babylon slew the sons of Zedekiah before his eyes…*

…Then he put out the eyes of Zedekiah." Zedekiah was then put in prison until he died. What a sad punishment: the last thing he saw before losing his sight was his sons being murdered, then his eyes were blinded to allow them to never see another good sight. His memory in prison would always be the last sight he had, of his sons' deaths. In a way, it is a picture of eternal torment, where people will endlessly "play back" the scenes that will haunt them. "Why did I not serve God when I had the chance?" they will say. It is also a picture of our conscience, which continues to bring back to our "mind's eye" the scenes we wish we could forget; it is an effective torture we put ourselves through until, hopefully, we repent and find a way to make restitution. For Zedekiah, he had plenty of time to repent in prison, and to be reconciled to God, as he had nowhere else to go. Samson, when his eyes were gouged out, had only thoughts of revenge for his eyes (Jud. 16:28), and died through suicide to avenge his anger and to kill his enemies. Both men were in a sad condition, but God's purpose for them, or for any of us, is first to bring us to repentance. Samson showed no real signs of repentance, and we don't know about Zedekiah. How easy to seek revenge, and how hard it is to repent! Do we, like Zedekiah, sit and think of "how evil they were to kill my sons and blind me", or do we think, "How well I deserve this punishment for failing to obey God"? Bitterness blinds us, so all we can see anymore is this scene before our eyes. Forgiveness allows us to be healed so that even if our eyes are gouged out we can see new and beautiful things. This was God's mercy to Zedekiah.

**…better… than to have two eyes and be
thrown into… hell** (Mt. 18:9 – NIV)

THE LORD IS LIKE AN ENEMY

(2:5)   The Lord was as an enemy: he hath swallowed up Israel...

Bad News! Let anybody else be like an enemy, but as long as God is on my side I will not fear. But what can I do when God is like an enemy? On February 17th of 1991 I felt this way. Even my prayer, I felt, was a sin to God. I had tried all my best to do something pleasing to God, even just finishing a 40-day fast, but God was not interested in my religious efforts. Total emptiness and blackness was all I could look forward to: it was frightening; it was a horror. Even my repentance with tears was not acceptable. Then, where else can I go? The Lord himself was an enemy! Not until we can feel this unrelenting fury of God can we understand what he poured out upon Jesus at Calvary. God hates sin with a perfect hatred. In the day of God's wrath, there is no pity (Ezek. 5:11). What enemy will pity one who continues to refuse terms of peace? If God poured out all of his wrath upon Jesus for our sakes on the cross, then he will be like an enemy to us on Judgment Day if we have not made peace with him. Israel is a picture to us that God means business: stop sin or have him for an enemy! Never mind just going into captivity, but torment for eternity. The worst sin can only be done by those who have known God (Heb. 10:26-31), and have willfully "fallen away". They will find "the Lord was as an enemy", and no place of repentance. Repent now while you are able. Don't be God's enemy. Neither be blind to your sin, but let God's Holy Spirit show you where you have sinned. Don't assume God is your friend and on your side, if you continue to treat him as an enemy.

**It is a fearful thing to fall into the hands
of the living God.** (Heb. 10:31)

WHY HAVE YOU FORSAKEN ME?

(5:20)   Why do you always forget us? Why do you forsake us so long? (NIV)

I suppose everyone must ask God "Why?" sometimes. I've been sick for 17 days, losing weight because I can't eat. I feel continually nauseous, like being "seasick", and persist in asking God "Why?" If it is punishment for sin, I deserve it and that is enough. We sin and reap the results. It may be worry over the big change of plans – to move back to California and leave India and missions. It may be hepatitis (or "jaundice") according to the doctors – I'll find out tomorrow. At any rate, the condition remains every day, unabated. Whether I pray, or complain, or suffer quietly, it is there. People, like Job's friends, all have their ideas, but nothing changes it, so, I ask, "Why do you forget me, Lord?" But this I know: God has a purpose, and "…all things work together for good to them that love God, to them who are the called according to his purpose" (Rom. 8:28). In Lamentations, the prophet Jeremiah cries out for Judah. There is no doubt that they sinned, and they can't say nobody warned them. We feel, though, that as soon as we see our sin and repent, God has to "call off the dogs". But, there is a necessary time of reaping the consequences of our sins, sometimes even of justice, for others who have been hurt or affected. When Miriam spoke against Moses and became leprous, she was immediately repentant, but God said, "If her father had but spit in her face, should she not be ashamed seven days?" (Num. 12:14). Even Jesus on the cross said "My God, my God, why hast thou forsaken me?" (Mt. 27:46), but God promises never to forsake us. We must trust him and receive both good and evil at his hands. He will surely return again in mercy.

…I will never leave thee, nor forsake thee. (Heb. 13:5)

FOLLOWING MARY'S LITTLE LAMB

(1:12)   Wherever the spirit would go, they would go... (NIV)

It sounds like the nursery rhyme: "Mary had a little lamb, its fleece was white as snow; and everywhere that Mary went, the lamb was sure to go." In God's Kingdom, all are in submission to God's will, regardless of consequences or threats to personal safety. These "living creatures" went, as the Spirit of God directed them, wherever he went. Mary, the mother of Jesus, submitted to God, so that she could bear the Savior, the "Lamb of God". This Mary also "had a little lamb" whose character was "white as snow". As a child, he learned submission to his parents (Lk. 2:51) so that later, "wherever the spirit would go, [he] would go". Ezekiel, as a prophet, was told to speak to rebellious Israel (2:3-8), whether or not they would listen, and like many other prophets, obedience would mean persecution and possibly death. We are saved from sin for a purpose: to be willing and obedient to God's Kingdom and then to lead others into the Kingdom. Although our "sins be as scarlet, they shall be as white as snow" (Isa. 1:18), that we also may be obedient as sheep, led by God's Spirit. Until his baptism, when the Spirit of God anointed Jesus for his mission, everywhere that Mary went, the Lamb was sure to go: until his public ministry began, Jesus was content to learn godly submission to his parents. Then, he graduated into submission only to the Spirit. Ezekiel saw "cherubim" going as they were led by the spirit. They would not have to suffer persecution, as we must suffer, to enter into God's Kingdom. But, neither will they ever know the mystery of God's salvation (1 Pet. 1:12), and "the fellowship of his sufferings" (Php. 3:10).

**The right thing to do is to dare to
do the right at any cost.**

SCAVENGER HUNT

(6:13)　...when their slain men shall be among their idols round about their altars...

Those who ask "If God is so loving, how could he ever create a place like Hades?" are asking the wrong question. They may as well ask "How could a civilized society ever create garbage dumps?" God says plainly "I have no pleasure in the death of the wicked; but that the wicked turn from his way and live..." (33:11). There is no joy for God in seeing idolaters' dead bodies strewn around the altars and idols to which they have bowed. Even madmen like Hitler didn't really derive pleasure from seeing six million Jewish bodies lying dead – he was looking for the glory of controlling the world. God's glory is not in tormenting people, but in saving men from what they already deserve. When prophets like Ezekiel speak to captive Israel, they are calling them out of the trash heap to come to their senses. "Ye are the salt of the earth: but if the salt have lost his savour, wherewith shall it be salted? It is thenceforth good for nothing, but to be cast out, and to be trodden under foot of men." (Mt. 5:13). The point is that men who reject God <u>should</u> be thrown out as refuse, being useless to God's Kingdom, and that includes all of us, until God's grace calls us to repentance. It is no glory to God to destroy Satan, who continues to oppose him, but it shows God's justice when such blatant rebellion is finally punished. Idolatry is worship of anything else than God alone. Idols belong in the trash bin, and those who worship them deserve the same treatment. Those who see themselves as God's helpless prey, being thrown out as garbage, have an exalted view of themselves. We are really only useless trash until the grace of God salvages us from sin.

In victory the hero seeks the glory, not the prey.

DON'T BOAST IN THE FLESH
WHEN IT'S IN THE POT

(11:3) …let us build houses: this city is the cauldron, and we be the flesh.

We all like "happy" proverbs, like "every dark cloud has a silver lining" or "it's an evil wind that blows no good" or "born with a silver spoon in his mouth". We like to think of God as being always happy with us, so we ignore warnings of true messengers of God calling us to repentance. Judah felt secure from Babylon – after all "we are God's people". Jerusalem was a cauldron, and they were the choice meat inside, protected from the flames that God would control and use to bring them to perfection; how nice! But Ezekiel was saying something different, and it didn't sound so nice, so they listened only to the "nice" prophets. Even if Ezekiel was telling the truth, "the days go by and every vision comes to nothing" (12:22 – NIV) was their new, happy proverb, or as Peter quoted in his day "Where is this 'coming' he promised? Ever since our fathers died, everything goes on as it has since the beginning of creation." (2 Pet. 3:4 - NIV). Foolish people! Don't we learn from history? Judah was like the frog in the cauldron, never quite sure as the temperature climbs that it is about to be cooked! A much more appropriate proverb would be "out of the pot and into the fire", but they were too preoccupied with "building houses" in the pot and getting cozy, and failed to feel the approaching heat of God's judgment. What can we learn? A) It is always good to listen to the prophet who speaks of repentance; B) "a watched pot never boils" so listen to the watchman and you won't get boiled; C) "Too many cooks spoil the broth" so get rid of false prophets, before your goose is cooked. (Out of the cauldron - unto the Chaldeans!)

**People who live in brass cauldrons
shouldn't stow thrones.**

MUD DAUBERS

(13:10)   ...one built up a wall, and, lo, others daubed it with untempered mortar.

A few years ago in Bangalore, India, a three-story building fell over during a heavy rainstorm because only mud was used to lay the bricks. It was then covered over with a thin layer of white-wash so it would look good. It lasted for years, until a soaking rain caused it to "melt". Fortunately, the tenants got out in time. Now it is discovered that many of the buildings were done that way to "cut corners", and to save time and money, cheating the financiers. When the church is built in this way, with no cement to hold us together, it may be built fast, but it won't last. We are the church, and each of us is a "lively stone" in the wall (1 Pet. 2:5), held together by the tempered mortar of truth and love, and by the Spirit of God. When any of this is missing, it becomes the "untempered mortar" of false teaching that whitewashes over sin, and the integrity of the wall begins to crumble. If we all will unite without truth, heresy will destroy us, but if we try to unite over truth without love and the Holy Spirit, we will destroy each other in doctrinal battles. Fortunately, "God hath tempered the body together... that there should be no schism in the body" (1 Cor. 12:24-5) but, as God said through Ezekiel (13:14), "So will I break down the wall that ye have daubed with untempered mortar...so that the foundation thereof shall be discovered..." Christ is our foundation, and the Holy Spirit and God's Word are the mortar that holds us together. Be careful to inspect the walls before you move into a home. Whitewash may look good, but it won't hold walls together.

United we stand, divided we fall.

FRUIT IN THE FACE

(17:23)   *...it will produce branches and bear fruit*
            and become a splendid cedar... (NIV)

This short parable is about Jesus the Messiah who was to come and reign in Israel. He is called "the Branch" in many other prophecies (Isa. 4:2, 11:1, Jer. 23:5, 33:15, Zec. 3:8, 6:12), and Jesus said of himself, "I am the vine, ye are the branches: He that abideth in me, and I in him, the same bringeth forth much fruit..." (Jn. 15:5). When Jesus cursed the fig tree (Mk. 11:12-14), it was to show a sign that Israel and Judah had willfully separated themselves from "the Branch" and were without any fruits because of it. Jesus himself is life and anyone who is connected to him will also be alive, and bring forth life in others. "Fruit" means several things to us as Christians. The fruit of a Christian is bringing forth other Christians, just as a mother bears children. It is also the "fruit of the Spirit", which will be an obvious manifestation from the life of one who lives in the Spirit. The "fruit" is the visible proof of what is inside, either of life or death, so that an evil person will also bring forth evil fruits. Similarly, our face is a mirror of what is in the heart, like fruit on a tree. When Christ is in the heart, there will be joy in the heart in even the worst of circumstances. Even a clown can smile at all times, as when someone throws fruit in his face, but without Christ in his heart, it will only mean pretense and hypocrisy to the clown, when he must appear to be happy at sad times in his life. I remember in my own life deciding to be happy for the last year before my conversion. I listened only to happy music and stayed away from heavy, depressing conversations. But, it only showed me the empty life I had because, like a clown, I knew I was putting it on. Repent of religious pretense, and come to Jesus.

**A merry heart maketh a cheerful
countenance...** (Pr. 15:13)

SUCCESSFUL FAILURES

(20:32)   ...we want to be like the nations... who serve wood and stone... (NIV)

Such ignorance, coming from the nation that knew the true and living God! The reason: because "success is the sole earthly judge of right and wrong". We all like to succeed, so when worshippers of other gods seem to get ahead of us, there is the tempting thought that "maybe they are right, after all". Many people flock to gurus, or after religions and cults that are growing fast, because success seems to imply correctness. But, history shows us that many have succeeded who were wrong. Satan was a success at getting Jesus crucified, but he was not right, and who would say that Jesus was wrong because he didn't become a financial or political success before he died? The Mafia succeeds in organized crime. Many groups like Jehovah's Witnesses, or the Mormons, Muslims and Hindus have become successful, and some have lasted for centuries. Some of them are among the richest people on earth, yet they can't all be right. Shall we begin to "serve wood and stone" if we see idolaters winning over us? Wouldn't it be better to learn that God continues to be right, and that temporary success in business, war or religion, doesn't mean right (even if "temporary" lasts for a long time)? God will be the final judge of right and wrong, and our earthly success will have nothing to do with that. The world will continue to judge right and wrong by success stories, but God says real success comes to those who will meditate upon and follow his holy Word (Jos. 1:8), the only judge of right and wrong.

Success is the sole earthly judge of right and wrong.

But I Found None!

(22:30)   And I sought for a man…that would…stand in the gap before me …

In prophesying against Israel, Ezekiel speaks for God: "Though these three men, Noah, Daniel, and Job, were in it, they should deliver but their own souls by their righteousness…" (14:14), but now in his appeal to Jerusalem, the center of all Judaism, God asks for just a man and cannot find one! Ezekiel is one man who takes this upon himself, as we must do. Prayer is our contact with God, to stay his wrath and identify, in intercession, with the sins of the people. We are to be that one man, while all are blindly going to destruction, and cry out for mercy for their sins. Noah, Daniel and Job were righteous men, but may not have been intercessors [cf. Gen 18:23-33], so they could only deliver themselves from God's wrath. It is certain that God's wrath will come, and so intercessors are what God looks for, to bring his kingdom <u>by man's will</u> to the earth. A hedge is for protection, and the gap is between God and man. Jesus came as that "one man" for the sake of the world. He wept tears of intercession over this same city of Jerusalem, and offered his life for their sins and the sins of the whole world. Now, he looks for one man who will represent his redeemed people who are still lost in sin, and pray for their salvation. Without an intercessor, God's "hands are tied" from saving anyone. We must enter into this great work, as well as into evangelism, and finally laying down our lives for this world's salvation, to see it come to pass. Otherwise, God will destroy it, saying "I sought, but I found none". Preach as if it all depends on man's decision to turn from sin, but…

Pray as if it all depends on God.

NOT HAPPY NOW, WILL NEVER BE

(23:5)   *And Aholah played the harlot when she was mine...*

Much like Adam and Eve, Aholah (Samaria) and her sister Aholibah (Jerusalem) had the exalted honor of a relationship with God, their Creator. Who could possibly seek for more? And yet, Adam and Eve lost their relationship with God when they chose to sin, as did Samaria and Jerusalem. Was it worth it? Were any of these happier now? No, and as they had decided to reject God, they would never again know true happiness and peace. Aholah couldn't be satisfied when God was with her, and she "played the harlot when she was mine", and so she would never be content when God was not with her. Harlots are never happy people, being in endless pursuit of satisfaction, but always empty inside. "Such is the way of an adulterous woman; she eateth, and wipeth her mouth, and saith, I have done no wickedness" (Pr. 30:20). Her life is filled with bitterness as she blames men for her sad estate. Her only hope is to repent, stop blaming God and men for her sad condition, and return in humility to her husband, if he will take her back. God showed through Hosea and Gomer that he would take "Aholah and Aholibah" back, and restore them to their place of honor, if only they would break and repent. "I gave faithless Israel her certificate of divorce and sent her away because of all her adulteries", yet God says "Return, faithless people," declares the Lord, "for I am your husband" (Jer.3:8, 14 - NIV). If God has extended that much love to us and we still reject it, then there is no hope for us, and we will die in our sins. We will not find happiness here, nor ever, in eternity.

Not happy now, Will never be.

A Change Of Mind

(25:5)   And I will make Rabbah a stable for camels...

"Rabbah of the Ammonites" was a city whose name meant "great", and it seems to be of equal stature with Jerusalem as a great city (21:19-20), situated close by on Israel's border. Rabbah was the place of the thirteen and a half foot long iron bed (or was it "coffin"?) of the giant Og, king of Bashan. This city remained undefeated until they insulted David's men (2 Sam. 10) who were sent with gifts to them. That led to a siege of the city, and finally it was defeated by Joab's forces, just at the time that David and Bathsheba's sin changed the course of David's life. It sounds like a great change for this great city to become "a stable for camels", but God's interest is in people, not cities and stables. Rabbah stands to this day as a city, once called "Philadelphia", and is still the capital of Jordan, now called "Amman" (from Ammon?) God used this city to change David in an area of weakness, and David's original idea of blessing this great city left him broken, after his adulterous and murderous affair. Meanwhile, people changed, but the city of Rabbah remained. You may be great, like this city, with ancestors who were "giants" resting in the big chambers of your ego's memory. But, if men of God should come with good tidings of peace from the city of God, don't send them away with shame. Your pride and greatness will be brought low, because God wants you, not your reputation, to live on. God will make you great in his way, or he will destroy you, but your own greatness must go. "I had rather be a doorkeeper in the house of my God, than dwell in the tents of wickedness" (Ps. 84:10).

Things do not change; we change.

MORTAL GODS

(28:9)   Will you then say, "I am a god," in the presence of those who kill you? (NIV)

About a year ago, somebody tried to kill Sai Baba, a self-proclaimed 'god' [not just 'a god', but he claimed that he was the Almighty God!] He escaped, and some others were killed, but it raised the obvious question: "Didn't he know about the plot, if he was <u>God</u>?" The next day it was business as usual with a 'darshan', although "god" had nearly died. Well, we might ask, didn't they also kill Jesus? Then how can he be God? True – but Jesus prophesied both his death and resurrection. He both <u>knew</u> about it and <u>overcame</u> it, as he is the true God, who chose to die for our sin. Pontius Pilate thought himself really something, saying "Don't you realize I have power either to free you or to crucify you?" (Jn. 19:10 – NIV). It amounted to "Will you then say 'I am a god,' in the presence of me, with the power to kill you?" But the resurrection proved that Jesus is God. Has anyone else tried to top that one? Even if one could "stage it", he would be again subject to death, like Lazarus who was raised from the dead. The Jews wanted to kill Lazarus again to end Jesus' popularity, and they could have killed him as he was still mortal. But Jesus was raised to life as a "spiritual body" – the first of the real resurrection that we look forward to. When he raises us up on the last day, we will never die again, but will live forever with him in heaven. We will never be God, and we cannot raise ourselves from the dead. Only God can do that, and Jesus did! If Satan, or the king of Tyrus, or Sai Baba or anyone else dares to proclaim "I am God", let him say it before "…him who, after the killing of the body, has power to throw you into hell. Yes, I tell you, fear him" (Lk. 12:5 – NIV).

Only a real fool says in his heart "I am God".

DUMB ANTI-ARMS LAWS

(33:22)   My mouth was opened, and I was no more dumb...

Why was Ezekiel "dumb"? Because God had said, "And I will make thy tongue cleave to the roof of thy mouth, that thou shalt be dumb, and shalt not be to them a reprover: for they are a rebellious house" (3:26). Now, the tables were turned. By strength of arms, Israel had bound Ezekiel so they would not have to hear the word of God, and God had complied with their wish. Paul the Apostle stated "I am suffering even to the point of being chained like a criminal. But God's word is not chained" (2 Tim. 2:9 - NIV). Jesus also was "brought as a lamb to the slaughter, and as a sheep before her shearers is dumb, so he openeth not his mouth" (Isa. 53:7). Jesus, however, will also return with his mouth opened, "And out of his mouth goeth a sharp sword, that with it he should smite the nations..." (Rev. 19:15). Like Ezekiel, Jesus will be vindicated when he returns as Judge of all the earth, but he will speak words of comfort, not judgment (as Ezekiel did), to those who are ready to hear and respond to his word. To those who continue to be a "rebellious house", who make laws to shut the mouths of God's prophets, there will be nowhere to hide from God's judgment, but like Job they will say "I am unworthy – how can I reply to you? I put my hand over my mouth" (Job 40:4 - NIV). Today, God's laws have been silenced in our classrooms and courtrooms by strong arm tactics of those who are "a rebellious house". But God's word is not bound, and God will be vindicated when he returns to judge the earth. Then, God's holy law will send them speechless from his presence, but that law will be dumb for those in the everlasting arms.

Laws are dumb in the midst of arms.

WOOLY BULLIES

(34:19)   Must my flock feed on what you have trampled... (NIV)

Sheep as bullies? Aren't they supposed to be submissive and meek? Yes, Israel's problems were not only with her leaders - even the strong-willed people spoiled life for the weaker ones. Jesus said, "Woe to you, teachers of the law and Pharisees, you hypocrites! You shut the kingdom of heaven in men's faces. You yourselves do not enter, nor will you let those enter who are trying to" (Mt. 23:13 - NIV). Scribes and Pharisees were not leaders, but simply men who proclaimed themselves to be holy keepers of the law. They were not kings, but simply bullies over people's spiritual lives. The good news of the kingdom should have been a cool drink of water to the weak and weary, but these men "fouled with their feet" (34:19) the good news, so nobody could enjoy it. Jesus leads us to "...green pastures..."and "...beside the still waters..." (Ps. 23:2), but these "wooly bullies" will always be there to spoil what they never enjoy themselves: they are too busy making sure others don't enjoy it. Paul later rebuked the Jewish Christians for muddying the clear water of the gospel with their demand of circumcision for the Gentiles. Today, there is "one fold, and one shepherd" (Jn. 10:16), but men who are themselves only sheep continue to muddy the water with their feet. For years in the Catholic Church, salvation was "clear as mud" to me: the Mass was in Latin, and we were told not to read the Bible, as only the priests could understand it. The blood of Christ was trampled underfoot (Heb. 10:29) by doctrines of salvation through scapulars, the Immaculate Heart of Mary, etc. It may be different today, but let us keep the water clean. Jesus alone is the Good Shepherd, and we are all sheep.

It's not you, but the bully who is insecure.

QUEEN FOR A DAY

(37:11)   …they say, Our bones are dried, and our hope is lost…

Today, doctors can do "miracles" through plastic surgery: things like face lifts, nose jobs, hair transplants, breast implants, false teeth and skin grafts. While the poor are happy to find a stick for a crutch, the affluent are able to perfect "prosthetics" to replace arms and legs. Cosmetic surgery has become a need, not a luxury, as our movies and advertisements portray beauty as the requirement for happiness in life. The truth is, beauty doesn't last long. "Miss America" captures only a brief moment of fame before she loses it to another, and many would-be beauty queens must "put their faces on" out of boxes and bottles daily. God looks much deeper for a beauty that comes from within, from a heart dedicated to him, which he sculpts for himself out of dust. God created Adam and Eve from dust, and he will raise his saints from corruption and decay to live in "the beauty of holiness" (Ps. 96:9). In God's eyes, Israel as "dry bones" was far beyond beauty being gone; they were dead, with the flesh rotted off the bones, and the bones dried and not even connected. A big challenge for a plastic surgeon who can do "miracles" might be to make an accident victim look good for his last viewing in the coffin, as people look upon his earthly remains for the last time. God is the only real miracle working surgeon, who can take us at any stage of dilapidation, or complete ruin, and make us alive and beautiful. Man may progress to one day be able to make a "Frankenstein" person out of body parts and dry bones put together, and he can even make it beautiful with plastic surgery, but only God can give life, and change a wicked heart into a good one.

Beauty is a short-lived reign.

255

DOG FOOD

(39:18) Ye shall eat the flesh of the mighty, and
drink the blood of the princes of the earth…

This is the language of God's judgment, spoken to "…every feathered fowl, and to every beast of the field…" (v. 17). Like a sacrifice, with a great banquet following, it will be a feast, not for man, but for all the vultures and scavengers of the animal kingdom. They will mindlessly gorge themselves and become drunk on the blood of man who used to eat them and have dominion over them. Each one of the "mighty" and the "princes" will be just another body to eat, to be thrown in with their horses and with "common" men. Similar language is used in Zephaniah 1:7 and in Revelation 19:17-18. But, is God really speaking this to birds and beasts? Of course not! It is to get the mighty men to see what <u>will</u> happen to them if they don't repent. The thought of judgment should do this to us also. "Therefore hell hath enlarged herself, and opened her mouth without measure" (Isa. 5:14). It is such an unthinkable existence, forever and ever; such a waste! Isn't man, the crown of all of God's creation, worth more than just to feed dogs and to stoke up a furnace? People laugh, and explain it away, saying "a loving God would never do that". But he surely will do it! Just as Jezebel became dog food for her sins, "Unless you repent, you too will all perish" (Lk. 13:3-5 - NIV). God's judgment will be complete and final. Jesus said, "…Except ye eat the flesh of the Son of man, and drink his blood, ye have no life in you" (Jn. 6:53). Which sacrifice will you take part in? If we seek the Lord and trust in Christ's sacrifice we "shall be hid in the day of the Lord's anger" (Zeph. 2:3). Don't be found at the wrong sacrifice, where you are the meal and not the guest!

For the Lord hath prepared a sacrifice,
he hath bid his guests. (Zeph. 1:7)

THE WALL

(42:20)   ...to separate the holy from the common. (NIV)

The temple was a picture of how man must approach God, so it was ordered to be built by God's pattern. Strictly following God's laws would bring a person into at least an outward show of humility and submission to God's will, but it could not change the man's heart. The wall separated "between the sanctuary and the profane place" (KJV), to show how much God hates sin, and that he cannot be approached when sin is not covered by the blood of the atonement. Because man's sin against God's law had made a wall of separation between him and God, this wall was made to show men how real that wall is. Only those who will come under God's law are allowed inside the wall and even inside only priests may go into God's presence. Man's will must be broken by the severity of God's law before the goodness of God can bring repentance (Rom. 11:22, 2:4). The world outside the wall has its own laws which will exalt "self" instead of God, and so "the sinful mind is hostile to God. It does not submit to God's law, nor can it do so" (Rom. 8:7 - NIV). In such a state of enmity against God, for man to enter his presence would profane the temple, or God's presence in heaven. Sin cannot exist in God's presence, just as darkness must be dispelled by light. "...the law is not made for a righteous man, but for the lawless and disobedient..." (1 Tim. 1:9), and so a place outside the wall is reserved for the lawless, separate from the sanctuary. That will be Hades, ultimately, because if a man will never submit his will to God, he would be unable to live with him. That place will be filled with those who have lived outside of God's law, although they may have strictly kept their own selfish laws.

Lawless are they that make their wills their law.

UNJUST GAIN

(45:10)   You are to use accurate scales... (NIV)

Cheating, stealing, coveting and gambling are all related forms of a root sin. This chapter begins with the division of the land by lottery, which is meant to give everyone an equal chance at the more desirable spots, although God is really in control of it (Prov. 16:33). A lottery in which all involved are looking to God for a just solution is one thing; but one in which people throw in money to gamble, in hopes of winning more, is something quite different. That one is trusting in "luck" and not in God, and it encourages us in dishonesty. Coveting often leads to gambling as a quick way to gain money, then cunning people contrive ways to rig the system to play upon the greed of unsuspecting gamblers. That leads to organized crime, which finds legal loopholes to stay in business, and is really just a cleverly concealed system of robbery. God has called for "just balances" which means no tampering with the weights on the scales that weigh out our purchases. "Unjust gain" (Prov. 28:8) may mean more than just money swindled from the less clever. It may include gambling proceeds, which are not earned by work. Two months ago I went to purchase a truck, and made a fast decision to sign a paper, taking responsibility of getting its smog certification done. It was a gamble, to save a little time and money, and I lost. It didn't pass. But, for the man who sold it to me, it was beyond a gamble if he cleverly cheated me into buying his truck and got himself off the hook with a piece of paper. It is still not resolved; may God have mercy on his soul.

The best throw of the dice is to throw them away.

THE RIVER

(47:1)   …and I saw water coming out from under the threshold of the temple (NIV)

After about seven chapters of description of the temple, this vision comes as something "other worldly". A river flowing out of a temple? It signifies life, and not dead religion. It even makes the Dead Sea alive again! Joel (3:18) says "…a fountain shall come forth of the house of the Lord…" and Psalm 46:4 says "There is a river, the streams whereof shall make glad the city of God". It is God's presence in his temple (now, his people) that always brings life. Jesus said, "He that believeth on me, as the scripture hath said, out of his belly shall flow rivers of living water" (Jn. 7:38), possibly referring to Isaiah 12:3, in which it says "…with joy shall ye draw water out of the wells of salvation". So, "living water" has to do with salvation [see John 4:13-15]. If "the kingdom of God is within you" (Lk. 17:21), then the river from under the altar, or from the throne (Rev. 22:1) will also flow out from our belly. We will become "streams in the desert" (Isa. 35:6) to the lost, and water from a rock (Ex. 17:6) – an even more unlikely place for a river to originate. But all of these show it is from God himself that life originates, so of course there will be a river of life coming out of God's throne – where else could these healing, life-giving waters come from?! Who could think of the "Dead Sea" becoming full of life again? But this is what our salvation is all about: life from God given to dead people and to dry bones. The temple signifies that there is only one true God to come to, but the river shows that all life emanates from his presence. As we approach this life, we first "get our feet wet", but eventually find we can be totally immersed in it; we cannot fathom it, as we cannot fathom God.

There's a river of life flowing out of me.

THE STONE

(2:34)　A rock was cut out, not by human hands. It struck the statue on its feet (NIV)

The image in Nebuchadnezzar's dream indicates the four great kingdoms of the world, and the rock denotes Christ. He is the precious cornerstone (Isa. 28:16) who is rejected by the builders (Ps. 118:22), and faith in him is the rock upon which the church is built (Mt. 16:18). "Not by human hands" means it is of God's doing, just as heaven is made without hands (2 Cor. 5:1). Jesus defeated the kingdoms of this world "without lifting a hand", simply dying on the cross. In the story of <u>The Princess and Curdie</u> by George MacDonald, Curdie causes the bad guys to be incapacitated when he hits them on the feet with a stone hammer. Likewise, the whole foundation of the statue, the feet, causes the whole thing to fall. Babylon, the golden head, was defeated by other inferior kingdoms, and Rome finally ruled with its power, as iron. But as the iron was mixed with clay, there was weakness in the feet, and its strength became its downfall [as in Psalm 2:9, breaking the clay pot with a rod of iron]. But again, the real reason for all the kingdoms falling is that the rock, cut out without hands, is coming back to reclaim the earth as his footstool! He destroys the feet that have no right to stand on his footstool. A stone is such an insignificant thing, yet it will destroy the great beauty of gold and silver kingdoms because of their weak foundation. The stone will grow into a mountain, and it will fill the whole earth. None will oppose him, as he is God himself. God delights in using base things (a stone) to destroy the greatness of this world (gold).

**The stone the builders rejected has become
the capstone.** (Ps. 118:22 – NIV)

FAIRY TALE ENDINGS

(4:37) All those who walk in pride he is able to humble. (NIV)

This picture of Nebuchadnezzar eating grass as an animal, with long hair and claws like a bird seems an extreme punishment but it is a picture of madness. In pride and rebellion, even I myself grew my hair long and at some points lived like an animal sleeping under bridges and in fields, eating out of dumpsters, just like the prodigal son. Then, after several years when I had enough, I came to my senses (4:34, Lk. 15:17), as God in his mercy saved me. This is the kind of story that makes great fairy tales or fables, like <u>Beauty and the Beast,</u> or Scrooge in <u>A Christmas Story</u>. Wouldn't it have been a nice story if Saul finally came to his senses, and was able to live out his days as the king, with David serving as his understudy? But all stories don't end like fairy tales. Manasseh and Ahab were the worst kings in Judah and Israel, and both were humbled, and repented at some time, but neither was a fairy tale ending as they still left behind an ugly legacy. I wish that all went well in my life after my being humbled, but God has had to do it over and over in my life, which in itself is very humbling. But the point is, it is more honoring to God, who always shows he knows how to humble the proud. Heaven is almost too good to be true but it is no fairy tale. Hades is a horror story ending for those who will not stop hardening their hearts. But both glorify God! Regardless of how the Bible stories end, God is exalted in them all. Our love for good endings should drive us to repentance. God delights in making the basest of men into rulers, and turns our hearts from the evil we long for and towards loving him. The Bible ends with God's redeemed people living forever with him. That is a good ending.

All's well that ends well.

IRREVERSIBLE DECREES

(6:15)　...no decree nor statute which the king establisheth may be changed.

Compare this with Hebrews 2:1-3: if even an earthly king's decree can't be reversed, what hope do we have of God's mercy if we have no payment for our sins? Herod killed John the Baptist to keep his word. In Esther, an irreversible decree went out against the Jews. Jephthah made a rash vow and had to keep it. All these kings and judges had to keep their word, but sought a way to turn back their decisions. No way! God made his decree for Adam and Eve: eating from the forbidden tree meant death. God also had to keep his own decree, but found a way to save Adam and Eve, and all their posterity. But the law remained in effect. Daniel went to the lion's den, but God "shut the lions' mouths", (6:22), just as for us, "Thy God, whom thou servest continually, he will deliver thee" (6:16). Jesus went to the cross for us and took the penalty of God's punishment. Darius prayed and fasted for Daniel and saw him the next morning, alive. Then, he threw to the lions those evil men who conspired to kill Daniel, just as Haman was hung upon the gallows he had made for Mordecai. The Jews then killed those (by a new decree) who would have killed them. Satan was defeated by the same gallows (cross) that he'd hoped would destroy Jesus. God's decree of the curse of the law was nailed to the cross (Col. 2:14). God's mercy can only come after justice has been fulfilled. "The die is cast", like a metal "die" being cast and set in a mold, or one "die" of two "dice" being cast for a decision, or colored dye in clothes being cast and setting a permanent color, so the dye of Christ's blood has been cast upon our sins. If we miss God's decree for salvation we will "die" and be "cast" from Heaven.

The die is cast.

SON OF MAN

(7:13)   ...one like the Son of man came with the clouds of heaven...

Even more than the term "Son of God", "Son of Man" is a messianic term, as we can see by Christ's use of it (Mt. 24:30, 26:64). The "Ancient of Days" is God, the Eternal Father, but the "Son of Man" is the one who, <u>in the form of man</u>, is given dominion over all nations, forever! Is this possible for a man? Jesus is both the "Son of God" and "Son of Man", and was crucified upon his usage of the term "Son of Man", after he was asked if he were the "Son of God". Both terms are unmistakable – Jesus is God by his own admission and by virtue of his being raised from the dead (Jn. 10:18), and <u>by his own power</u> (Jn. 2:19)! But an equally unmistakable claim is that of being the "Son of Man", and the Jews understood it perfectly. Jesus, the eternal son of God became the son of man (mankind) to unite man again with God. God will not share his glory with another (Isa. 42:8), but because Jesus is himself the eternal God, he can say "Father, glorify me in your presence with the glory I had with you before the world began" (Jn. 17:5 - NIV). Also, because he is the "Son of Man" he can share that glory with those who believe among all mankind (Jn. 17:22). The Son of Man is a mystery, as all of God's nature is a mystery. If we reject Jesus' claims, then we must crucify him as a blasphemer. But he is, in fact, Son of Man/Son of God. Daniel saw him coming with the clouds of heaven, one who was "like the son of man", which was important to say because only a heavenly being, or God himself, could come like this, and yet he looked like a human being. This shows that the Son of Man had to be also the Son of God. That makes him the perfect mediator between God and man.

**...the Son of Man sitting on the right
hand of power...** (Mt. 26:64)

DIM BULBS

(12:3)   *"Those who are wise will shine like the brightness of the heavens...*

...and those who lead many to righteousness, like the stars for ever and ever" (NIV). The brightness of the heavens is the stars, which shine all the more brightly against the blackness of a night sky. Diamonds are displayed on black velvet to show off their luster. Even so the saints will shine against the background of the blackness of sin in the world, and those who shine most brightly will be those who have led many others out of darkness and into the kingdom of God. "He that winneth souls is wise", said Solomon (Pr. 11:30), and Paul was "crafty" and used "trickery" (2 Cor. 12:16 - NIV) to become "all things to all men" to wisely win souls (1 Cor. 9:22). Jesus said, "The people of this world are more shrewd in dealing with their own kind than are the people of the light" (Lk.16:8 - NIV). We who have light should wisely use it to win eternal riches in heaven, and a crown that won't fade away. God puts a premium upon human souls, and reserves a place of glory for those who wisely win souls [see also Jas. 5:19-20]. But this glory is not just reserved for us to shine in heaven; there everyone will shine. Rather, we "are the light of the world" (Mt. 5:14), and it is here in the darkness, "in the midst of a crooked and perverse nation..." that we "...shine as lights in the world," (Phil. 2:15). All the world lies in darkness, waiting for us to shine and without light there is nothing to see, but all is blackness. Shall we let the lost sinners perish, being "more shrewd...with their own kind" (Lk.16:8 - NIV), than we who have the light of truth? If they use their worldly wisdom to get by in the world, let us be wise and use our wisdom to win these lost souls into God's kingdom. Let us awaken the light in them so they may be saved.

**Darkness cannot drive out darkness:
only light can do that.**

SHAME TAKES THE BLAME

(2:10)   And now will I discover her lewdness in the sight of her lovers...

Verse 3 says, "Lest I strip her naked..." which taken literally would be a very shameful punishment. Before the first sin was committed, "The man and his wife were both naked, and they felt no shame" (Gen. 2:25 - NIV), but sin brought an immediate awareness of both shame and nakedness. Nothing else had changed outwardly, as they were already naked, but shame over sin made them want to cover themselves. God's desire is not to expose our nakedness, but to cover it, but before he can cover us, there must be shame, remorse and some understanding of how hopelessly lost we are and then a plea for forgiveness. Otherwise, the shame for what we have done will continue to drive us to look for a way back to peace with God. If Israel was not able to feel the shame of exposing her nakedness to her many lovers, then why should she now feel ashamed? Simply, because if God, as her husband, was ready to "strip her naked" she would have to admit to herself what she had become, and each of her "lovers" would know that she had been pretending fidelity to each of them. The use of the word "Lest" means there is room for us to repent before God has to strip us naked to our shame, to break our pride. In the story The Emperor's New Clothes, a king was convinced that he was dressed elegantly when in reality he was naked. That is the true nature of our condition before God: we are as naked as Adam and Eve and oblivious to our sin, until the law comes like a mirror to show us that we are naked and shameful in God's sight. Let shame over sin keep us from shameful punishment.

The shame is in the crime, not in the punishment.

BENT TO BACKSLIDING

(11:7) And my people are bent to backsliding from me"

My favorite picture of "backsliding" is Hosea's, when he says "the Israelites are stubborn, like a stubborn (backsliding: KJV) heifer" (4:16). The picture it summons to mind is that of a cow or donkey on a rope, being yanked by the neck, but sitting down on its hind quarters to resist. We think of a backslider too often as a poor, unfortunate and weak person who keeps sliding back down a slippery sliding board on his upward struggle to heaven. Hosea says they are "bent to backsliding", meaning that the real problem is strength and not weakness. Jesus said to Peter, as he struggled to "watch and pray" in the garden of Gethsemane, "The spirit is willing, but the body is weak" (Mt. 26:41). For the backslider, the opposite is true: "The spirit is unwilling, and the flesh is strong". C.S. Lewis wrote about "That Hideous Strength", which is a good descriptive phrase for strength that is not submitted to God's will. We should not pray "God, give me strength", but "God, make me willing", because as David says, "thy people shall be willing in the day of thy power" (Ps. 110:3). When God's Holy Spirit comes upon us, it is time for revival. God commands us to do his will, but we find ourselves failing to do it, even when we feel willing to do it. To do God's will, we need God's Spirit to live in us, to conquer our contrary wills, and to establish his rulership in our hearts. Our own strength and will power will not bring about God's kingdom, because pride results, and we, too, will soon be bent to backsliding. What we need is to have God's Spirit work his will into our hearts. When God's will motivates my strength, I will be bent to taking on his yoke (Mt. 11:29), not to backsliding.

People do not lack strength; they lack will.

TRUMPET BLAST, SILENT FAST

(2:15)   Blow the trumpet in Zion, sanctify a fast, call a solemn assembly.

Not "Blow a trumpet to call a feast" as one might expect. Where's the excitement of a fast, in response to a trumpet blast? It may seem incongruous, but the fast is really the more exciting response, as this is what will get God's ear, while feasting is an abomination to God if our hearts are not first pure. Likewise, for someone to "sound a trumpet… as the hypocrites do in the synagogues and on the streets" (Mt. 6:2) will only produce a reward of honor here on earth. The kind of fasting referred to here is that of a national fast for mourning over sin. Fasting will always put us in a better frame of mind for going before God in earnest prayer. Personal fasting is to be done in silence, so that nobody else knows, but corporate fasting will unite the hearts of all of God's people, to seek his face in unity. Sometimes silence speaks louder than many words, and sometimes fasting from food to silence our appetites will give us more hunger for God. It is like a pause for emphasis, a "selah" that calls God and ourselves to serious attention. "Silence is deafening" at the appropriate time, and fasting will blow a trumpet that God will hear, when we are in earnest. There will be plenty of time for feasting, when God has heard and answered a sincere prayer with fasting. It is a tool that we must develop as we learn to communicate with God, and to hear his voice. When we come to the "valley of decision" (3:14), it will be God's decision, and not ours that decides our fate. On that day, it will be a day of silence for those whose mouths will be stopped by the terror of God's law. Let us learn before that how to communicate with our Maker, and to listen for his voice.

Silence is one great art of conversation.

ROOTS AND FRUITS

(2:9)   ...I destroyed his fruit from above, and his roots from beneath.

"Roots and fruits" – that is total destruction. The Amorites were appointed to destruction from God, being from the sons of Canaan (Gen. 9:25, 10:16) but the immediate reason was for refusing to let the Israelites pass through their land (Num. 21:24). They were destroyed "lock, stock and barrel", and we never hear about them again once they are gone. Their "root", or stock (their lineage of kings down to Sihon), and their "fruit" – even their children, were wiped out, so they would cease to exist. If God did this to a great and tall and strong nation, can he not do it to his people Israel, and to us, if we continue to be rebellious? Jude says, "They are... autumn trees, without fruit and uprooted – twice dead" (Jude 12 - NIV), as he speaks of false "brothers", or false prophets who creep into our assemblies. They are twice dead because they have no fruits (of righteousness, or fruits of the Spirit), and are not rooted in Christ, and so are spiritually dead. They will also be twice dead as "their place will be in the fiery lake of burning sulfur. This is the second death" (Rev. 21:8 - NIV). Jesus cursed a fig tree for showing its foliage but having no fruit. It withered and never bore fruit again, "dried up from the roots" (Mk. 11:20). When God curses and plucks someone up from the roots to throw him into Hades, that is total destruction. John the Baptist preached "Produce fruit in keeping with repentance... the ax is already at the root of the trees, and every tree that does not produce good fruit will be cut down and thrown into the fire" (Mt. 3:8,10 - NIV). "Even though we speak like this, dear friends, we are confident of better things in your case – things that accompany salvation" (Heb. 6:9 - NIV). Thank God!

**No branch can bear fruit by itself; it must
remain in the vine.** (Jn. 15:4 – NIV)

FIGURING THE FUDGE FACTOR

(8:5)　...skimping the measure, boosting the price...

. . . and cheating with dishonest scales (NIV). Figures will not lie, unless they have been falsified through tampering, and liars have always found ways to tamper to their own advantage. This verse speaks of one of the oldest methods of deceit in the book, using altered weights when weighing out food on a scale, or putting the balance off center. People who cheat their way through this life often suppose a similar "weighing scale" will be used on Judgment Day, and hope that they may again be able to cheat their way into heaven. Supposing good deeds will be balanced against bad, they hope to "fudge" their way into heaven, using lead weights instead of gold. More sophisticated and "fool proof" systems are being developed every year to insure honesty, but enterprising crooks will always find a way to crack the system, so why worry that the "Day of Final Reckoning" should be any different? Well, it will be different. Only the blood of Christ will outweigh our sins, and no amount of good works will make the slightest difference. Figures will not lie on that day when God who knows all displays a record book of all our sins. But foolish liars will go into eternity figuring on "falsifying the balances by deceit" (KJV), making their pound of sin look small, and the ounce of good works look great. Too bad for them, God's figures will not lie, and they cannot be tampered with or made void, except through the blood of the cross. That alone will outweigh all our sins, small or great. What a deal, what a bargain! But liars will figure and lose it all, because no amount of fudge will nudge the Judge, or make him budge.

Figures won't lie, but liars will figure.

269

TEN POINTS FOR SUCCESSFUL PREACHING

(3:2)　*Go to the great city of Nineveh and proclaim to it the message I give you (NIV)*

Jonah saw possibly the greatest evangelistic response that has been seen in the history of the world, but what was the secret of his success? His eight word <u>message</u>? Or maybe the <u>way</u> he preached it? (Anger against Nineveh!) Did Jonah have <u>faith</u> that results would come? (You bet he did, and he hated the thought of God being merciful to Nineveh!) He knew God would save them in his mercy. I think <u>God had already decided</u> he would save Nineveh, and had <u>prepared</u> (Phil. 2:13) their hearts beforehand. But still he needed a <u>preacher</u> (Rom. 10:13-15). Even a hateful, reluctant preacher would do, just someone who would open his mouth and speak what he was told to say. Even just eight words, and even if he said the words with anger! Not a word about the <u>love of God</u>. Not even the <u>Ten Commandments</u>, but just "the judgment is coming in forty more days!" Not a "<u>positive mental attitude</u>" (he wanted them to be killed). It's obvious that "Salvation is of the Lord" (2:9), and God will save when he wants to, for his own glory. Jonah failed in anybody's book on "Ten ways to prepare for revival". Jonah didn't even have an "<u>altar call</u>". He didn't <u>pray</u> for them to be saved – if he prayed at all he would have liked to pray against them. Jonah's heart was wicked and full of anger, so even <u>his own heart</u> was not prepared to make way for revival. But this was not "revival" – these were Gentiles who had not been saved before. This was God's own sovereign move upon a city to bring them to repentance. Two of these 12 points were the "secret" of Jonah's success: it was God's sovereign design and preparation. The rest were what we want to think will work.

Salvation comes from the Lord.

GOD, THE MESSIAH

(5:2)　...whose origins are from of old, from ancient times. (NIV)

This is quite a messianic prophecy, fulfilled in Jesus, who was the "King of the Jews", born in this little town of Bethlehem. But look at this: the KJV says "whose goings forth have been from of old, from everlasting". To any thinking person, the meaning is obvious: that the messiah is God himself, as even angels were not from eternity. And yet, "out of you will come for me" (5:2 - NIV) means it is someone external to God, about whom God is speaking. Is this messiah God, or not God? Could anyone else but God be eternal? Certainly not. Then, what is the meaning of this enigma? These hints are throughout the Bible, to tell us that the messiah is a man and yet is God. The mystery of the "Trinity", never spoken of as such, is also throughout Scripture, in such obvious clues that the person of integrity who will search with honesty the Scriptures will find it must be the true nature of God. How unassuming and typical, then, for God to choose a small place like Bethlehem to hide away the messiah, that only the honest seeker would ever find him. God has "hid these things from the wise and prudent, and hast revealed them unto babes" (Mt. 11:25). So, likewise, like Bethlehem, which was no great place in comparison to a thousand other towns, anyone who humbly believes in the truth of Jesus, the God-man, will be saved. We can understand who God is only through his revelation of himself to us in this life. And, it is finally in Christ that we see the perfection of God in a life we can see and feel. None compares to Jesus for perfection, so he is the proof of who the real God is.

Thy throne, O God, is for ever and ever. (Ps. 45:6)

GAZING STOCK

(3:6)   I will pelt you with filth, I will treat you with
contempt and make you a spectacle... (NIV)

...or "a gazing stock" (KJV), which was the worst type of humiliation. A person who had done a crime was put into a "pillory": his head and hands locked into a wooden frame, and people who passed by could jeer or throw dirt and filth upon him as he became a 'gazing stock' to them. Paul used a similar image, saying "We [apostles] are made a spectacle unto the world, and to angels, and to men" (1 Cor. 4:9). This was now to be the shame of Nineveh, that proud city which 100 years before had repented at the preaching of Jonah. Now their pride was put in the pillory. A person in prison can rattle his cage, but he is still inside, if those who hate him want to jeer at him. The person in a stock or pillory cannot even move his hands or head if someone wants to spit on him, or throw dirt or dirty remarks; he's helpless, and Nineveh deserved this derision. And, as sinners, so do we all! But this is what Jesus did for us – he was nailed, hands and feet, to the pillory of the cross, where people walked by and spat upon him, and threw dirt and filth, and cursed at him. He could not even move a hand to cover his nakedness, or to defend himself. He became a "gazing stock" for you and me, for <u>our</u> sins, not any sin in himself. Paul said correctly that the apostles were made to be a spectacle and we as Christians will also bear Christ's reproach (Heb. 10:33), if we will carry our cross and follow. But, through this, the world will see their own guilt and shame. Let us gaze upon Christ, and take stock of our own sinful condition, before we become a gazing stock as the punishment we deserve.

Looking unto Jesus the author and
finisher of our faith... (Heb. 12:2)

How Long?

(1:2)   O Lord, how long shall I cry, and thou wilt not hear!

"How Long?!" Time seems to drag on for so long when things are not going well, but life is so short when we are enjoying it. Yet, time just goes on at the same rate for everybody. A better question might be, "Why am I here, and how could I make better use of the time I have?" Habakkuk gets this answer when he asks why the bad guys don't get punished: "See, he is puffed up; his desires are not upright – but the righteous will live by his faith" (2:4 - NIV). Many who are faithful to God may die young, while many who live for themselves live to a ripe old age. "Woe to him who piles up stolen goods and makes himself wealthy by extortion! <u>How long</u> must this go on?" (2:6 - NIV). When we die and enter eternity, "How long" will take on a whole new meaning for the good and the evil. Eternal life in heaven will joyfully go on forever, but a day in Hades will seem like eternity, and "How long" will only be answered with silence. How we live here on earth is important, not <u>how long</u>. Don't be overly concerned or envious when you see evil men prospering: "For like the grass they will soon wither" (Ps. 37:2 - NIV). On Judgment Day, how long we lived will not be as important as how we lived. When we say, "How long, O Lord, must I call out for help, but you do not listen?" (1:2 – NIV) we are crying out to God who <u>does</u> hear <u>immediately</u>. Those who don't know God, who never cry out to him, are the real losers, who one day will cry out "How long" to a God who no longer listens. We should pray for them that they may be saved and ignore our present affliction.

How we live is important, not how long.

WHEN IT RAINS, IT POURS

(1:15)   That day is a day of wrath, a day of trouble and distress...

"When it rains, it pours". Originally, that was not meant as an expression of free-flowing salt, but of troubles coming one after another. When Job was hit with his troubles, they came in waves, one after another. This saying means, "When we need rain, it doesn't come, but when it finally comes it is a torrent that destroys crops, not a helpful watering rain." Job's troubles could be called 'misfortune' because he didn't deserve such trouble, but when God's judgment comes, it will be deserved by everyone who receives it, and it will come in waves. Like a woman who forgets to take a birth control pill after taking them for a long time, she may suddenly find herself the mother of quadruplets! How we view misfortune will no doubt color it when it comes. Those with a "Murphy's Law" mentality might see life as a long string of misfortunes to be expected and dealt with. But "...to them that love God, to them who are the called according to his purpose" (Rom. 8:28), God's blessing is seen behind the misfortune. Shouldn't quadruplets, triplets or twins be considered as a blessing from God, instead of misfortune? "When it rains, it pours" finally had a good meaning, when Morton Salt adopted it: "Thank God, when it rains, the salt still pours!" When everyone else is complaining about no rain, or too much rain, we should continue to be the "salt of the earth", to remind others that God will turn our misfortune into waves of blessing if only we will turn back to him in our hearts. Don't wait for the day of wrath, when misfortune will multiply.

Misfortune and twins never come singly!

PAPA AND GOD CAN DO ANYTHING

(3:7)   If thou wilt keep my charge, then thou shalt also judge my house.

If we could see with God's eyes, how different would be our estimation of the mundane and simple jobs that we do daily! Zechariah says it another way: "For who hath despised the day of small things?" (4:10). Those who remain faithful in what they are put in charge of will one day be exalted, and the great men of the world have gotten there by doing simple things well. Many will never be "great" in the world's eyes, but God's Kingdom is run on a different standard of what is "great". Brother Lawrence, who wrote <u>The Practice of the Presence of God</u>, found greatness in a kitchen, where he learned to enjoy washing dishes and other menial tasks. Mother Teresa of Calcutta, India, may be considered great now, but she still works for nothing among the poorest and most destitute of people. Jesus was never rich, never married, and had only three and a half years of time to be known at all, but who would deny that he was the greatest of men, at the very least? Maybe you feel trapped as a parent, or as a lowly housewife or a 'henpecked' husband, but God may be seeing you as the greatest living human being, if you are faithfully doing what he has put in your life to do. Maybe the child you are raising will be your ticket to greatness, so pour yourself into that young life. It is your charge from God, so rule the world with God in your little corner. My brother Christopher once said, "Papa and God can do anything!" You are your child's first glimpse of what God is like, and with a charge like that, be sure to live up to it.

The hand that rocks the cradle rules the world.

THE GIFT THAT KEEPS ON GIVING

(8:13) ...as ye were a curse among the heathen...ye shall be a blessing...

In what way were the Israelites a curse and a blessing? Long before they were a nation, a promise was given (Gen. 12:2-3) to Abram that he would be father to a nation that would bless all the nations of the world. But, God would also curse those that cursed Israel, and they saw both blessings and curses in their long history. There is nothing wrong with receiving blessings, and God loves to bless his children so they will joyfully bless others. The problem comes when we begin to enjoy receiving so much that we forget to be thankful, and forget <u>why</u> we are being blessed. It seems that Israel enjoyed receiving so much that she started receiving from the nations their idolatry, instead of blessing them by sharing God with them. Today, America is doing that same thing, forgetting God who blessed her, and taking in all of the religions of the world, and now wonders why things are going wrong. Once known as the real center of blessing to the world, America is now a leader in crime, drugs, abortion and divorce, and now exports cults like Jehovah's Witness, Mormons and the Children of God to the world. Israel may again become the channel of blessing to the world if they will return to the true God of their Scriptures, and receive Christ, their promised Messiah, and share his good news with others. Just like the real joy of "Christmas", we must discover the true joy in giving and seeing others blessed as they receive, not false religions and bad gifts, but God's blessing.

It is more blessed to give than to receive. (Acts 20:35)

BEAUTY AND BANDS

(11:7)   Then I took two staffs and called one Favor and the other Union. (NIV)

The King James Version calls them "Beauty" and "Bands", Beauty for the covenant we have with God, and Bands for our brotherhood as his children. Not a "rod and a staff" (Ps. 23:4), but two staffs, signifying our relationships with God and man. Jesus said all of the commandments are summed up in these two: to love God supremely, and our neighbors as ourselves (Mk. 12:28-34). The Old Covenant Ark contained a rod symbolizing God's supreme authority, as a master over slaves, but the New Covenant came as a new relationship of love in marriage, with God as our husband. This had always been there for God's people, but few had entered into the "Beauty of Holiness" (Ps. 29:2). The rod and the law could lead to the fear of God, but "Beauty and Bands" came through God's goodness and grace (Jn. 1:17). God broke these two staves of covenant and brotherhood when Israel and Judah strayed from him, but Jesus came with a new and eternal covenant, written in his own blood on the cross. In the cross we see the two staves bound together inseparably, showing God's covenant holding up the crosspiece of brotherhood, and Christ being sacrificed on it. The cross didn't conquer him, but Jesus conquered the cross as he rose up from the grave. Let us embrace the 'old rugged cross' and enter the eternal marriage covenant with God, taking all of his blood-bought children as our brothers and sisters. If love conquered the cross, we too can love and conquer in him.

Love conquers all; let us too yield to Love.

ROBIN HOOD

(3:8)   Will a man rob God? Yet ye have robbed me...

When we rob God, we rob ourselves. God has designed the world and all of creation to operate on giving, not on receiving. Although we are all receivers, still we must practice and cultivate the principle of giving, or ultimately we will find that things will start to break down. Christians are not some exotic form of religion, but are people who do the practical and normal giving of their time, money and energy to see the Kingdom of God run as it is meant to run. When Paul the Apostle quotes Jesus as saying, "It is more blessed to give than to receive" (Acts 20:35), or says that "God loveth a cheerful giver" (2 Cor. 9:7), he expresses God's attitude toward giving, and the attitude we should have as his children. The kingdoms of this world all run on taking, not on giving, and that is an endless and frustrating pursuit. The people that learn the joy of giving, of passing on their blessings to others, are those who find peace and contentment. A robber will never be content, and God compares us to robbers when we refuse to give cheerfully while saying we are of his Kingdom. Tithes and offerings are Old Testament concepts that still have a prominent place in a great number of churches today, but that is only a beginning. God wants all of us – money, time, life, possessions, affections and all of it – to be given first to him as Lord of it all, and then to others as he directs us. Being a cheerful giver will lead to a long and satisfied life. Try it! Robin Hood, with his 'merry men', "robbed from the rich, to give to the poor" and was applauded as a selfless champion of good, but be careful not to steal from God, thinking to make yourself rich. That is selfish and will only end in misery.

Robbin' who'd make merry men?

HEROD AND HITLER'S HOLOCAUSTS

(2:16) *...and slew all the children that were in Bethlehem...from two years old and under...*

Imagine, if Jesus had come back to Bethlehem, he would have had no classmates in kindergarten, or all through his years of school, that were his age. If that seems like a funny thought, then consider "Roe v. Wade" and the abortion issue. "Jane Roe" (an alias), who became a figurehead for the "pro-choice" (or pro-death) movement, recently changed her mind publicly, while her lawyers and other abortionists quickly slammed her as a "turn- coat" or traitor. With very little foresight, she and many of us who took "choice" over "life", destroyed a whole generation of innocent children. Somebody decided to check, just one short generation after the "Roe v. Wade" decision, and found a sharp drop in the number of kids enrolled in the first grade class. Why? Simply, the would-be parents of that class were aborted and killed just 20 years before. Now, when it is too late, we see our crimes, and our arms ache, wanting to hold and love these sweet children destroyed by a selfish whim. Now, we change our minds, and only God and our guilty consciences know which of us are guilty, as the evidence died years ago. America's collective guilt is now paying the price, as another godly country is on the verge of ruin. Yes, Herod and Hitler's holocausts were bad, but who will cast the first stone at them on judgment day? All of those innocent children will be there on that day, with a foresight to God's judgment.

Vengeance has no foresight.

JOKE ONLY

(5:37)   Simply let your 'Yes' be 'Yes' and your 'No,' 'No'... (NIV)

Say what you mean to say in all your dealings with God or man. In the Philippines, people say "Joke only" when caught in the act of stealing or some other deceit. How sweet! (A cute one on a tee-shirt: on the front "Marcos for President"; on the back "Joke only!") But most joking hurts people. We laugh at others' pitiable situations, instead of having compassion, making it easier to learn deceit. A cute smile and "Joke only" is supposed to excuse us when we are caught lying. Proverbs speaks of two kinds of insincerity: "Joke only" and "Holy jokes". The first is compared to a madman throwing firebrands into a crowd (Pr. 26:18-19), not funny because it kills people. Like Jesus' assessment of murder and adultery beginning in the heart, joking this way is also killing people emotionally. The second "Holy joke" is even worse: "He that blesseth his friend with a loud voice, rising early in the morning, it shall be counted a curse to him" (Pr. 27:14). Don't try to cover your real intentions with an appearance of holiness. Hypocrisy is a thin veil over an evil heart, and people can see through it. It is worse than "joke only" because we try to bring God into it and hide behind a holy front, making God look bad. It is cowardly. Better to slap the person if you want a fight. God says, "let your 'Yes' be 'Yes', and don't make enemies with him or your neighbor by speaking falsely. Let your words be few, and don't make oaths to God that you might change your mind about someday. If you say "I do", then do, and stay married! And don't ever say "Joke only" to God.

Keep your oaths, even when it hurts.

No Expectations

(9:2)   he said to the paralytic, "Take heart, son; your sins are forgiven." (NIV)

Sin has brought about all of the evils and sickness in this world, and God is under no obligation to help any of us. If anyone receives God's grace in any form, he should fall on his face and weep for joy that God has even taken notice of him. Whether we are rich or poor, well or sick, we are all beggars before God, in need of what only he can give us. This paralytic man may have desired first to be told, "Arise and walk", but Jesus came to him and gave him a full pardon from his sins, which is the greatest need for all of us. When the lame man at the Beautiful Gate asked for alms, Peter and John gave him something he didn't ask for, but which was more needful for him, saying "arise and walk". Beggars can't be choosers! In India, I gave some bread once to a beggar who had come to our door. I looked back at him a minute later and saw him throwing it on the ground. Apparently, he wanted money, but he wasted our bread. Others have frowned when we gave less than they had hoped for, instead of receiving anything they got at all with thanks and gratitude. The paralytic did not sulk or feel slighted because he was not healed. And suddenly he <u>was</u> healed, besides having his sins forgiven. Some beggars in India make more money than those who carry rocks on their heads all day long. The beggars who scowl at me for their disappointment are not likely to receive anything next time, are they?

Beggars must not be choosers.

SHEEP AMONG WOLVES

(10:16)   *"I am sending you out like sheep among wolves. Therefore be...*

... as shrewd as snakes and as innocent as doves" (NIV). <u>Little Red Riding Hood</u> is the story of a wolf in Grandma's clothing trying to eat up the little girl, possibly taken from Jesus' statement about false prophets coming as wolves in sheep's clothing (Mt. 7:15). It is tender sheep that "ravenous wolves" (Acts 20:29 - NIV) love to devour, yet this is how Jesus came, and how he sends us out. "If wolves can come in sheep's clothing", some have thought, "then let's be sheep in wolves' clothing!" They dress, look and speak so much like the world, and impersonate worldly music, it soon becomes hard to tell them apart. Some backslide. But Jesus sends us out as sheep, without disguises, and that is dangerous among wolves! Serpents are wise, but are also harmful; doves are harmless, but without much wisdom. So, in this evil world, we must be wise to survive, but harmless if others will ever see Christ in us. We are counted as sheep for the slaughter, but we also know what we are doing. Little Red Riding Hood was at least wise enough to recognize a wolf, even when it was in her Grandmother's clothing. Can we tell the "wolves" from the Christians when they look so much alike? Don't be fooled by appearances; test their fruits. But don't let fear of the wolves turn you into a wolf or a serpent. Be wise and harmless. Remain as a sheep, and don't be conformed to the world of wolves. I was once a wolf, but was transformed by the gentle nature of sheep, and soon became another sheep. Wolves may devour us someday, but remember Jesus sent us as sheep, so others may also become part of his Kingdom.

...be...wise as serpents, and harmless
as doves. (Mt. 10:16 – KJV)

HEAVYWEIGHT DESIRES

(13:17)   *...many prophets and righteous men have*
          desired to see those things which ye see...

Most of us wouldn't mind seeing a few things that the prophets saw, either. They had some pretty stunning attainments in their lifetimes, like calling down fire from heaven, stopping the mouths of lions, parting the Red Sea and even raising the dead, so what was Jesus talking about? He did say "many prophets", so he may not have been referring to the real "heavyweights", but I don't think that is the answer. Even the greatest of the prophets could only give glory to God for any of their triumphs, but Jesus came and did it all on his own. The desire of all the "prophets and righteous men" of all ages has only been to see God glorified, and not any personal success. Paul said it well, after he recounted all of his personal achievements: "But whatever was to my profit I now consider loss for the sake of Christ. What is more, I consider everything a loss compared to the surpassing greatness of knowing Christ Jesus my Lord..." (Php. 3:7-8 - NIV). When Jesus came, it was God walking in a human body, and to see and hear and know him was something all the prophets had desired; they would have gladly forfeited the privilege of seeing miracles done by their own hands if they could only have seen Jesus, the promised Messiah in their lifetimes. Tonight, as I was finishing this, I watched a good quarterfinal tennis match in which Andre Agassi won two sets, then lost the next and nearly lost the fourth against Petr Korda. I remember when he gave glory to Jesus as a young man, and I wonder now if his desire to glorify God will remain. May that be our desire, not pursuing miracles. That is how prophets dreamed.

We live in our desires rather than in achievements.

LASTING FAME

(16:13)   Whom do men say that I Son of man am?"

Jesus was not checking his popularity ratings by asking this but was priming the disciples before he asked them the same question. At this point, he had done nothing particularly heroic, but had done lots of things that were sensational. Miracles are good crowd pleasers, as are witty comebacks to overly stuffy, self-righteous Pharisees. Based on these, and his authoritative style of teaching, Jesus could have won a landslide victory in any election. Many were saying he was a great prophet like Elijah, and Peter gave the great confession that he is "the Christ, the Son of the living God" (v. 16). But moments later, when Jesus spoke of the soon coming suffering and crucifixion, Peter was caught completely off guard. How could such a dynamic person as Jesus even talk about crucifixion? Look at another example: The "Beatles" became very famous for several years, until John Lennon said, "We're more popular than Jesus". Suddenly, their shallow basis of fame came crumbling down overnight, and soon John sang, "The way things are going, they're gonna crucify me!" Talking about it, for the Beatles, became a stench that they couldn't undo, but when Jesus spoke of crucifixion, he was prophesying his death, the most heroic deed in history. Had anyone asked Peter just after the Savior's death "Who is Jesus?" he may have hesitated. But, after the resurrection, the full impact of Christ's death became obvious. Real lasting fame belongs to real heroes.

Fame is the perfume of heroic deeds.

BREAKFAST OF CHAMPIONS

(17:21)   Howbeit this kind goeth not out but by prayer and fasting

My father used to say, "You have to feed your body if you want your soul to stay in it". It's true that without food we cannot continue to live for very long, but there are times when it's more important to our overall health to fast than to eat. When the disciples could not help this young man, they asked "Why could not we cast him out?" referring to the other (demonic) soul inside him. They probably expected "Did you eat your Wheaties today?" But, spiritual strength seems to be helped more by <u>not</u> eating than by eating. When Jesus was tempted in the desert, he was physically weak, but spiritually very strong. When the devil tempted him to "command that these stones be made bread" Jesus answered "It is written: Man shall not live by bread alone, but by every word that proceedeth out of the mouth of God" (Mt. 4:3-4). Apparently, when dealing with demons in someone else which are especially long established or strong, the maxim is now, "You have to starve your body if you want his soul to stay in it [and the demonic soul to leave]". Life is more than just living to eat, though we must eat to live. Man is not a body alone, but has a soul and a spirit that must be made alive by communion with God. And, we are responsible for the spiritual health of others. If someone took the time to pray and fast for me, to see me enter God's Kingdom, I should count it a privilege to do the same for others. I am "my brother's keeper" (Gen. 4:9), and what I cannot do for others by eating a bowl of Wheaties, I may be able to do by giving up breakfast. The real champions in God's Kingdom may not look like Arnold Schwarzenegger, but they get the job done.

Man shall not live by bread alone... (Mt. 4:4)

IT IS WRITTEN

(22:29) *"Ye do err, not knowing the Scriptures, nor the power of God"*

Those who desire power, and yet deny that the Scriptures written by God's prophets are really His Word, are missing the boat, and those who pride themselves in having the Scriptures, but don't take the time to study the meaning, are on the boat without a compass. The power of God is the source of all power, and to be untrained in God's Word is a grave disadvantage for anyone. The Jews who hated Jesus, and finally had him crucified, erred greatly by not knowing what Scripture said of Christ: that he would rise from the dead. Many other religious groups have developed since the time of Christ, claiming to be God's latest prophet, with the message of the hour, but "erring greatly, not knowing the Scriptures" that came before. When the religion of Islam came along with "the prophet of the sword", many of the teachings sounded like the Jewish Scriptures, but as usual, Christ became the stumbling block. The sword of Islam conquered much of the world, and continues today to strike fear into people's hearts. But, "the pen is mightier than the sword", and God's true message of grace through the blood of Christ's sacrifice is "…the power of God unto salvation to every one that believeth…" (Rom. 1:16). The sword has the power to kill, but the pen of the prophets speaks of the resurrection for the blood-bought. "…My tongue is the pen of a ready writer" (Ps. 45:1), as I quote the truth of Scripture to those who have erred from the truth. God's power has not come to kill, but to save; but, if you live by the sword, you will die by the sword.

The pen is mightier than the sword.

SHAME FOR HIS NAME

(24:9)　"Then you will be handed over to be persecuted and put to death,

...and you will be hated by all nations because of me" (NIV). Why would anybody persecute and kill Christians? Or hate them? Aren't Christians supposed to be the best of all citizens, and kind to everyone, even while they are being treated wrongly? Yes, and the history of the world is filled with God's people, both Jews and Christians, being treated unfairly. Peter says, "If you suffer as a Christian, do not be ashamed, but praise God that you bear that name" (1 Pet. 4:16 - NIV). Persecution is most real when it is aimed at those who are suffering unjustly, and it is designed to bring shame not only to us as Christians, but to Christ himself, and to his righteous kingdom. The real shame, though, will come upon the persecutors, as we take affliction as God's opportunity for us to glorify him. When Jesus suffered and died, it was a most shameful death, but history has shown the real shame is to those who unjustly crucified him. If we despise the shame of the cross as Jesus did, and suffer when we are wrongly subjected to it, God will turn the shame back upon those who are doing the injustice. Peter wrote from experience, remembering how he and the other apostles, having done no wrong, were beaten and commanded to stop preaching Christ. "And they departed from the presence of the council, rejoicing that they were counted worthy to suffer shame for his name" (Acts 5:41).

To do injustice is more disgraceful than to suffer it.

A FRIEND INDEED

(26:49)   ...Judas said, "Greetings, Rabbi!" and
kissed him. Jesus replied, "Friend..." (NIV)

The treachery of Judas continues for all time as the most graphic example of friendship betrayed. Though it happens every day, and it is the worst kind of pain for those who are betrayed, usually it is done unwittingly. Peter betrayed Jesus, but it was not planned. Judas was called "friend" even at this point of pretense, when a kiss was used as a sign that he was the one to be taken. How many times could Jesus have revealed Judas' identity as the betrayer to the other disciples?! And yet, the bond of friendship would not allow it. This is the thing that hurts the most when marriages end in divorce, often because of unfaithfulness to the marriage vows. Marriage should be the closest bond of friendship on earth, yet there are marriages ending every day because of a lack of truthfulness between spouses. Premeditated acts of adultery, with dishonesty when confronted about them, are the hardest to take, because it is one's best friend who has done the betrayal. From an enemy we could expect it, but now "Even my close friend, whom I trusted, he who shared my bread, has lifted up his heel against me" (Ps. 41:9 - NIV). While it is easy to judge Judas as an evil man, we must also be careful to judge ourselves, if we have not been guilty of the same pretense. God has invited us all to be partakers of his divine nature, and has called us friends. How much more evil is it for us to pretend to be God's friends, and to continue to play with sin, when he knows what we do! Be a friend indeed!

In friendship there should be no pretense.

ALL OR NOTHING

(27:19)   *"Don't have anything to do with that innocent man" (NIV)*

Pontius Pilate's wife spoke these words, and they are the only hint of sanity among all the activities leading up to Jesus' crucifixion. Her husband had said, "What is truth?" (Jn. 18:38), but was really not interested in an answer. He was too busy being the V.I.P. Governor to really care about truth. Soldiers mocked and spat upon Jesus (27:27-31) and cared only about who would win his garments, with not a thought about who Jesus really was. The disciples all cared more about saving their skins than about saving the one who was going to save not only their skins but their souls. Judas was in it only for the money. The Jews wanted only their precious positions to continue, and killed their own Messiah. The multitudes had followed Jesus, who is truth itself, but only to be fed and to see miracles (Jn. 6:26-7). The thieves crucified next to Jesus seemed only to care about getting out of their due punishment, not about the truth hanging between them, who would soon be their judge. Herod, like the earlier Herod (2:3), was only afraid of losing his throne if it were true that Jesus was a King, but now that he was in his hands, he wouldn't mind seeing a miracle. If you and I were this close to the truth, would we also be so caught up with trivial pursuits that we would completely miss him? If so, we had better "have nothing to do with this just man" if we are planning to try to be rid of him. But, truth seekers will have all to do with him.

Truth lies beyond our selfish pursuits.

SILENT STRENGTH

(1:35)   Jesus…went off to a solitary place, where he prayed. (NIV)

"Quiet times", when the noise of the daily routine of life is silenced, are a most necessary part of the Christian life. Jesus took strength from daily times alone, in solitary places. His life was not all "flash" and miracles, but much of it was spent alone, in prayer to God. He had learned from his thirty years of "silence", working as a carpenter, that his time alone with God was the place of depth and strength. He began his ministry with forty days of fasting (1:12), alone in the silence of the wilderness, and later, often went for whole nights alone, praying for important decisions. When performing miracles, he usually told them, "See thou say nothing to any man" (1:44), instead of looking for public acclaim. And, it was because he practiced so much at silence that he could refrain from speaking in his own defense as he was on trial to be crucified. His silence showed real strength and conviction, not weakness and panic. He had spent his life preparing for the cross, and he would trust in God his Father, who always heard his prayers. If you are lacking in strength for what you must go through, have you had any good quiet times with God lately? Those who make a lot of noise to get attention are probably doing so to make up for their lack of power. When Jesus, having spent time in prayer, commanded unclean spirits to go, he said simply, "Be quiet! Come out of him!" (1:25 – NIV) Silence! No great noise was needed, but just a word to silence them. When we face the God of all power, "Be still, and know that I am God!" (Ps. 46:10)

In silence there is strength.

BESIDE HIMSELF

(3:21) ...they said, He is beside himself.

C. S. Lewis wrote concerning Jesus that he must have been "a liar, a lunatic, or Lord of all". All of these were thoughts people actually had of him, and here is a good example. The meaning is, of course, "he is crazy", as when the Jews said, "He hath a devil, and is mad; why hear ye him?" (Jn. 10:20). In this case, his own family and kinsmen saw him inviting so many people home, he could barely even eat. "Beside himself" is a funny expression: did it mean (King James' time) "by the side of himself" or "in addition to himself"? The first would imply something like a split personality (another version of himself alongside him). The second could mean, "Besides himself, there is another [demon] inside of him". The Scribes (v. 22) decidedly opted for the second, but Jesus shows it is rather <u>they</u> who have "entertained angels unawares" (Heb. 13:2). "The Fool on the Hill", (an old song by the Beatles) showed one who was considered mad by everyone, who was actually the only one with his right mind [see Job 2:8 & Eccl. 2:12]. Jesus said, "For John came neither eating nor drinking, and they say, 'He hath a devil'" (Mt. 11:18). So, those who do the will of God will always be out of step with the world. We will be accused of the same if we choose to follow Jesus. Paul spoke "as a fool" (2 Cor. 11) to show others they were really the foolish ones. He was accused of being "beside thyself" by Festus (Acts 26:24), but he spoke only wisdom. Christians are "beside themselves" in a good sense, because there is one "besides ourselves", even Jesus, who lives inside us.

**There is a friend that sticketh closer
than a brother.** (Pr. 18:24)

OFF WITH HIS HEAD

(6:16)   *"John, the man I beheaded, has been raised from the dead!" (NIV)*

Sin will come back to haunt you, and Herod's sin is a good example. He married his brother's wife, but God sent John to him to speak conviction for his sin. Fittingly, a husband is called "the head of the wife" (Eph. 5:23), so Herod had already beheaded Philip from his wife. He was guilty of adultery, but now his sin led him to the ugly consequence of silencing the voice of his conscience by beheading John. Herodias was no doubt also responsible for tempting Herod to marry her, and now for John's death. Maybe Herod was already having dreams that John the Baptist was risen from the dead to haunt him. Herodias' guilt led her to ask for the head of John but, like Adam and Eve, Herod gets the responsibility for the crime as her new head. Divorce and adultery are as evil as Herod's crime: if we do these, some innocent person will lose a head and the sin will come back to haunt us in our dreams. So, it was not an accident that John should be beheaded. He became a sign for the church, whose head is Christ. As an adulterous wife, Judah and all Israel had gone off from God, their faithful husband, and Jesus was the head they cut off by crucifying him. But, he came back to haunt them by rising from the dead! A story was told of a drunken man who, in a stupor, shot and killed his barking watchdog. The dog was warning him that a robber was coming in. God has given us a conscience to warn us of sin at our doors. Before your sin drives you to an even worse sin, listen to the voice of your conscience. Don't try to lock it up in jail, and don't silence it. It is your faithful aid to turn you from sin. Repent, and return to God.

A bad conscience has a very good memory.

GET THEE BEHIND ME, SATAN!

(8:33) *But when he had turned about and looked*
on his disciples, he rebuked Peter...

What could bring such a strong censure from Jesus against a statement from Peter, who had just made the most important confession that Jesus was the Christ? It was his denial of the cross (as he first rebuked Jesus!) "Such 'wisdom' does not come down from heaven, but is earthly, unspiritual, of the devil" (Jas. 3:15 - NIV). Any doctrine that denies the cross, though it appeals to our earthly senses, is from the devil. We like prosperity doctrines and religious works that exalt our egos, but the cross is the death of all these selfish ideas. Satan even tried to sell Jesus on the idea of worshiping him, to skip the cross and still gain the whole world. Today, the world is filled with religions that exalt 'earthly, sensual, devilish' doctrines "denying the Lord that bought them" (2 Pet. 2:1). "For the preaching of the cross is to them that perish foolishness; but unto us which are saved it is the power of God" (1 Cor. 1:18). Religion, be it ever so holy in appearance, is devoid of any heavenly wisdom if it denies the cross, "having a form of godliness, but denying the power thereof" (2 Tim. 3:5). Power to overcome sin is not within us – it comes only by the cross: both Jesus' blood and our death with him. We must have this attitude firmly in our hearts, so we will not be swayed by false comforts. If Jesus and so many disciples have embraced the cross, shall we not follow our Lord and be conformed to his death? Our immediate response must be "Get thee behind me, Satan!" when we are tempted to get away from the cross in our lives, or we cannot follow Christ.

The cross before me, the world behind me.

WHAT DO YOU WANT?

(10:51)   "What do you want me to do for you?" Jesus asked him. (NIV)

Wasn't it quite obvious what 'Blind Bartimaeus' needed? We might think, "Can't you see he's blind, and needs his sight?", but what he kept saying was simply "Jesus, thou Son of David, have mercy on me!" Jesus made him speak out whatever he felt he had faith to ask for. This shows us an important aspect of prayer: be specific, and ask for it specifically. Jesus asked the same question of his disciples just before this (10:36), but here it was not at all obvious what they wanted: "we want you to do for us whatever we ask" (NIV). Earlier, Jesus didn't ask at all, and he said to a man lowered through the roof on a bed, "Son, thy sins be forgiven thee", and only afterwards he healed him of paralysis. At the pool of Bethesda, Jesus asked an invalid "Do you want to get well?" (Jn. 5:6 - NIV). Now that seems like a silly question! Of course he does, so why does Jesus ask these things? Not for his information, but to let them see into their own hearts. Jesus said to the band of priests who came to take him in Gethsemane, "Who is it you want?" (Jn. 18:4,7 - NIV), knowing it was for himself that they came. But, each time they said his name he answered "I am" (the Name of God) (Jn. 18:5,8). When we come to Jesus, we must know who he is, and what we are asking for, and ask for it with confidence, and specifically. God knows what we need before we even ask (Mt. 6:32) and will give us "immeasurably more than all we ask or imagine" (Eph. 3:20 - NIV), but still requires that we ask. Sometimes, we may ask for "whatever we shall desire" and the question "What do you want?" makes us see that we don't really know what we are asking for. My dying friend Ric Carlson said it well:

"Ask intelligently"

294

MY WORDS WILL NEVER PASS AWAY

(13:31)   Heaven and earth shall pass away: but my words shall not pass away.

Isaiah (40:8) says, "The grass withereth, the flower fadeth: but the word of our God shall stand for ever". Only God can make such a true statement about his words, so this becomes another proof text that Jesus is God. Although the heavens and the earth seem so eternal to us, "what is seen is temporary, but what is unseen is eternal" (2 Cor. 4:18 - NIV). The words of Jesus have eternal importance, and will certainly come to pass when they involve prophecy. Faith in Jesus' words will also have the eternal consequence of life in heaven, just as rejecting his words will result in eternal banishment from heaven (Mt. 5:17-20). Jesus' words are in harmony with all the law and prophets, and he himself came to fulfill the whole law for us, as well as to fulfill many prophecies. But Jesus did more than speak eternal words – he is "the Word...made flesh" (Jn. 1:14), so that he is himself eternal, as God. John "...saw a new heaven and a new earth: for the first heaven and the first earth were passed away..." (Rev. 21:1). Still Jesus was there, to talk to him, and we will be judged by Jesus' words, whether we have rejected, or believed and lived by them. Jesus' words are the expression of himself, just as he, the word of God, is the exact expression of God, the invisible Father in heaven. Jesus spoke only what he heard from the Father, so his words have the power and eternity of God in them. We must choose to believe and obey his words, if we are to enjoy eternal life with him.

The word of our God shall stand for ever. (Isa. 40:8)

COME DOWN FROM THE CROSS

(15:30)   Save thyself, and come down from the cross.

Among all his other sufferings, Jesus had to endure this mocking, which was spoken in front of his friends who stood and watched. He had already answered this one with a question in the garden of Gethsemane, saying "Do you think I cannot call on my Father, and he will at once put at my disposal more than twelve legions of angels?" (Mt. 26:53 - NIV). But, it was with purpose that he set out to go to the cross, and predicted it many times. It was the love of God for worthless, helpless sinners that held him there, and would give worth to sinful men. Muslims say he <u>did</u> save himself from the cross, or that "God snatched him away" just before the cross. If that happened, nobody would ever be saved as it is only the blood of this perfect, sinless sacrifice that can save us from our sins. Jesus told his disciples, "if any man will come after me, let him deny himself, and take up his cross daily, and follow me" (Lk. 9:23). Our cross will not be a wooden one but something that will be a constant embarrassment to us (in the world's eyes), like doing God's will and suffering for it, when we could easily give up and get out of the suffering. People will call us "stupid" for what we're doing, and so add further pain to our cross. They might say "save yourself (embarrassment) and come down from the cross". The shape and nature of the cross doesn't matter, but it will kill your selfishness and crucify your sin, and will allow Jesus to shine through your life to others. Don't come down from your cross; let it kill your pride. The worst part will be the insinuation that it is worthless, but God knows the truth.

**...Be faithful, even to the point of
death...** (Rev. 2:10 – NIV)

BLESSED VIRGIN MARY

(1:42)   Blessed art thou among women…

Who was this young woman, really? The Catholic Church has exalted her nearly to the point of idolatry, and the Protestants have, in reaction, lowered her to something less than she was, as just another woman. She lived with the stigma of "bearing a child before she was married", as though she had sinned, though she was spotless from any such sin. She had quite a cross to bear with her 'blessing'. True, she was honored to be the one to bear God's Son into the world, but to her "…a sword shall pierce through thy own soul also" (2:35) at his crucifixion. As a mother, she loved Jesus as her son, yet was constantly in turmoil in her heart, not understanding his mission (2:50, Mt. 12:46, Jn. 2:3). Still, she humbly accepted all of this, not knowing what it would be when she told Gabriel, "I am the Lord's servant. May it be to me as you have said" (1:38 - NIV). "Blessed art thou among women, and blessed is the fruit of thy womb" (1:42) was a joyous thing to hear from her cousin, but when a woman told Jesus, "Blessed is the womb that bare thee", he answered, "…rather, blessed are they that hear the word of God, and keep it" (11:27-8). Jesus, "the fruit of her womb", was blessed of God as well, but he said later, "Blessed are… the wombs that never bare…" (23:29) when tribulation comes. So, when did the "Blessed Virgin Mary" finally receive her blessing? Mary prayed, "My soul doth magnify the Lord, and my spirit hath rejoiced in God <u>my Savior</u>" (1:46-7). On the day of Pentecost, after Jesus' ascension to heaven, she was filled with the Holy Spirit, sent by Jesus, her Savior! The Catholic prayer begins with Gabriel's greeting: "Hail, thou that art highly favored, the Lord is with thee" (Lk. 1:28) …

Hail, [Mary], full of grace, the Lord is with thee.

THE PRINCE AND THE PAUPER

(2:7)   She wrapped him in cloths and placed him in a manger... (NIV)

The King of all kings, when he was born, was laid in a feeding trough for animals. No "silver spoon in his mouth"! By way of contrast, look at how the king of Tyrus was born, "perfect in beauty... every precious stone was thy covering... perfect in thy ways from the day that thou wast created" (Ezek. 28:12-15). But, like Satan, his beauty and gold corrupted him. You can clean up a pig, and put a gold ring in its snout, but he will return to the mire when he sees his chance (Pr. 11:22, 2 Pet. 2:22). And, you can put a real prince in prison and in rags, but he will continue to act like a prince (Gen. 39:20). Jesus in a manger, or in a carpenter shop or on a cross could not lose his glory, and Satan's evil is not hidden by the world's gold. When he tried to tempt Jesus with it (4:5-8), we see the real story of the prince and the pauper. Satan, called the "prince of this world" (Jn. 14:30), had nothing to offer Jesus that could be of any worth to him. Jesus, born in a manger, was still Lord of all the riches in creation, and all the riches of the world can't buy Satan a one-way ticket out of Hades. Where are your treasures laid up? (Mt. 6:19) On earth or in heaven? In heaven, paupers will walk on gold streets, while many princes will curse their earthly riches that could not follow them to where they go. Come with the shepherds to the feeding trough if you want to find real gold. Come with the wise men and lay your worthless gold at the feet of the Son of God, and he will give you true riches. "You say, 'I am rich; I have acquired wealth and do not need a thing.' But you do not realize that you are wretched, pitiful, poor, blind and naked. I counsel you to buy from me gold refined in the fire" (Rev. 3:17-18 - NIV).

All that glitters is not gold.

THE REASON FOR MIRACLES

(5:24)   *...that ye may know that the Son of man*
           hath power upon earth to forgive sins...

Here is Jesus' answer to the question, "Why do you do miracles?" He performed them, not to be a sensation, but as a personal statement to <u>individual</u> people, so that each one would believe and be saved. Often, he said to "Tell no one!" He didn't need advertisement, but came to save individuals, in body, soul and spirit. The Scribes and Pharisees correctly said that <u>if</u> Jesus is not God (5:21), it is blasphemy for him to say that he forgives sins. The only alternative is that he is God. Jesus here wisely comes to the real point: that they may know that he truly does have the power and authority to forgive sins, thereby concluding (if they are logical and honest) that Jesus Christ is God! But, Jesus was not interested in saving masses of people in his lifetime; he only called a few disciples, and showed them how to reach others. When (and if) God gives his servants power to perform miracles and healing, it is so that the few that see them will know that there is also power <u>through the name of Jesus</u> for their sins to be forgiven. "Who is this which speaketh blasphemies? Who can forgive sins, but God alone?" (5:21) Well said, teachers of the law! This is Jesus, who is God. When John the Baptist began to question his faith as he languished in jail before he was beheaded, he asked, "Art thou he that should come? or look we for another?" (7:19). Again, Jesus pointed to his miracles as proof of his identity as the Messiah. John wanted to make sure he wouldn't be deceived by anyone less than the Messiah of God. Miracles are for individuals, to bring them to faith in the living God.

Miracles happen to those who believe

THE GOLDEN RULE

(6:31)   *"Do to others as you would have them do to you." (NIV)*

This is such a well-known saying, people like to make their own funny version of it: "Do to others before they do (bad) to you", or "the Golden Rule is, 'he who has the gold makes the rules'". People are afraid to do good to others, so they water down compliments like this: "You do nice work... just not a whole lot of it!" Our nature goes against doing good to others, because we don't trust people, and that is because we know ourselves to be untrustworthy. But, Jesus' meaning is that we do <u>good</u> to others <u>first</u>, before they do anything (good or bad) to us, and it will make them want to do good to others, too. Hospitality in India makes me ashamed of how inhospitable I am, but it also encourages me to change. Envision a good world in which everyone treats one another well, and begin living as though it were already here. "You are either part of the solution, or part of the problem". In a sense, "he who has the 'gold' (the godly type of character that blesses others) is the one who is able to change the rules of the game". The world runs on cutting down others, cheating, getting ahead and all other sins, but he who has the gold of God's Kingdom is he who dies to his own desires daily on the cross. This is the principle of the cross, and of love, and of God's Kingdom. This alone will establish God's Kingdom "... in earth, as it is in heaven" (Mt. 6:10). Imagine a heaven where selfishness reigns: we cannot – it would be the opposite of heaven. Let us live with the godly attitude of heaven while we are here, and see heaven come.

**Do to others as you would have them
do to you.** (Luke 6:31 - NIV)

FAMILIARITY BREEDS CONTEMPT

(8:35) ...sitting at the feet of Jesus, clothed, and in his right mind...

This is such an extreme story that most of us forget why it was written. The situation may have been different, but for each of us the destination is just the same. I will remember always the night when I first "sat at the feet of Jesus, clothed and in my right mind". Like the "prodigal son" (15:11-32), I wandered far from God, and from my home until suddenly, unexpectedly, one day I was confronted by Jesus concerning my ungodly life. He clothed me with the robes of righteousness and gave me the mind of Christ. But, why do some people suddenly repent, while others are around the truth all the time, and still they never repent? The older brother of the prodigal son had everything at home but, like the Jews, "familiarity breeds contempt". None of the people who saw the man with the legion of demons had ever been "unclothed or out of their right minds", as far as they knew, but neither did they sit at Jesus' feet. In fact, they told him to leave! Maybe it is the suddenness of meeting Jesus that causes repentance. Like the demoniac, if I can't be with Jesus always, at his feet, I should return home to family and friends, to "show how great things God hath done unto [me]". It is acquaintance with Jesus, and not just long-standing familiarity with religion, that will bring repentance. Even Jesus' own mother and brothers, through familiarity, almost missed repentance! (8:19-21).

Sudden acquaintance brings repentance.

LEGAL LOOPHOLE LOOKERS

(10:29)   But he, willing to justify himself, said unto Jesus, And who is my neighbour?

Like this man, we are always ready to justify ourselves by looking for "legal loopholes" in the law. Jesus was even talking to a lawyer here, who was a "legal loophole looker". Lawyers are sought after for this, as they spend their lives seeking new and creative ways to re-interpret laws, instead of telling the law as it truly is. A lawyer may make big money by taking a case that he knows is wrong, and finding a way to get his client "off the hook". Lawyers should be the most upright and honest among men, but even in Jesus' day, many used their clever skills to justify others and themselves. Jesus said that even our most hated enemies are our neighbors, and so that is the end of the argument. America has been ruined by clever lawyers who have re-interpreted the good laws to make them say things they were never meant to say, and so America has undermined itself from within. Peter speaks of Paul's writings, "which ignorant and unstable people distort, as they do the other Scriptures, to their own destruction" (2 Pet. 3:16 - NIV). We must return with true hearts to the law, and to its accurate interpretation, or we will be responsible for society's destruction. Like Cain and Abel, we are our neighbor's keeper, and as such, are responsible before God. When "lawyers" become "liars", where can we go for justice? We, as Christians, are the lawyers the world looks to for the correct meaning of God's laws. Let us be honest, and give the world a standard to live by that shows justice.

Honesty is the best policy.

BARN-Y RUBBLE

(12:18) ...This will I do. I will pull down my barns, and build greater...

The problem, Jesus says, is not in being rich, but in being "not rich toward God" (v. 21). Any wise businessman or farmer is right in trying to make his business grow. After all, didn't Joseph also "pull down [his] barns and build greater" when the grain of Egypt began to increase (Gen. 41:49)? Jesus speaks much in this chapter concerning the need to be prepared. He commends wise and faithful stewards like Joseph who prosper in the business they are in: "He will make him ruler over of all that he hath" (v. 44), as Pharaoh did with Joseph. However, "That servant, which knew his lord's will, and prepared not himself, neither did according to his will" will get the "the worst" that he didn't prepare for. Solomon built some great buildings, and amassed great riches and built greater and greater "barns" to house all of his possessions, but it all turned to be "vanity" when he was not rich toward God. Today, many churches are like that. When a "revival time" comes, we are ready to "pull down the barn (or meeting hall) and build greater". That is fine, so long as the good news is still going out from there to the lost, but a better idea would be to send out a "daughter church", made up of some mature members, who will later also plant another church or more. If your only desire is to have the biggest and richest church around, God calls you a 'fool'! Prepare for the worst, while you continue to hope for the best, or else the worst will certainly take you by surprise.

Hope for the best and prepare for the worst.

LEAVES DON'T COUNT

(13:7)   "Cut it down! Why should it use up the soil?" (NIV)

What good is a fruit tree that doesn't bear fruit? Like so many other parables, this one of the fig tree was directed against God's own people the Jews, or today, to the church. Jesus came as the owner of the vineyard and of the fig tree, and for three years as he preached the Kingdom of God, his ideas were rejected by the Jewish leaders. While they were proudly "tearing down barns to build bigger ones" (12:18 – NIV), to contain all the riches of their crops, God was ready to tear them down. In God's eyes, there was no fruit at all. Jesus cursed the fig tree (Mk. 11:13) which produced lots of leaves but no fruit, and unless you are putting tobacco into your barn, leaves don't count. Being God's people has always meant listening to God's voice and obeying him. If the Jews had not closed their ears to hearing from God, they would not have crucified Jesus. But, his words brought fear to those who wanted God to fit into their religious program. Why would a fig tree ever stop bearing fruit? It would stop if there were no life-giving nutrients coming into it, as was the case for the Jews who chose to reject Jesus' ideas. I once heard a story that Mordecai Ham, the preacher responsible for Billy Graham's conversion, asked a hateful and belligerent man to consider Jesus. The man said he would never in a hundred years turn to Christ, after cursing him. Mordecai finally told him that if he really meant that, there was no point to living any longer. The man fell dead, and no longer wasted his space on the earth. Be careful that what you take pride in doesn't blind you to your purpose of giving God his due.

Fear of ideas makes us impotent and ineffective.

INCREASE OUR FAITH

(17:5)   And the apostles said unto the Lord, Increase our faith.

People quote this verse for getting answers to prayer, but Jesus was speaking here about forgiveness. The first ten verses of this chapter are one thought, and Jesus' response to their request for increased faith. Jesus demonstrated that to forgive constantly and consistently every time anyone sins against us is nothing more than our duty. We don't need to increase our faith in order to forgive another person; all we need is to do our duty. Like the servant coming back from the field, we deserve no special treatment for doing our duty (to forgive others), and should say simply, 'We are unprofitable servants: we have done that which was our duty to do' (v. 10). As this parable shows, we cannot even eat in God's presence until we have done our duty to forgive others (Mt. 5:23-4, 1 Cor. 11:28), and God won't thank or reward us if we do. It is simply our duty: we must forgive. We should think, as Jesus says, that telling a tree or mountain to be thrown into the sea requires little faith. If we are faithful in our duties, God can do anything through us. But for us, forgiveness requires the greatest of faith – Why? Because it seems so hard to forgive when we've been wronged. It seems impossible! But, in God's perspective, it is simply our duty: say it (speak it) and it is done (v. 6). Again, in the next chapter, it is our duty to give up riches if they hinder our faith in God (18:18-27), and again, "The things which are impossible with men are possible with God" (Lk. 18:27). Don't say "Lord, increase our faith", but joyfully "I will do my duty". It is the mark of a Christian to forgive others.

Forgiveness is our duty.

SMALL CHANGE

(19:3) ...because he was little of stature.

Why did this item of information about Zacchaeus make its way into Scripture? We are told he was also chief among the tax collectors, and rich. The first, most obvious lesson is that "it is not how long and tall we are, but how well-to-do that matters". But, far beyond such mundane thoughts as that, the Bible preserved a man like Zacchaeus for us to consider in another way. Jesus said, "Which of you by taking thought can add one cubit unto his stature?" (Mt. 6:27). But, we are commanded to change some other things which are equally impossible. "Can the Ethiopian change his skin, or the leopard his spots? Then may ye also do good, that are accustomed to do evil" (Jer. 13:23). Although Zacchaeus could not "add one cubit unto his stature", something in his nature had begun to change by meeting Jesus. He was resourceful enough to climb a tree to add to his stature, and apparently the acceptance of Jesus had shown to him something more important than riches, which prompted him to make things right where he knew he had wronged others. None of us can add one day to our lives either, but if you knew you had only two more months to live, would you try to "live it up" and "enjoy the pleasures of sin for a season" (Heb. 11:25), or would you cry out to God for mercy, and try to right some of the wrongs you previously have done? Only the grace of God will make us react like Zacchaeus, who no longer tried to make up for his stature by his "financial stature", but was converted in his heart. With God, all is possible!

It's not how long, but how well, we live.

By What Authority?

(20:2) Tell us, by what authority doest thou these things?

Which things? This question, in each gospel where it is recorded, closely follows the cleansing of the temple, and Jesus poses another question in response, "The baptism of John, was it from heaven, or of men?" (v. 4) What was he getting at? By the Jews' failure to reply, we see the true nature of their hearts. They had no fear of God, nor any interest in spiritual things. They believed neither John nor Jesus, as they both spoke the truth about God, and spoiled their system of control over the people. They were afraid of the power of the people if they were to speak against them, and so Jesus showed them their hypocrisy. The same question of authority was posed to Peter and John (Acts 4:7), possibly by the same group of scribes and elders, Pharisees and Sadducees. All authority in heaven and on earth comes from God, and was given to Jesus, who sends us out to preach the gospel in his authority. When those who seem to be in authority can't even answer about the authority of John's baptism, they don't deserve an answer to their question, as they are out of submission to God. Peter and John gave a similar answer, to show their own submission, and the Jews' rebellion against God. Jesus cleansed the temple of the moneychangers, without permission of the Pharisees or temple priests, and John baptized without their permission, because his authority came straight from God, like the Old Testament prophets. But, the Jews wouldn't even pray and ask God from their hearts, or search the Scriptures to see if John and Jesus were from God. Therefore, their own authority was out of order. Jesus pointed them back to God alone.

**If you wish to know what a man
is, place him in authority.**

SNOOZE YA LOSE

(22:57)   And he denied him, saying, Woman, I know him not.

Here is an ironic situation. Peter, fearing that he would also be taken and crucified, thought to save his life by denying that he knew Jesus. It was a momentary lapse of reason, due to fear. He had heard Jesus' words, "But whosoever shall deny me before men, him will I also deny before my Father which is in heaven", and "He that findeth his life shall lose it, and he that loseth his life for my sake shall find it" (Mt. 10:33, 39). Fortunately, the rooster crowed and, like an alarm clock, woke Peter to reality, and he wept. The lie had to die for Peter to live. Eventually, he did die in exactly the same way, anyway, but having denied the lie instead of denying Jesus, he will live now forever. Many of us have lied at different times to save our skin, but God has given us a conscience that screams at us like a rooster, and will not shut up. If we don't kill the lie, the lie will kill us. Some try to kill the rooster to have peace again. 'Meditation' is an attempt to 'transcend' above the voice of a guilty conscience, but neither that, nor drugs or alcohol, can free us from the consequences. A lie is never 'the perfect crime' because God knows the truth. If you are caught up in a lie, confess it and tell the truth, and have peace again in your heart. If you are living a lie, you are dead even as you live. You may fool others for a long time, but you can't fool your own conscience. When the rooster crows, don't hit the 'snooze' button, but wake up and live for Christ.

A lie never lives to be old.

BOAST BUSTERS

(24:19) ...Concerning Jesus of Nazareth, which
was a prophet mighty in deed and word ...

Cleopas spoke this to Jesus in the past tense, because Jesus was still dead, in his mind. While he was on the cross, at least three times he heard words like, "If thou be the king of the Jews, save thyself" (23:35, 37, 39). People want to see action, not just words. Jesus never boasted anything he could not perform, and refused to boast about even the things he could perform. The devil had tempted him also with the words, "If thou be the Son of God..." (Lk. 4:3), and followed them with three challenges to show off what he could do. Anybody can claim to be the Christ, the Son of God, or the King of the Jews, but the boast should be followed by proof, if the skeptics are to be convinced. It was one of the thieves next to Jesus on the cross that said "If thou be Christ, save thyself and us" (23:39) which is just the thing he was about to do. Coming down from the cross was not the problem, but death and resurrection was the real test, and by doing so Jesus "saved himself and us". Had he just died, he would still have been "a prophet, powerful in word and deed" as Cleopas had said, but Jesus was something far greater. He is the Lord over life and death, and proved it by raising himself from death. Many prophets are mighty in word, without a fraction of action. Proud boasters can shout at a man nailed to a cross or tempt a man who is hungry with fasting, but which of them could do what they asked of Jesus, or would lift a hand to help him? Jesus did more by staying on the cross than by getting himself down. He made good on his "boast", and rose to save us.

Actions are mightier than boastings.

OMNISCIENCE

(2:24-5)   But Jesus did not commit himself unto
them...for he knew what was in man.

It is God alone who "searches every heart and understands every motive behind the thoughts" (1 Chr. 28:9 - NIV). Jesus, as God, saw through the shallowness of man, who would make him a king only because of his miracles. Many times it is stated that Jesus "knew their thoughts" (Mt. 9:4, 12:25, Jn. 6:64, 16:30), which only God can do (Rev. 2:23). Jesus had many opportunities to be made king through popular opinion, but he had a mission to accomplish because he "knew what was in man" which is <u>sin</u>. No matter how good man appears by his good works, he is a sinner before God, needing a Savior to free him from his sin. As with Paul, who one minute was nearly worshipped as a 'god', and soon after stoned and left for dead (Acts 14:11-20, 28:4-6), Jesus knew the fickleness of men's evil hearts, who would call out to him "Hosanna" and "Crucify him!" both in the same week! Our desperately wicked hearts (Jer. 17:9) don't even know that we are dead in sin. But God does, and so he did something about it, sending Jesus to die for all of man's sins. Jesus committed himself only to the Father, not to man, but commands all men to commit themselves to him, because the Father "hath committed all judgment unto the Son" (Jn. 5:22). Jesus did not know from experience the sin that was in men's hearts, as we do in our consciences, but as God, he was aware at all times of not only the general fact of man's sin, but even the specific thoughts in the minds and hearts of men. Knowing the plot in Judas' heart to betray him, he did not retaliate, but committed himself to the crucifixion done by man; but, in reality, he was committing himself to the Father.

I the Lord search the heart and examine
the mind... (Jer. 17:10 – NIV)

CONTEND FOR CONTENTMENT

(3:29) ...That joy is mine, and it is now complete. (NIV)

To what joy was John referring here? His own disciples expected him to be sad and disappointed that so many were leaving him to follow Jesus. For most of our leaders today, this would be a devastating defeat, to see their own congregation leaving to join another. John said, instead, that this was the very thing that brought joy to him. Real happiness cannot come to those who are given to feelings of jealousy, envy or covetousness. Paul wrote to the Philippians, "I have learned to be content whatever the circumstances" and also, "whatever was to my profit I now consider loss for the sake of Christ" (Php. 4:11, 3:7 - NIV). Had John's own happiness been only wrapped up in his ministry growing, he could not have responded as he did, but his joy and expectation was to see Jesus' ministry succeed. Those who are not content become contentious. Do you find yourself becoming angry or contentious when a friend succeeds and you don't? For John, "gain for me" (keeping all his disciples) would be "loss for Christ". He knew his disciple had to go on with Christ, so he never became contentious about it. When Paul stood in chains before King Agrippa he began to speak, saying "I think myself happy" (Acts 26:2), because he was in God's will and knew it. If you also "think yourself happy", you will be, if you know you are walking in God's light. John knew he would not be judged by how many disciples he was able to keep, but by his faithfulness to God, which fulfilled him, too.

He is happy who thinks he is.

CLOSE, BUT NO CIGAR

(6:54)   Whoever eats my flesh and drinks my blood has eternal life... (NIV)

When Jesus gave this most important truth to his disciples and followers, they responded by saying "This is an hard saying; who can hear it?" (6:60 – NIV) Jesus was explaining the most profound truth concerning his sacrificial death for sin, that it is a covenant of blood, the most sacred and binding of all agreements known to man. But, men heard it and rejected it, and "many of his disciples went back, and walked no more with him" (6:66 – a familiar number). Ultimate truth is dangerous ground to tread upon, and only the pure in heart can receive it. All the world appears to be looking for the ultimate truth, but why then don't they find it, and what are they finding instead? In man's rebellion against God, he will refuse to admit his sin and need of a Savior, so when "ultimate truth" is offered without the cross, men flock to it, no matter how hard or ridiculous it may sound. A guru may call himself a "savior" when he himself is a slave to his own lust for money, power or sex. The Buddhist says "all is nothing", which is his ultimate truth. But these are not the worst deceptions. That worst category is reserved for those who know the truth, but mix a little error with it. To hear the teaching and see the lifestyle of Jesus, and to hear him offer eternal life in his flesh and blood, and then to say he didn't really die, or to try to add some of our own works to improve upon his sacrifice, that is the ultimate error, so near, and yet so far.

The ultimate truth is penultimate to a falsehood.

A NEW HERITAGE

(8:44)　Ye are of your father the devil..."

Jesus also said of himself, "If ye had known me, ye should have known my Father also" (v. 19). We can tell a lot about someone by observing his children. In the Law it was written, "I the Lord thy God am a jealous God, visiting the iniquity of the fathers upon the children unto the third and fourth generation of them that hate me" (Ex. 20:5). It is not that God punishes children for their fathers' sins, but that children continue to practice the same sins their fathers did. It is a chilling and sobering reality that we should learn early in life. When we become born again into God's family, we have a new heritage, and no longer need to continue in our fathers' and grandfathers' sins. God is the true Father of us all, as he created us, but because of sin we are born into this world as children of Adam, and we naturally do the sins of our forefathers. Until we are born again, we are "of our father, the devil", who rules this world, but when the Spirit of God begins to change us from the inside, we suddenly have a new heritage. We are "predestined to be conformed to the likeness of his Son" (Rom. 8:29 - NIV). Now, instead of doing the lusts of our father the devil, we begin to "offer the parts of [our] body to [God] as instruments of righteousness" (Rom. 6:13 - NIV). Others can tell whose children we are because our father's image lies within us, whether it be that of God, or of the devil. Jesus came as the Son of God, to reveal the image of the Father to us in a human body, and to recreate that same image in us who receive his Spirit. If you continue to sin, making excuses for it and not fearing consequences, "ye are of your father the devil". Take heed and repent!

In the child the father's image lies.

JESUS IS GOD

(10:24)   *If thou be the Christ, tell us plainly*

People say, "If Jesus is God, why wouldn't he ever say so?" Here is a good example why. Whenever he even implied that he is God, they tried to kill him. He said, "I and my Father are one". Then the Jews took up stones again to stone him (v. 30-31). He offers a good explanation later, when given the same ultimatum at his trial (Lk. 22: 67): "If I tell you, ye will not believe: and if I also ask you, ye will not answer me, nor let me go". It was self-evident, but if spoken, it would lead to his death, because of their assumption that man cannot be God (Jn. 10:33). Although it is true that man cannot become God, God can certainly become man, as he can do all things. Jesus had nothing to gain by saying plainly "I am God". His sheep would know it anyway, by revelation of God, as Peter did when he confessed "Thou art the Christ, the Son of the living God" (Mt. 16:16). Even then, Jesus told him, whatever you do, don't tell anybody! Jesus telling us he is God would be like the Queen of England or the President trying to convince me who they are; if I don't know, then their telling me won't convince me either. Jesus couldn't say plainly who he was until his "hour had come", or it would have hastened his death. When the proper time came, there was still no point in saying it, as people still wouldn't believe or let him go. When people said "tell us plainly", they really did not want to know the truth, but had decided already that Jesus could not be God. So, it doesn't matter still today that Jesus didn't say exactly "I am God". If we have already made up our minds, we will never be convinced.

"Before Abraham was, I am!" (Jn. 8:58)

HANDS ON EXPERIENCE

(13:15)   For I have given you an example, that ye should do as I have done to you"

During prayer this morning, I got a picture of my father training me years ago in carpentry work. He used to put his arms around me and his hands on mine as I held a jack plane. All the power was supplied by him, but I felt the wood being planed as curls of wood shavings fell to the floor. He did the whole job as he showed me, and made sure much later that I did it just right, when I finally got to do it myself. He still is my teacher in all this – he's the master, I'm the student. This is how Jesus taught the disciples, by "hands on" example. I used to wonder each time, "when will he let me do it alone?" as he showed me the right way, start to finish. Whether washing feet or building cabinets, we all learn by example and later teach by example. But, washing feet is more humbling for us, just as it is for the master. God, in Christ, humbled himself just by coming to earth, so foot washing was only another step. If it is humbling and hard for me, God has his arms around me, and supplies the power, so I have only to obey and learn. Yesterday, we saw "be my witness" as simply watching what God is doing and joining him in it; again, learning by example. We feel the power of God as we witness what he does, using us as his instruments. But, we never do progress to "doing it on our own". God will never leave or forsake us, but will guide us in "hands on" experience to perform his pleasure. . "And the things that thou hast heard of me among many witnesses, the same commit thou to faithful men, who will also be qualified to teach others" (2Tim. 2:2). Be a hands-on learner and teacher.

You are the potter, I am the clay.

CLOAK AND DAGGER

(15:22)   *"Now they have no cloak for their sin"*

Ever since Adam and Eve's sin, man has tried to cover his sin, to hide his guilt from God. They sewed together fig leaves but God wasn't fooled. God provided another cloak of animal skins, after what must have been the first blood sacrifice, done by God himself. Man was naked and unashamed before he was a sinner, and man today feels unashamed by his sin until he becomes convicted by the perfect Law of God. Jesus begins here by saying, "If I had not come and spoken to them, they would not be guilty of sin" (NIV). This doesn't mean any man was ever without sin, only that "before the law was given, sin was in the world. But sin is not taken into account when there is no law" (Rom. 5:13 - NIV). So, the law brings the knowledge of sin, and the conscience shows our guilt. Jesus is our sacrifice for sin, and we are covered by his blood as a cloak for our sin. Jesus did not come into the world to condemn, but to save man, but now man continues in his sin as he rejects God's offer of forgiveness; this is the crowning sin of all sins. Men who do bad deeds usually wait for the "cloak of darkness", and a "cloak and dagger" operation means hiding their sinful intention in a cloak. The Jews were not guilty in the eyes of the people, but now these Pharisees were exposed as the light of truth shone upon their wicked hearts. Their self-righteousness was only fig leaves sewn together, and God wasn't fooled. Judas "…went immediately out: and it was night" (13:30): his betrayal could not be done without a cloak, so God provided darkness, though the evil couldn't be hidden from his knowledge. God is too holy to behold evil. In the end outer darkness will cloak sin, if not Christ's blood.

Everyone who does evil hates the light… (John 3:20)

WHAT IS TRUTH?

(18:38)   Pilate saith unto him, What is truth?

Coming from Pontius Pilate, a Roman governor, what did this question mean? If it was out of <u>plain ignorance</u>, then how did he get to be governor? If a question of <u>philosophy</u>, then what was the basis for Roman government? Was it spoken out of <u>disdain</u>? Then what is worth living for if not for truth? Was it possibly <u>disillusionment</u>? No doubt! The Romans probably had no time for "truth" when power was everything. Maybe <u>unbelief</u>? Yes. He couldn't believe anyone could still have such an archaic belief as in truth. "Is this guy from this planet?" Actually, Jesus said, "My kingdom is not of this world" (v. 36 – NIV), so it would be a good question. Still, to his credit, he knew there was no fault in this man, and said so three times (18:38, 19:4,6). Before Pilate's "What is truth?" Jesus had just said, "Every one that is of the truth heareth my voice", so the question puts him outside that category. How about us? Are we on the side of truth? When we are confronted by someone who shows up our sin, do we pass it off with "What is truth"? That may be excusable for a Roman "heathen", but not for one who professes faith in God. Truth is a person, not a philosophy. Only truth could endure suffering and death at sinners' hands and forgive them and then rise up again from death. Truth was staring Pilate in the face, and he was blind to it. Jesus said, "<u>I am</u> the way, <u>the truth,</u> and the life" (14:6). That is Jesus the Son of God, who was crucified for our sins. Believe the truth and live, or reject him and perish. The truth doesn't change, so we must change and agree with the truth, or join the perishing.

**In a time of deceit, telling the truth
is a revolutionary act.**

THIRD TIME'S THE CHARM

(21:17)   *The third time he said to him, "Simon, son of John, do you love me?" (NIV)*

"Three times" seems to be a kind of trademark or "in-joke" between Jesus and Peter. There may have been a hint of it when Peter asked on the Mount of Transfiguration if he should put up <u>three</u> shelters for Jesus, Moses and Elijah. God spoke and told him to listen only to Jesus (Mt. 17:4-5). The first "three times" was when Jesus foretold that Peter would deny him three times before the rooster crowed. Before Peter fulfilled this, he joined James and John in falling asleep three times in the Garden of Gethsemane, failing Jesus in his hour of need. Then, he denied him three times, as predicted. After the resurrection, Jesus asked Peter three times if he really loved him, until it grieved Peter. Was this Jesus' way of reminding Peter of his denials, or maybe rather, establishing a pattern for Peter? If so, then imagine the reaction of Peter when he saw the vision of unclean animals lowered three times in a sheet coming down from heaven. It would have had, for him, the stamp of Jesus upon it, as well as a reminder not to "blow it" again but to listen to what God was telling him, and not repeat his old pattern of failures. God's way is not to condemn us, but to teach us the right way and encourage us to walk in it. God reveals himself in the Trinity, and is worshiped with "Holy, holy, holy" by the angels. Peter responded correctly to the three-times-repeated vision, and understood that salvation had come to the Gentiles as well as the Jews. We are all "hard of hearing" like Peter, and need multiple reminders before we respond, but God uses the weakness of man to glorify his grace and to convert sinners.

If at first you don't succeed, try and try again.

GAZING INTO HEAVEN

(1:11) Why stand ye gazing up into heaven?

Like the people saying "Who was that masked man?" as the Lone Ranger rode into the sunset, or like those staying to watch the last credits on the screen after an incredible movie, the disciples stood, hoping to get one last glimpse of the end of the story. But, the angels were there to say, "Get on with it! This is just one chapter ending to start a new one." The book of Acts begins and ends like that – it is one "chapter" in the continuing story of God's acts among men, and it is left open so we will enter into it, like the "Never Ending Story" movie. Today was one of those days in Srinagar, Kashmir, India, watching the acts of the Holy Spirit. We met Sister Basil, a Catholic nun who prays eight hours a day for peace in Kashmir. Then we went to repair the cross on top of the abandoned St. Luke's church steeple, but we had only a 14-foot ladder and a barefoot carpenter to get to the top of a 40 or 50 foot steeple! Somebody came by and saw our Mickey Mouse operation and said, "Why don't you get the Fire Department to bring a truck with a big ladder?" Amazingly, that's exactly what happened in less than two hours, and in front of an all Muslim crowd of cheering onlookers! We were again "gazing up into the sky" at what God had done. Faith is dynamic and one thing simply follows after another as we stand in awe of what God can do. God spoke to Moses at the Red Sea: "Tell the Israelites to move on (Ex. 14:15) [read the Living Bible for a good laugh!]. Again, as the angels in Acts said, God is just moving on, so stop scratching your heads and get with the program!

Get right or get left!

HOW DO THE WELL FARE?

(4:35)   *...and distribution was made unto every man according as he had need.*

"The love of money is a root of all kinds of evil" (1 Tim. 6:10 - NIV), so that man is always in danger of being ensnared by it. Jesus said "You cannot serve both God and Money" (Mt. 6:24 - NIV). This "welfare system", devised by the apostles and other disciples for the good of the newly-forming Christian community, was the spontaneous result of people being led by the Holy Spirit, giving to the needs of others. Any good system can be corrupted, though, and Ananias and Sapphira (5:1-11) became the first to yield to this temptation. Interestingly, they were not tempted with anyone else's money, but by their own! When Achan was tempted by silver and gold (Jos. 7:21), he then took it and hid it, and it affected the welfare of the whole of Israel, causing men to die. Money itself is not the root of all evil, but the lust for it in men's hearts, and those who have money are just as susceptible to greed as those without it. Just as surely as a "wet paint" sign will tempt somebody to touch it, so an open door tempts a robber. Welfare in California has become a corrupt system, and many are "living off the fat of the land", who are able to work, but clever enough to beat the system, and so they take money they don't need and corrupt the welfare system. A typical Ananias and Sapphira today will give money to the poor to look good to others, but will do it for selfish motives like "tax breaks". Welfare makes a political party look good to the poor, but corruption within the system will kill the good that is done. Welfare often leads those who fare well to say "Farewell" to their consciences.

An open purse tempts a saint.

SANITATION ENGINEERS

(6:2)   It is not reason that we should leave the word of God, and serve tables.

Reason tell us a lot of things, like priorities. This passage doesn't belittle "serving tables", nor does it say the study of God's Word is the most important of all things, for everybody, and at all times; but sometimes, even a menial task like serving tables can become a platform for a great ministry like Stephen's. Brother Lawrence, who wrote <u>The Practice of the Presence of God</u>, was a 17th century Carmelite monk who served as a dishwasher, but his insights to Christians have spanned the centuries. The point here is simply that we should do what is most necessary with our talents at all times, for the good of the Body of Christ. 'We' was the apostles speaking, and it was necessary to continue with table serving, but it wasn't necessary that <u>they</u> do it, as the Word of God for new believers was a more needed job for them. Others were prepared by God and filled with his Spirit for the ministry of waiting on tables, and they turned the tables on these apostles, making the job into a godly ministry. Cleaning toilets or attending to dying men in India may seem unimportant, but people like Mother Teresa have elevated these simple tasks to greatness in the world's eyes. Jesus made fishers into "fishers of men" (Mt. 4:19), and he can transform my mundane job into an enviable one when I am submitted to him, full of faith and of his Holy Spirit. Serving is always the way to greatness in God's Kingdom. The best thing is not to "leave the word of God", but to bring it into our mundane daily jobs, and to let God provide an avenue of ministry for us in these jobs.

Treat menial tasks as meaningful tasks.

SON OF GOD

(9:20)   ...he began to preach in the synagogues that Jesus is the Son of God. (NIV)

Ananias laid hands upon Saul, and "scales" were removed from his eyes, he was filled with the Holy Ghost, and immediately he preached "that Jesus is the Son of God" (NIV). This is the result of the Holy Spirit coming upon us: that a revelation of who Christ is fills our hearts. It can only come by revelation of God, as it did to Peter when he said "Thou art the Christ, the Son of the living God" (Mt. 16:16). Nobody would argue that Christ was a good man or a prophet, but only the Holy Spirit can reveal Christ to us in all of his glory. He is God himself, "And declared to be the Son of God with power, according to the spirit of holiness, by the resurrection from the dead" (Rom. 1:4). Some stumble at his being God, others with the title "Son of God", and many say "How can he be both?" Philip preached to the Ethiopian eunuch, and when he was asked for a statement of his newfound faith the eunuch said, "I believe that Jesus Christ is the Son of God" (8:37). Even the devils confess him as "Jesus, thou Son of the most high God" (Mk. 5:7), and Jesus was crucified because of this confession, which he did not deny in order to save his life. This confession, and the changed life that results from it, is the only way a man can be saved from sin, death and destruction: "But these are written, that ye might believe that Jesus is the Christ, the Son of God; and that believing ye might have life through his name" (Jn. 20:31). "Who is he that overcometh the world, but he that believeth that Jesus is the Son of God?" (1 Jn. 5:5). No one can make this confession unless the Spirit takes the scales from his eyes.

**You are my Son; today I have become
your Father.** (Heb. 5:5 – NIV)

PAIN RELIEVERS

(11:19)   Now they which were scattered abroad upon the persecution...travelled...

This is a further move after Stephen was stoned to death, when people "went every where preaching the word" (8:1-4). The principle of death bringing life is apparent in all of life, and especially in the Christian life. When Paul says, "And we know that all things work together for good to them that love God, to them who are the called according to his purpose" (Rom. 8:28), he is certainly <u>not</u> saying that all things will go well for the Christian. Persecution will come, as well as the normal trials that everyone has to endure, but God uses <u>all</u> things, good and bad, to bring about his purposes. Being "scattered" and having to set up a new household and make new friends is one way that God makes us into witnesses of the gospel, to people we would otherwise never meet. "No pain, no gain" is a favorite expression of body builders, whose bodies hurt from exercise, but who gain size in the process. The pain of persecution also builds strong character in individuals, and strong, growing churches. We don't need any church growth programs when we are facing daily persecution for our faith. Churches like Laodicea (Rev. 3:14) may pride themselves with being rich and needing nothing, but their growth will be in superficial people who will fall away as soon as persecution comes. Neither do we need to be poor to see real gains in churches, but if we are filled with God's Holy Spirit and ready to preach anywhere, pains and gains are sure to come.

No pain, no gain.

CLEARLY STATED

(13:39) *"And by him all that believe are justified...*

...from all things, from which ye could not be justified by the law of Moses." When preaching the gospel, we have a choice of making a clear statement, and thereby provoking a debate, or else saying what people want to hear, and being accepted by all. India has gurus who win converts by doing the latter, and then condemning any who would do the former as being "divisive and unloving". Had Paul stopped with the first statement, "And by him all that believe are justified", the Jews could have felt the Moses, too, offered justification through the works of the law. But, when Paul added, "from all things, from which ye could not be justified by the law of Moses", <u>that</u> was a clear statement, stepping on the toes of the Judaizes. In India, I have seen "I am the way, the truth, and the life" (Jn. 14:6a) written on the walls outside of church buildings, and nobody objects, thinking "yes, and my religion is also another way, truth and life". But, when someone decides to complete Jesus' statement, "no man cometh unto the Father, but by me" (Jn. 14:6b), it would then be a clear statement that would provoke an argument. Jesus said, "I came not to send peace, but a sword" (Mt. 10:34), not to bring harmony to all the religions, but to make a clear statement about man's lost condition and the only possible solution to it. No Jew, Muslim or Hindu likes to hear that his religion doesn't work, and will not bring salvation to a follower, but because that is true, we must make it plain to those who are lost.

Clear statement is argument.

To The Unknown God

(17:23)   Now what you worship as something unknown
I am going to proclaim to you. (NIV)

This is a classic example of an interest door for evangelism. These Athenians were so superstitious that, after worshiping all the possible 'gods' they could think of, they felt "just in case, let's have an altar to the unknown god, to cover all the bases". Paul used their title to open the conversation: God is not unknown but only to those who don't yet know him (he is not "unknowable", or their meaning may have been "were unacquainted", or he is "the invisible god", or simply "whichever god we forgot to worship" – if there were many, let them fight it out, but each 'god' can think we intended him!). India's Hindu gods are much the same: people keep adding to their collection to "try to hit the lucky number". Man in his sin is the same everywhere: as long as God remains a mystery and superstition, man is not responsible to his own conscience because he doesn't really know <u>what</u> God wants. Paul blew away the cloud of ignorance and preached to them the God who has revealed himself in the person of Jesus. God, who is invisible, is by no means unknowable. We are expected "to know God and to make him known" (YWAM motto), as man is responsible to come out of his ignorance, though God once "overlooked" it (v. 30 - NIV). God is not the least bit honored when we keep him as "unknown". Jesus revealed God's character and his hatred toward sin, and love to all who will believe. Man is now counted guilty for his sins and must make a decision that he will receive Christ's forgiveness, or perish forever.

To know God, and to make him known.

But Who Are You?

(19:15)   Jesus I know, and Paul I know, but who are ye?

The evil spirits who spoke knew more about Jesus and Paul than these Jews knew, who so proudly spoke their names. What a dignified exit they made: 'They fled out of that house naked and wounded' (v. 16) after the possessed man called their bluff, but as Paul says in another place, "We, however, will not boast beyond proper limits...by boasting of work done by others" (2 Cor. 10:13,15 - NIV). Boasting is so unbefitting to a man who is not submitted to God. Man was given dignity by God in the beginning, but sin has caused man to seek for that dignity without submitting to God. These words of the evil spirits, "but who are ye?" are like Paul's words, "But who are you, O man, to talk back to God?" (Rom. 9:20 - NIV). Man, who boasts of anything apart from God, is on dangerous ground. Again, a most undignified performance is seen a few verses later when the Ephesians "all shouted in unison for about two hours: "Great is Artemis of the Ephesians!" (v. 34 - NIV). Their boasting was in an idol made by man's hands, which lowers man's dignity to something below even the stone he carved, because now he is bowing down to it. "All who worship images are put to shame, those who boast in idols – worship him, all you gods!" (Ps. 97:7 - NIV). By contrast, when Apollos, who "was a learned man, with a thorough knowledge of the Scriptures" (18:24 – NIV), heard from Priscilla and Aquila, he did not respond with pride and boasting, but learned from them in humility and became an even more powerful preacher. When we are asked by someone, "who are you", we speak too often of our professions, and not of <u>whose</u> we are.

Where boasting ends, there dignity begins.

GOD'S BLOOD

(20:28)   *Be shepherds of the church of God, which*
          he bought with his own blood. – (NIV)

God's blood! Some manuscripts say, "the church of the Lord", which lessens the effect of this verse. Surely it was Christ's blood, but the implication is still that Christ is God. Other similar statements appear in Scripture, such as, "…and the Word was God …and the Word was made flesh, and dwelt among us" (Jn. 1:1,14). Thomas said, "My Lord and my God" to Jesus (Jn. 20:28 – another 20:28). Paul wrote of "Christ, who is God over all, forever praised!" (Rom. 9:5 - NIV), and "the glorious appearing of our great God and Savior, Jesus Christ" (Titus 2:13 - NIV), [and surely the invisible God will not appear – the Father, whom Christ came to reveal!] Peter speaks of "the righteousness of our God and Savior Jesus Christ" (2 Pet. 1:1 - NIV). People argue away these plain declarations of Scripture, but it seems much harder to try to be consistent with Scripture and to believe that Jesus is <u>not</u> God, than to accept these clear statements and to change one's theology, if need be. Still, the Holy Spirit seems to have felt it was more important to mask this truth, and to have men seek after it, than to state it any more directly. History is evident enough to show that believers have always come to this by revelation of God's Spirit when they become truly born again. How we perceive Christ will determine how we respond to the gospel. Only God himself could provide blood of a perfect sacrifice for our sins. Jesus was a perfect man, but he was also God in the flesh, who gave blood, and it is only God's blood that is a perfect solution for sin.

Jesus Christ is God.

UNSEASONABLY HOT

(24:25)   *"When I have a convenient season, I will call for thee"*

With these words, Felix left Paul in prison for more than two years. Although he did call him from time to time, he never again came so close to the gospel changing him. Many, like Felix, "have no time for the gospel right now" because the conviction of sin fills them with the fear of God's wrath. Such people are like disobedient children who are afraid to be truthful with parents or teachers concerning something they have done wrong. Some of us carry a load of guilt for a lifetime over some unconfessed sin, and hope at some "convenient season" to deal with it, but it will never come. It is never too soon to deal with a guilty conscience, but someday it will be too late. Some say "I will make my peace with God on my death bed", so they may continue "to enjoy the pleasures of sin for a season" (Heb. 11:25). Paul may have been inconvenienced by this man's dragging of his feet, and may have been two years late for something God had planned for him to do. But, Paul was not dragging his feet, as Felix was. Someday, Felix would be one minute late, standing before God's judgment seat, and without an excuse for his tardiness in dealing with sin. While we have time, "Let us therefore come boldly unto the throne of grace..." (Heb. 4:16), having dealt with our sin and guilt by the blood of Christ. Those procrastinators who say, "Never put off until tomorrow what you can do the day after" will be surprised by seeing God sooner than they wished. Come sooner and not later to make things right with God. Now is the season.

Better to be three hours soon than one minute late.

A CERTAIN DEAD MAN

(25:19)   ...about a dead man named Jesus who Paul claimed was alive. (NIV)

Our eternal destiny depends upon how we think about "a certain dead man" named Jesus. To the Jews, who killed their own Messiah, that's all he was, but to Paul, who was on trial for this, Jesus was no longer dead and buried, but alive forever more, and Lord of all the earth. To many today, Jesus is just another historic "dead man". All men, even great men and the leaders of religions that dominate the world, will end up as "a certain dead man" when it is all over. As for the Jews, they got rid of him by crucifixion, and all that remained for them was to dispute about certain 'points of dispute' (25:19 – NIV) with Paul. But Jesus is not a dead man – he's alive, with all power to raise us up who believe in him. The world in unbelief sees only a historical figure and a dead man. They are themselves dead in sins, and without hope. Dead religion sees only a dead crucifix, and deifies, at best, that which they are afraid of. Jews killed prophets, and then whitewashed their graves, happy that they couldn't hear their words any longer. But, Jesus will return to judge the living and the dead. To the dead, he is a dead man, but to those who will live, we know he is alive. The world thinks that death is the end, but Jesus changed that when he rose from the dead. Unfortunately, like King Agrippa in the next chapter, nobody will be fully persuaded to believe in the truth, even if a certain dead man were to rise from the dead, as Jesus said after his story of Lazarus and the rich man (see Luke 16:31). Thanks be to God that he takes us dead men and makes us alive in Christ, and that along with him we will never die again.

Follow me; and let the dead bury their dead. (Mt. 8:22)

ALL HOPE GONE

(27:20)   …we finally gave up all hope of being saved. (NIV)

This is the point to which God is constantly trying to bring us, that we may see our true spiritual condition. Compare this with Psalm 107, where four times the people are despairing of life before the Lord saves them. As Peter, walking on water, called out to Jesus, "Lord, save me" (Mt. 14:30) when he began to sink, so we only call out of a sense of desperation to God. At most times we are oblivious to our lost state. While we are in health and prospering, we tend to forget God instead of thanking him, but God knows how to get our attention. Only when all hope is gone do we call out for God's mercy. In the law we see how far we are from God's standard, and it drives us to the cross. "Religious" people, who should be closest to God, are the farthest away. The book of Acts ends with Paul's rebuke to the Jews who reject the gospel, whose hearts are hard and eyes blind to the truth. Maybe from jealousy they will come when they see Gentiles worshiping their God, but presently they don't see their hopeless condition. The Law of God must reveal it to them, and we must use the Law to whittle away all false hopes, that men may cry out to God. Fear of death is a powerful motivation – fear that there is no hope of being saved. Again, consider the plight of Jonah and of the Philippian jailor who were hopeless before crying out for God to save them. Wisdom will show us how to impress upon sinners their hopeless state, and then "the goodness of God leadeth [them] to repentance." (Romans 2:4)

Hope is faith holding out its hand in the dark.

ICHABOD

(1:28)   ...they did not like to retain God in their knowledge...

One of the most chilling thoughts in this chapter is when "God gave them over" (v. 24,26,28). As frightening as the wrath of God may be, God's silence is more so. Those who wish God would stop talking to them may very well get their wish. Since creation, God has spoken to man "at many times and in various ways" (Heb. 1:1 - NIV), and especially to the Jews, his covenant people. Often he spoke loudly and clearly through prophets, acts of nature or even miracles. Finally, he sent Jesus as the clearest and most perfect picture of his will for man, but those who stopped their ears to the truth put him to death on a cross and got the silence that they wanted from God. When man continues in his rebellion and sin against God who calls out to him daily, God says "My Spirit shall not always strive with man..." (Gen. 6:3). When King Saul continued to sin against God in his headstrong way, "He inquired of the Lord, but the Lord did not answer him by dreams or Urim or prophets" (1 Sam. 28:6 - NIV). When God's Spirit departs, it is "Ichabod...the glory is departed from Israel" (1 Sam. 4:21). Psalm 107 is the description of Israel's recurrent history of God withdrawing when they forgot him. The silent treatment works! But, when have we gone too far? God has now been silent for nearly two thousand years to the Jews who rejected their own Messiah. The silence of prophets is deafening and very disquieting, but God knows how to get our attention. When God "gives us over" to our own desires, we should wonder, "have I gone too far?"

**Behold, your house is left unto
you desolate.** (Mt. 23:38)

STAR TREK

(4:18)   Against all hope, Abraham in hope believed… (NIV)

There is an element of courage necessary for those who will walk in faith. Abraham is remembered as the Father of Faith, because he believed God, not only as he waited for the promise of a son, but in two other great tests also. The first was in leaving his country to go to an unknown place (Heb. 11:8-10), "to boldly go where no man had gone before". That was not a physical place, but "a heavenly one" (Heb. 11:16 - NIV), and his journey was in following the God he could not see, while others worshiped idols. After the second test, he still had to brave the third, offering his only son to the God he could not see. Here is the real "star trek" as Abraham trekked with God where no man had gone before, and offered his miracle son so that he could pioneer the way of faith for the multitudes who were to follow, "so many as the stars in the sky" (Heb. 11:12). Those who want to make this star trek, to a place not in this world, but a heavenly place, must follow this example of faith in what they cannot see. Jesus on the cross also pioneered that trek for us, daring to die for the crowd he could not see, "the just for the unjust" (Rom 5:6, 1 Pet. 3:18). We count men and women to be brave who would venture to die to save someone from a fire or from drowning. "But God commendeth his love toward us, in that, while we were yet sinners, Christ died for us" (Rom. 5:8). Now, "he that holdeth the seven stars in his right hand" which are "the angels of the seven churches" (Rev. 2:1, 1:20) has received the fruits of his trek on earth. Wise men once made a trek, following a star and finding Jesus. Now, "those who are wise will shine…like the stars", leading others to Christ (Dan. 12:3 - NIV).

Live long and prosper.

BRAVE HEART

(8:17)   we are...co-heirs with Christ, if indeed we share in his sufferings... (NIV)

Is it suffering that makes us joint-heirs, or is it that being joint-heirs with Christ causes us to suffer with him? Either way, it seems that "the fellowship of sharing in his sufferings, becoming like him in his death" (Php. 3:10 - NIV) is part of being a Christian, and only the brave will come to "know Christ and the power of his resurrection" (8:17 – NIV). Scripture suggests that otherwise timid men and women become brave when the Spirit of God comes upon them. Of course, many who don't even know Christ do brave acts, but there is a quality in those who "suffer with him" that elevates their bravery above that which might be rooted in selfish motives. The word 'suffer' is used often in the King James Version to mean 'to allow' [e.g. Mk. 10:14, 1 Cor. 10:13, Ex. 22:18] which implies that to suffer in other passages may carry with it the possibility of <u>not</u> allowing. Many brave men and women avoid suffering by sheer strength and will power. Some learn martial arts, not because they are brave but because they are afraid of suffering. Christians are those who, knowing they could avoid suffering by renouncing their faith in Christ, "choose" rather to suffer and die than to deny him. [cf. Heb. 11:25] There are many who 'suffer' simply because they don't know how to get out of it, and there is not necessarily any bravery in that. The best of the sufferers are those who "suffer with him", taking up their own cross every day and doing it for the sake of Christ and his Kingdom. Esau may have been much more "brave" than Jacob in his life, but God chose Jacob (Rom 9:13), and made him learn how to suffer. "All that will live godly in Christ Jesus shall suffer persecution" (2 Tim. 3:12).

The best hearts are ever the bravest.

DISCIPLES OF ANTS

(12:16)   Be not wise in your own conceits.

Paul begins this teaching with "Mind not high things, but condescend to men of low estate" (12:16) or "Do not be proud, but be willing to associate with people of low position" (NIV). When we are open to it, we can learn great lessons from the most unlikely places. The Jews should have learned from the children to praise Jesus as the Messiah (Mt. 21:15-16), but they were too proud. Jesus himself had learned obedience, and many things that made up his parables, in the woodshop. The wise man is able to learn from anyone, and by doing so he increases his wisdom. Balaam learned from a donkey, and Jonah from a whale, so we should be able to learn from less humbling means. The writer of the Proverbs said, "Do you see a man wise in his own eyes? There is more hope for a fool than for him" (Pr. 26:12 - NIV). He also said, "Go to the ant, thou sluggard; consider her ways, and be wise" (Pr.6:6). The caste system of India has forced men and women into different levels of elevation and degradation, based originally on skin color, and the revival of Arianism under Hitler took its whole insidious system from that abomination. I learned much more language in India by sitting with the "low caste" children than by sitting in more formal classrooms. God's advice to us comes in humble ways, too, if we are ready to hear it. If we have our own agenda, and choose only "high caste" friends, we may well miss the "still small voice" of God (1 Kings 19:11-12), as we want to hear a much bigger and more powerful voice. The Jews would have received much more than the ability to overcome the Romans, had they received the word of God through a carpenter from Galilee.

To accept good advice is but to increase one's ability.

THREE LITTLE PIGS

(3:12) If any man builds...using gold, silver, costly stones, wood, hay or straw (NIV)

This reminds me always of the children's story about the "Three Little Pigs" who built houses to be safe from the "big bad wolf". One was of straw, one of sticks and one of bricks, and only the brick one could stand up to the wolf as he tried to "huff and puff and blow the house down". Our works that are built on the foundation of Christ will be tried by fire on Judgment Day, not by the big bad wolf, nor by Satan, but by God himself. Fortunately, if we are built on the foundation of Christ, we will be saved, no matter what we build with, but only will be rewarded for the good works of value. Not only our salvation, but our works must be founded on Christ. If the "Three Little Pigs" analogy could be stretched, they were sure to be saved because the reader wants good to prevail over evil. Pigs, being unclean animals, could be the Gentiles who trust in Christ, but whose works are being judged. We must be as Paul, a wise master builder (3:10), who built the congregations on the foundation of Christ. In fact, the building of which Paul is speaking is the Church, the congregation of saints. If it is built upon man's ideas or false doctrines, then the big bad wolf, the devil, will prevail against it. The foundation, which is Christ himself, will remain even after false doctrines cause churches to split. Churches built with gold, silver and precious stones (not buildings, with stained glass and gold and silver, but believers in fellowship, based on the Word of God) will endure trials by fire. We are to build the church to last, and all share the rewards.

**Except the Lord build the house, they
labor in vain that build it.** (Ps. 127:1)

CONSUMED WITH CONSUMPTION

(7:37)   ...having no necessity, but hath power over his own will...

The writer of Ecclesiastes wrote "...God hath made man upright; but they have sought out many inventions" (Ec. 7:29). In both good and bad ways, it is true that "necessity is the mother of invention". God made man with no need of anything and placed him in a perfect garden, and even gave him a wife when he saw that "It is not good for the man to be alone" (Gen. 2:18). Wherever there is a need, God has provided a good answer to it. Why, then, was man tempted into sin? The answer is that Adam and Eve were first convinced that they had a need, which was not true. Man, in subjection to God, has all of his needs met by a loving God who "will meet all your needs according to his glorious riches in Christ Jesus" (Php. 4:19 - NIV). In the West, where clever advertisers have succeeded in convincing us daily that we need their products, we have become "consumed with consumption". That was the serpent's strategy in the garden because "having no necessity, [Adam had] power over his own will". Are you tempted in any area to sin? The battle is always in the mind first, where we must decide firmly that "unless God supplies it, I don't need it!" Buddhists attempt to do away with their desires so that they may be satisfied, having no desire for anything; but that is emptiness. God's way is fullness, with God himself being the fulfillment of all of our desires. Many inventions have come through the diligent work of those who look for easier ways to meet man's needs, but without seeing God as the source, we are consumed only with consuming.

Necessity is the mother of invention.

SHADOW BOXING

(9:26)   I do not fight like a man beating the air. (NIV)

Shadow boxing is alright for a boxer-in-training, who is practicing his jabs, but it is totally out of place for a trained boxer in a real fight. During the "Gulf War" or "Operation Desert Storm" in early 1991, the Iraqi armed forces shot up hundreds, and quite possibly thousands, of expensive missiles and various rounds of ammunition, blindly hoping to hit something. It was a sheer act of desperation, and probably did more damage to themselves than anything. It was obvious in no time at all who had the advantage. Saddam Hussein boasted many proud things, and made some rash judgments which caused many of his own young soldiers to perish unnecessarily, and many others fled and defected. It was General Schwarzkopf who became the hero of the war, and he did so with no rash moves or words; the orderliness of his strategy is a model for the history of wars in the world, and there were nearly no casualties for the troops under his command. Jesus came as Commander-in-Chief of God's forces, and he came with a plan. Those who fight on his side will live forever, even if they might suffer and die terrible deaths on this earth because the strategy of Christ's plan will even conquer death (1 Cor. 15:55)! Satan may call out many rash and proud things, but he is fighting a losing battle, and many of his best soldiers are defecting to Christ's side while there is still time. Satan continues to throw his fiery darts by the thousands, hoping to hit something, but true Christians have the advantage of spiritual armor which can extinguish them all (Eph. 6:16). Don't be like Satan, shadow boxing and beating the air. Know the enemy and join the winning side.

Advantage is a better soldier than rashness.

LOUD AND CLEAR

(14:8)   If the trumpet does not sound a clear call, who will get ready for battle? (NIV)

The trumpet, or 'clarion', is known for its loudness and its clarity. In fact, the word clarion comes from 'clar' meaning clear. Trumpets were used for this reason to summon troops to battle, but what good is a trumpet which is loud but not clear? The Psalmist wrote, "My tongue is the pen of a ready writer" (Ps. 45:1), so when a tongue becomes a pen, a pen becomes a clarion. Those who are speakers often become writers, that their message may be heard, loud and clear, by a greater audience. But, when a message is muffled and unclear, it will be unintelligible, just as a self-centered voice becomes like a "sounding brass", discordant and irritating (13:1). We hear and read things every day which have some bearing on our lives, but we must become discerning as to what is good and helpful, and what is bad. Fortunately, the prophets not only spoke, but they wrote down their prophecies so that we also could benefit from them, and their words were loud and clear to those who had ears to hear. If today's Christian leaders muffle the message, "who will get ready for battle" against sin? The "brass section" sounds loud enough, like the "hypocrites do in the synagogues and in the streets" (Mt. 6:2), sounding their trumpets to advertise their piety before people. The gospel has to again become loud and clear when we speak and write, to turn men from self-righteousness to repentance over their sin. Let us become clear in our understanding of the gospel before we become loud in proclaiming it.

A pen becomes a clarion.

RAISED FROM THE DEAD

(15:12) ...how can some of you say that there is no resurrection of the dead? (NIV)

Personally, I've never had a problem with how God will raise the dead. I figure that if God could make me along with a whole universe out of nothing, raising up my dead body should be a piece of cake. Even Adam was formed as a dead body out of clay, and God simply breathed life into him, so what is the problem to do the same for our dead bodies? But when I first heard about the "rapture" as it is commonly called, I felt that was a worthy problem for God to deal with. Never mind "How are the dead raised up?" (15:35), but how are those who are still alive going to be "raised up" to heaven, with bodies that still function? When this was written, Jesus had already raised several people from death, as did Paul and Peter, and then Jesus was raised bodily to heaven. Of course, his was a "spiritual body" (15:44), and Paul states that even the live bodies in the rapture will be changed to these spiritual bodies, prepared for heaven. So, there is God's answer for how it will be. But Paul's question has more to do with 'why' the dead must be raised. God made us to live forever, but that was lost through sin, and the hope we have is to be raised to new life after this one is over. This life is filled with pain, suffering and all the evils that are the result of sin, and without deliverance from sin, we would only be raised up to an eternal life of more suffering and pain. That is what Hades will be. Christ was raised to be the first of all mankind that will spend eternity in a perfect heaven with our Creator, and our resurrection must follow if we are to be there with him. Faith that does not believe in Christ's resurrection leaves us lost in sin.

**If Christ has not been raised, your
faith is futile.** (15:17 – NIV)

FOUND NAKED

(5:2)   Meanwhile we groan, longing to be clothed with our heavenly dwelling (NIV)

…because when we are clothed, we will not be found naked (v. 3). A nightmare I've had several times in my life is that I'm walking somewhere and suddenly I notice that I've forgotten to put clothes on! Like Adam and Eve after they sinned, we feel ashamed to be found naked, yet we are born naked and without shame. Even our bodies are clothes for our spirits, and though we grow old and lose our hair, teeth, sight, strength and beauty, we are awaiting our new and incorruptible bodies, to clothe our naked spirits when we die. If we go to heaven, we will be clothed with a "robe of righteousness" (Isa. 61:10) that will clothe our nakedness. We will again be as Adam and Eve before sin brought shame: "The man and his wife were both naked, and they felt no shame" (Gen. 2:25 – NIV). To pay for our sins, Christ was stripped of his clothing and was nailed in shame before all to see. He died to take away our shame, and was stripped of his clothing so nothing could hide the shame of sins he bore for us. God turned his face and disowned him, that we should never be abandoned. While carrying the cross, Jesus prophesied of the Day of Judgment when many would stand in the nakedness of their sins, crying for even the mountains to "Fall on us; and…Cover us!" (Lk. 23:30). Anyone who appears before God on that day not having the clothing of Christ's righteousness will have to suffer the greatest shame imaginable as he is thrown into Hades. Seeing that "Everything is uncovered and laid bare before the eyes of him to whom we must give an account" (Heb. 4:13 - NIV), take care "so you can cover your shameful nakedness" (Rev. 3:18 - NIV).

**…longing to be clothed with our
heavenly dwelling.** (5:2 – NIV)

UNWISE COMPARISONS

(10:10)   *...his bodily presence is weak, and his speech contemptible.*

I got both of these assessments two days ago, and it's amazing how a little "negative reinforcement" can affect us! First, a girl said (in Kannada language, as I tried to communicate with her), "You're killing Kannada!" Then, as I drove in a rickshaw with one of my students (as we passed a wall with Sanjay Dutt written on it) he said, "Before Sanjay Dutt took steroids, he looked as bad as you, even worse than you!" The devil couldn't have said either of these any better; my natural reactions would be to give up on languages and on building up my chronically unhealthy little body, as well as to go into a tailspin of depression and rejection. But, in this chapter, Paul shows how he addressed these thoughts, "Casting down imaginations" and "bringing into captivity every thought to the obedience of Christ" (v. 5). Paul knew who he was in Christ, and didn't give in to fighting these fleshly attacks. "They measuring themselves by themselves, and comparing themselves among themselves, are not wise" (v. 12). Two things I'm learning: 1) Watch your tongue – it's easy to mindlessly wound a friend and 2) Even <u>if</u> I do this, others will still say hurtful things, so I'd better know who I am in Christ, and care only for God's assessment of me. I'd like to learn so many languages and to be physically fit, and I try to spend some time daily with these, but priorities make me spend more time in the Bible, praying, witnessing and fasting, so often it's a losing battle. What I <u>won't</u> do is to give in to the world's mold of "greatness" and start on steroids to make me less insecure. Thank God if you look like Sanjay Dutt!

But by the grace of God I am
what I am... (1 Cor. 15:10)

SUBTLE SUGGESTIONS

(11:3) …just as Eve was deceived by the serpent's cunning… (NIV)

We have all wondered at times how the serpent could have succeeded in beguiling Eve. Wasn't the life in Eden, and actually walking with God daily, enough for Adam and Eve? How could Eve be so easily tricked into hearing and obeying the suggestions of the serpent over the word of God? The root of the problem was pride, the same root that had been the downfall of Satan. "If I had been there, I wouldn't have sinned!" Paul says, "If you think you are standing firm, be careful that you don't fall!" (1 Cor. 10:12 - NIV). It is not the external suggestion, but internal pride that is the problem, and it is only the grace of God that will keep us from falling. Suggestion from a serpent worked because Eve didn't compare it with God's original command. In carpentry, we write "pattern" on one piece that is to be reproduced, and check each copy against the original. When the serpent enticed Eve with a good sounding new idea, it went against God's already revealed orders, but very subtly, or she wouldn't have fallen for it. Unfortunately, we still try to blame our sins and faults on suggestions from others, just as Adam and Eve did after their sin. Every false religion, cult and "new revelation" comes in the same way, and those who are corrupted by them make the same mistake. Check it against the original pattern and if it doesn't agree, throw out the new doctrine and not the tried and tested pattern! If you think that Moses' one infraction of striking the rock in anger (Num. 20:10-12), or Adam and Eve's sin of tasting the forbidden fruit, were punished too severely, then maybe you haven't dealt with pride yet. A suggestion is only as powerful as the pride it attempts to seduce.

Pride is at the bottom of all great mistakes.

ANOTHER GOSPEL

(1:8)   *"But though we, or an angel from heaven, preach any other gospel...*

...let him be accursed"! There is only one "gospel" – the good news of God's own answer for our sin, through Jesus Christ's blood on the cross. There is no other good news, as any other "gospel" will only exclude us from Heaven. Any angel who would dare to preach some counterfeit gospel belongs in Hades. John "saw another angel fly in the midst of heaven, having the everlasting gospel to preach unto them that dwell on the earth..." (Rev. 14:6). Everlasting, the gospel does not change, though "another gospel" my come, as preached by "another angel" than this one. If an angel, or apostle or prophet, or anyone else comes to you with "another gospel", do not be afraid to curse him in Jesus' authority. Though the whole world should go after another gospel, don't let it sway you away from the truth. The "Book of Mormon" has the subtitle "Another Testament of Jesus Christ", supposedly brought by another angel named "Moroni", and of course it corrupts the truth of the gospel. Anyone "who does not enter the sheep pen by the gate, but climbs in by some other way, is a thief and a robber" (Jn. 10:1 - NIV). Jesus is the only door to heaven, "through the curtain, that is, his body" (Heb. 10:20 - NIV). Once he has died on the cross to provide salvation, anyone who denies his death or brings "another gospel" is to be accursed! Shall a man who is saved from drowning say to the one who risks his life to save him, "I didn't need your help" or "I saved myself"? How much worse, when Christ has already paid Holy blood for our sins for us to say "Jesus didn't suffer and die", or that there could ever be 'another gospel' to save us?!

**Do not add to his words, or he will rebuke
you and prove you a liar...** (Prov. 30:6 – NIV)

A LITTLE LEAVEN

(5:9) "A little yeast works through the whole batch of dough." (NIV)

"One bad apple spoils the whole bunch". It will spread its rottenness to a whole box of apples if it is not removed, and yeast will cause a whole lump of dough to be "puffed up". That is an apt picture for sin which is used in many parables, because sin puffs us up with pride (see also 1 Cor. 4:6, 5:2, 8:1, 13:4, Col. 2:18). "Let us not become conceited, provoking and envying each other" (v. 26 - NIV). One of our most common sins is this one, and it affects the whole body as we indulge in it. I'm guilty of it all too often. This week, several of our team members (and myself) have felt the sting of jokes, or flippant remarks against us. It hurts, and some of the boys cried over it. One began counting the days until outreach is over. The whole team is affected by the spirit of it, and it is rooted in pride, causing rejection. How much better to speak encouraging words to one another, defeating "vainglory" and "envying" (5:26 - KJV) by esteeming others better than myself. Achan (Josh. 7:21) secretly took silver and gold when God had said to destroy everything, and he hid it in his tent: real "vainglory" – he couldn't even enjoy it! Yet, "one bad apple", and Israel suffered a defeat because of his one sin. In America, many are now divorcing their husbands and wives, but one good apple can also affect others around it. Adam's one sin affected the whole human race, but the obedience of Christ (also only one man) brought us salvation. Do not underestimate what your own obedience to Christ can mean. Stand up against sin and be a good leaven to those around you, and see God use it for good.

One bad apple spoils the whole bunch.

FULTON'S FOLLY

(5:15)   See then that ye walk circumspectly, not as fools, but as wise...

There are only two ways to choose as we walk in this world: God's way and the way of the world. Each of them has its own value system, and each one sees the other as foolish. To the world, the gospel is foolishness, but to the believer, who has walked in the way if the world before, the foolish way is the way of the world. Those who live only for this world may make great fortunes as they scoff at the world to come and by all appearances they are the real success stories, but are they? Jesus said, "What shall it profit a man, if he shall gain the whole world, and lose his own soul?" (Mk. 8:36). It is not that worldly fortune is evil in itself, but if one pursues that without having his heart set upon God, he will lose it all when he dies. Here on the earth, those who prosper without faith in God may feel they have conquered the world, and may laugh at Christians who are "so heavenly minded they are no earthly good". There is some truth in that, but the Christian may respond (as I saw on a church bulletin years ago) "For heaven's sake, what on earth are you doing?" Who is right? The wise person will use this world's money and things to prepare himself and others for the next world. If "the preaching of the cross is to them that perish foolishness" (1 Cor. 1:18), they will find themselves foolish when the final judgment comes. On that day, those who have laid up "treasures in heaven" (Mt. 6:20) will appear to be the real success stories. Just as "Fulton's Folly", the steamboat, and Noah's folly, the ark, proved to be their wisdom and good fortune, so those who "miss the boat" in the world's eyes may have their eyes on "that great big river boat in heaven".

The folly of one man is the fortune of another.

SUFFERING

(1:29) It has been granted to you on behalf of Christ not only to believe on him

"… but also to suffer for him" (NIV). In 1972, I was asked to try to lead a Bible study one morning, only a few weeks after coming to Christ. I spoke from a word study I did on "suffering", after they gave me a concordance and instructions on how to use it. We all used KJV at that time, and the phrase "Suffer little children, and forbid them not, to come unto me" (Mt. 19:14) caught my attention, and I saw a connection between this meaning and that of physical pain. Suffering seems to be different from affliction in that we <u>choose</u> to go through sufferings, while afflictions are put upon us against our will, and when we can do nothing about it. If this is the true meaning of suffering then it explains why Christ suffered – that he <u>chose</u> it, considering the end of it all, which was to save us from sin. We also, "on behalf of Christ", are to choose suffering over comfort when it will result in glory to God. Many have died martyrs' deaths "Choosing rather to suffer affliction with the people of God, than to enjoy the pleasures of sin for a season" (Heb. 11:25). Just as belief on Christ is a gift from God, so is suffering as we partake of Christ's sufferings as his body. Christ could have "come down from the cross" (Mk. 15:30), but instead of saving himself from pain, he suffered for me! "Allowing" these sufferings to be put upon us is different from putting ourselves through voluntary pain to show we are "spiritual". For instance, fasting is not suffering until it is done selflessly for someone else's benefit. In the Philippines, people have others beat and crucify them to pay for their sins. None of this "religious suffering" impresses God, but believing on him, we can share in his suffering.

**But join with me in suffering for
the gospel** (2 Tim 1:8 - NIV)

REMEMBER MY BONDS

(4:18)   I, Paul, write this greeting in my own hand. Remember my chains. (NIV)

The writer of Hebrews says, "Remember those in prison as if you were their fellow prisoners, and those who are mistreated as if you yourselves were suffering" (13:3 - NIV). Prison is a lonely place, but especially when nobody even remembers you are there. People can even stand torture, so long as they know others are at least thinking about them, and hopefully praying for them. Even if some are in prison for sins against society, we should visit them to show God's love and forgiveness, in the hopes of their repentance. But many are in prison unjustly, for crimes they never did and Paul was one who spent much time in prison, simply for believing in the true God of Scripture. Richard Wurmbrand, a Romanian pastor, spent fourteen years in prison for his faith in Christ, and became the "Voice of the Martyrs" to the world, saying "remember my bonds" (4:18 – KJV). If we are truly the Body of Christ, we must remember our faithful brethren who are suffering in such conditions, "as bound with them" (Heb. 3:13 – KJV), because it could as easily be you or I someday. Jesus said, "I was... sick, and in prison, and ye visited me not" (Mt. 25:43). It is not just laziness that keeps us from visiting prisoners – it is more often a guilty conscience. If we see what some are suffering, and realize they are no more evil than we are, we then become aware that "I could be that person in there!" Especially when it is Christians in bonds, we understand they are only inside for doing something we may be afraid to do. If we are not willing to preach, we must at least be willing to remember them that do, and pray for them when they are put into prison for it.

**Do to others as you would have them
do to you.** (Luke 6:31 – NIV)

MUG SHOTS

(2:15)   They displease God and are hostile to all men... (NIV)

This sounds like a description of Veerappan, a man in South India who poaches elephants, killing them for their tusks, and who has killed at least 104 men and beheaded them. But, this is a description of God's people, the Jews, "who killed the Lord Jesus and the prophets and also drove us out" (v. 15 – NIV). We may well ask, "How did God ever pick out a people as bad as this to be his people?" They belong on a bulletin board in a Post Office, with an "armed and dangerous" sign by the mug shots! But God chose them, and continues to call them his people. They are 'hostile to all men' like "Public Enemy #1", and don't even please the God they so proudly claim to serve. Jesus said of them, "You shut the kingdom of heaven in men's faces. You yourselves do not enter, nor will you let those enter who are trying to" (Mt. 23:13 - NIV). But, be careful! If we are not ready to suffer and die at the hands of such persecutors for the gospel's sake, we may very well become the same kind of people, as Paul was before his conversion. The Jews are typical "religious" people, and we must guard against becoming religious hypocrites, ourselves. Does my self-righteous attitude keep others from being saved? Do I kill people with my anger? Will I persecute and kill God's next move because I'm so sure I have the final revelation? Do I "Take great pains, and give them to ever body else?" (This is a pretty good description for a perfectionist!) This was written by way of warning to us by Paul, and is a chilling reminder of where religious pride can lead.

Pray for persecutors, lest you become like them.

I OWE, I OWE, SO OFF TO WORK I GO

(3:10) *... this we commanded you, that if any*
would not work, neither should he eat."

Paul spends a whole section of this letter on the subject of honest labor, and he himself followed the rule he set for others. Paul was a tentmaker who continued his trade while he preached the gospel. Paul was not idle at any time, being consumed with his call to preach the kingdom of God to the Jews, and especially to the Gentiles, but to work as a tentmaker on top of his other work was particularly appealing to his hearers. I worked in San Francisco for a 65-year-old man, who told me he would never ask me to do something he was not also prepared to do. He carried tools and heavy sheets of plywood up several flights of stairs, although he had been told by his doctor to slow down after a mild heart attack! It certainly made me honor him, and even want to do things for him. Paul, who was never idle, was also not a "work-a-holic" as some of us tend to be; there is a healthy balance. Paul's main objective was the gospel, and tent making never took priority over that, but neither was he dependent upon others for his livelihood. What does this say to us today? The gospel is also our primary objective, but too many are making an easy living from the gospel, and giving it a bad name. Hard work never hurt anybody and many of today's "evangelists and gospel workers" are fat and lazy, using the gospel as a money making scheme. Others, like David Brainerd and C.T. Studd, worked so hard it drove them to an early grave. Let us work hard at the things that will most promote the gospel among our peers and "...do the work of an evangelist..." (2 Tim. 4:5) when we see the opportunities come, and also look for whatever needs to be done physically, to open the hearts of the lost to Christ.

Honest labor bears a lovely face.

PARDON PRACTICE

(3:4)   One that ruleth well his own house, having his children in subjection…

Here is a wise and practical prerequisite for the person who wants to oversee a congregation of God's people. Anyone who has children will know the exasperation of trying to remain even-tempered when children are out of control. We have all been children, and have struggled with the need to obey our parents and teachers, and have learned much about forgiveness by the ways we have been forgiven. Moses had to learn to keep sheep in subjection before he could shepherd the flock of God's people in the wilderness. Priests in the Old Testament were chosen from among sinful men (Heb. 5:1,2), because an understanding of man's rebellious nature goes a long way in preparing a person to forgive the repeat offender. When children know their limits, it trains them to be obedient in all things, and parents will have daily confrontations with their children if they don't train them early, to break their stubborn self-wills. God has put us all into families so we can learn authority and submission, both as children and as parents. We may have to pardon our parents when they react in unloving ways, but as we understand they are also human beings, we can more easily accept their fallibility. We have all been rebels as children, until love breaks our stubborn wills and teaches us to be good parents. A judge must first learn to judge small claims cases, and someday he may even graduate to the Supreme Court, but his best training will come from training his own children at home. Jesus, who is the Supreme Judge over us all, "learned obedience through the things he suffered" (Heb. 5:8 - NIV), and is able to pardon us through having become acquainted with our struggles.

To understand is to pardon.

SHAMEFUL WAYS

(2:15) *"Do your best to present yourself to God as one approved...*

... a workman who does not need to be ashamed and who correctly handles the word of truth" (NIV). Paul speaks of several things in this letter that cause a person to be ashamed. We would all like to appear without shame before God and men, so we should consider what things cause shame and avoid them. Paul lists many sins that will be prevalent in the last days, which seem to be the opposite of shame (at least in this world) and pride seems to be at the core of all of them. Man, who proudly walks in his own selfish way, will finally be ashamed when he stands before God's Judgment Seat. But a worse shame comes to those who are being good outwardly for the praise of men, and are caught in hypocrisy. The Christian should be the most concerned about this, so he will not bring shame upon the gospel as he avoids shame to himself. Timothy was told to "Flee the evil desires of youth" (2:22 - NIV) which will cause shame when they are discovered before men and God, but again, these are not the most shameful things. Hypocrisy, as with "Jannes and Jambres [who] opposed Moses..." is folly that "will be clear to everyone" (3:8,9 - NIV), as God brings shame upon their pretended greatness. But these men were only pagans who were exalting themselves. The worst shame will come to those who try to appear as God's servants, as Christians who are models to others in their purity, and are found out for insincerity. That is why there was such an outcry against Jim Bakker and Jimmy Swaggart when they were discovered in blatant sins. We must learn to "correctly handle the word of truth" (NIV).

Nothing is more disgraceful than insincerity.

UNCLE TOM'S CABIN FEVER

(Ph. 16)   ...no longer as a slave, but better than a slave, as a dear brother. (NIV)

Why did Onesimus run away and also steal from Philemon? No doubt, Philemon was a good Christian man and a good master, but in Onesimus' mind, the place of a slave was less than ideal, or he would have stayed, being satisfied. He is like each of us, as we ran away from God and ruined our lives with sin, having no appreciation for how good God is. Man apart from God is like the "wicked and slothful servant" (Mt. 25:26) who saw his master as "a hard man" (Mt. 25:24). Until we are converted, God seems like an unjust ruler and we, like Onesimus, may try to run away, feeling it is the only way out of a bad situation, and even deceiving ourselves that we have done the right thing. <u>Uncle Tom's Cabin</u> shows a different attitude from a slave who was truly oppressed by an unjust ruler. Simon Legree beat Tom mercilessly, but Tom was free inside, knowing God was there and that Legree could not hurt the inner man. One way or another, God will not allow "unjust rule" to continue, either bringing us to our senses like Onesimus, or giving us a "way to escape, that ye may be able to bear it" (1 Cor. 10:13), as with Uncle Tom. The truth is, God is the best and kindest of all rulers, who goes out of his way to deliver us from the unjust rule of Satan, which we fall under when we run away from God. Again, Onesimus was like the prodigal son, who didn't know how good he had it until he ran away and had to live under the harsh rules of a hostile world. For Onesimus, his conscience was finally convicted through Paul's preaching, and he saw the error of his thinking and, by God's grace, was able to return to Philemon. His perception was changed: 'unjust rule' became fellowship.

Unjust rule never endures perpetually.

POWER IN YOUR SERVE

*(2:7,8)   You made him a little lower than the angels…
and put everything under his feet. (NIV)*

This quotation from Psalm 8:4-6 is spoken about man and refers first to Adam, who lost his sovereignty over creation through his sin. He had been given dominion over all earthly creatures, and was himself subject only to God. Now, authority comes in two ways: by inheritance, as is the case with Jesus, the Son of God, and by delegation, when it is given by God himself, or someone in a position of authority who delegates power and authority to those who are trusted because of their submission to the head. Christ, who is lord over all, has both of these kinds of authority, and came to earth to redeem us from the slavery to sin, that we could again fulfill God's original plan, and that God would "put all things in subjection under [man's] feet" (KJV). Power can also come by usurping it, as Satan did by deceiving Eve, and so became 'the god of this world' (2 Cor. 4:4) for a while; but because Jesus came, through his perfect, sincere obedience and service to God he fulfilled God's design for man, and got back for man the power and authority that Satan had seized. Now, man can again have "all things in subjection under his feet", by willing submission to Christ as Lord over all. We were designed by God to have such dominion, but it only comes in the way that Christ got it for man: through sincere service to God. The dominion of Satan could never last, as he would never serve God. "Whoever wants to be become great among you must be your servant" (Mt. 20:27 - NIV). Although we cannot be the natural sons of God, as Christ alone is, obedience, submission, and genuine faith in Christ will allow us to be adopted sons, and heirs with Jesus Christ.

Power comes from sincere service.

ETERNAL SECURITIES

(10:34)   ...you knew that you yourselves had better and lasting possessions. (NIV)

Putting trust in money and earthly possessions has a real fascination to people, and many spend a lifetime trying to have security through an abundance of riches and things. The problem is that security and significance will not last if they are based upon temporal things, and the wise person will think beyond this earthly existence if he wants to be truly secure. As Jesus said, "store up for yourselves treasures in heaven, where moth and rust do not destroy, and where thieves do not break in and steal" (Mt. 6:20 - NIV). The writer of Hebrews commended his hearers for having done this, who "joyfully accepted the confiscation of your property because you knew that you yourselves had better and lasting possessions" (NIV). Even the most sophisticated security systems can be broken into, and in the end "we can't take it with us". How much wiser it is to put confidence in those "better and lasting possessions" (NIV) which we can put in God's trust, and be "convinced that he is able to guard what I have entrusted to him for that day" (2 Tim. 1:12 – NIV). That is real security, and "confidence; it will be richly rewarded" (v. 35 - NIV). Those who hoard riches and possessions here on earth have little peace, not knowing the Prince of Peace. Howard Hughes became a recluse after making his great fortune, and was afraid to be seen by anyone for his later years. In the end he died, and could not take any of his riches into eternity. Although there is nothing evil in money itself, there is in heaven a substance that is "better and... enduring" (KJV). It is fine to have and use money, but don't put your trust in it. "Heaven and earth shall pass away, but my words shall not pass away". (Mt. 24:35)

Put not your trust in money, but
put your money in trust.

The Phantom Tollbooth

(11:26)   Esteeming the reproach of Christ greater riches than the treasures in Egypt...

If you feel you no longer enjoy life, learn from Moses. Here was a man who "had it all" and was not enjoying his life, but he knew there was something more to be enjoyed than the riches of Egypt. He gave it all up to suffer with God's people, and he had one of the most exciting lives recorded in the Bible. His formula "so that you may enjoy long life" (Deut. 6:2 - NIV) was to fear God and keep his commands. Anybody may live to a ripe old age and still not "enjoy" it if he misses the joy of serving God. As Peter wrote, "Whoever would love life and see good days...must turn from evil and do good...but even if you should suffer for what is right, you are blessed" (1 Pet. 3:10,11,14 - NIV). Jesus said, "And this is life eternal, *[not just length of days, but...]* that they might know thee the only true God, and Jesus Christ, whom thou hast sent" (Jn. 17:3). Are you bored with a humdrum life? Try preaching the gospel, and see how excited you will become with life. Norton Juster wrote a book for children called The Phantom Tollbooth in which a young boy, bored with his life, entered a land where letters and numbers came alive in the kingdoms of "Dictionopolis and Digitopolis". The admission was free, by just entering the phantom tollbooth in his toy car. We are offered a similar and more exciting experience by entering the "narrow gate", but sadly "only a few find it" (Mt. 7:13,14 - NIV), and many who do find it are scared away by the prospect of suffering and losing what earthly life has to offer. Those who are bold enough to enter will never again be bored with a dull life. Jesus paid our admission, and he himself is the door that leads to eternal life, and the reward on the other side (Jn. 10:9).

To enjoy life one should give up the lure of life.

DEADLY ERRORS

(1:16)   Do not err, my beloved brethren.

A parallel passage (Ps. 19:12-14) begins with "Who can understand his errors?" Errors are the first of five steps into sin, as we simply "wander" from the right way. If we can understand our errors, it will save us from worse sins. We soon progress to "secret faults" as we try to hide the sin from others. Then we become "presumptuous" – presuming it is alright to continue in sin, and that God will surely forgive us, even if we continue to sin. Next, sin begins to have "dominion" over us – we no longer can control our urges to sin, and it becomes our master. The final step is "great transgression". James gives a progression as Lust (*secret thought*), Temptation (*presumption: dwelling on the thought until we are enticed by it*), Sin (*dominion: giving in to action*), and finally Death (*great transgression ending in God's just punishment*). We must begin, with God's grace, to understand our errors and weaknesses, and then to militantly pray for freedom from sin's mastery over us. Job, who was a godly man, said, "I made a covenant with my eyes not to look lustfully at a girl" (Job 31:1 - NIV). This is being militant against sin at its very inception: don't even allow sin to start a thought. "We take captive every thought to make it obedient to Christ" (2 Cor. 10:5 - NIV). We tame the tongue by first taming the thoughts, "For out of the overflow of the heart the mouth speaks" (Mt. 12:34 - NIV). And so, David's prayer, after giving the progression of sin, is "Let the words of my mouth, and the meditation of my heart, be acceptable in thy sight, O Lord..." (Ps. 19:14). Finally, Proverbs addresses a young man caught in sexual sin: "Do not let your heart turn to her ways" (7:25 - NIV).

Do not err, my beloved brethren.

THE CHURCH AT BABYLON

(5:13)   The church that is at Babylon, elected together with you, saluteth you.

"Some want to live within the sound of church or chapel bell; I want to run a rescue shop, within a yard of hell!" (- C.T. Studd). It sounds pretty radical, and "the church that is at Babylon" sounds like "the church that is in Hades". Babylon has always been a symbol of man's rebellion against God, and Peter is probably referring to Rome. Babylon, which is still in Iraq, started out with the same reputation, being the first city built by Nimrod (Gen. 10:10), son of Cush, son of Ham, who was cursed by Noah. He also built Nineveh. Babylon, called "the great, the mother of harlots and abominations of the earth", sounds like a good place to stay <u>away</u> from, but the church's job is to "go ye into <u>all</u> the world, and preach the gospel to every creature" (Mk. 16:15), including cities like Nineveh (Jonah 1:2), Babylon, Rome (Rom. 1:15) and Amsterdam. I once spent a year preaching the gospel in San Francisco every day, going to the worst areas and giving out the good news. We even went once into a "transvestite bar" and came out with a soul for Jesus. Is there any place so evil that God cannot reach it? Even Sodom had a "church" in it, until Lot and his wife and daughters left. Spiritual warfare for God's kingdom means going into the worst and darkest reaches of Satan's kingdom here on earth and planting churches there, even if they must begin "underground". Jesus said, "...I will build my church; and the gates of hell shall not prevail against it" (Mt. 16:18). If Rome was the seat of Satan's kingdom in Paul and Peter's day, they went straight into the heart of it and planted a church. We must do the same today, (and we may die doing it) for "the church at Babylon".

Good intentions are not good unless carried out.

ONE FINE DAY

(3:10)   *...the heavens shall pass away with a great*
           noise; and the elements shall melt...

I first read this on Sunday afternoon, September 10, 1972 – my first Bible reading in my life. I was so struck with the up-to-date nature of this verse, and the whole letter, as I was only three days old as a Christian, that it put a real fear of God in me. I could envision something like an atomic bomb exploding in the air above the earth, so even the "elements" themselves melted as the hydrogen, oxygen, nitrogen and other basic atoms and molecules that make up the atmosphere were affected. This is reality as it will be "one fine day" when nobody expects it. That "they willingly are ignorant" (3:5), or "they deliberately forget" (3:5 - NIV) means willful unbelief in the true story of Noah's ark and the worldwide flood. No need for surprise, as nobody believed it then either, until the flood came. Likewise, few today believe God will really set the world and heavens on fire, but it will certainly come to pass, even if the whole world votes against it, or "proves" by science that it can't happen. Deliberate ignorance of the flood requires that today's scientists "prove" to us that a "big bang" is responsible for creation and, after millions of years have passed, life has naturally and spontaneously come into being and evolved to what it is today. "Scientists" need to get back to a basic fear of God and stop lying to people, pretending their theories are more logical than the truth of the Bible. The fact is that the flood did happen, and wise men will learn from history. One hundred years of Noah's preaching only resulted in his own family's salvation. Be wise and flee the wrath to come.

**But the day of the Lord will come
as a thief in the night...** (3:10)

ME BLIND THRICE

(2:11)   *"But whoever hates his brother is in the darkness...*

...and walks around in the darkness; he does not know where he is going, because the darkness has blinded him" (NIV). Paul was blinded by a light from heaven, until a man of God prayed for him three days later. People have been made blind by looking at the sun for too long, or by light flashes from arc welding, but is it really possible to be also blinded by darkness? Yes – by extended absence of light. I used to do cave exploration and once I saw fish in an underground stream in a cave that had no eyesight. They had the remains of what used to be eyes, but after generations of living in darkness they lost the ability to see, as there was nothing to see! We are much the same. Until the light of Christ came to the world, we had lost the ability to see. We went about hating one another because it was all we knew. Everyone did it. But, when light comes, darkness is dispersed, and all things become visible to those who have eyes to see. Still, God must now open our blind eyes, just as Paul needed the prayer of Ananias. Blind fish in a cave will not see suddenly when light comes, but must once again adapt the ability, because they have actually been blinded by darkness. We also have all the mechanism necessary, but don't know where we're going until God gives light, and sight to our eyes. One thing is certain: if we continue to hate our brother we cannot say we are born again. We cannot continue in willful sin and be Christians. It will keep us blind, that we won't know where we are going, thinking we are going to heaven, but actually going to destruction. Don't be blind fish, but fishers of men.

There is none as blind as one who will not see.

STICKS AND STONES

(Jude 10) ...these men speak abusively against
whatever they do not understand. (NIV)

This was Paul's error before his conversion, and later he called himself "chief of sinners" (1 Tim. 1:15), knowing how bad this attitude had been. Our words go much farther than our actions, for good or evil. God speaks of how evil it is to have "insulted the Spirit of grace" (Heb. 10:29 - NIV). Paul had been forgiven because he "did it ignorantly in unbelief" (1 Tim. 1:13), but those who insult the Spirit of grace and know what they are doing will find "no sacrifice for sins is left" (Heb. 10 26 - NIV). God can forgive any of our actions, knowing we are ignorant captives of the prince of darkness. We often injure others in our selfish ambition. As children, we used to say, "Sticks and stones may break my bones, but words will never hurt me". It is true that words cannot hurt the body, but they do much worse damage when we insult another's character. Those wounds go much deeper and are a lot harder to heal. Even insults against the Spirit of grace may be forgiven, if they are truly done ignorantly and in unbelief. But willful unbelief, and insults spoken when we know the truth, will never be forgiven, unless we repent from the heart and plead forgiveness. Jude spoke of men who "speak abusively against whatever they do not understand", but they are not the worst of sinners, and can find forgiveness. Sticks and stones could hurt Jesus, and crucifixion could even kill him, but he said, "Father, forgive them; for they know not what they do" (Lk. 23:34). He also said, "Be not afraid of them that kill the body, and after that have no more that they can do" (Lk. 12:4). Jesus forgave those who beat, insulted and even killed him in ignorance, but not an insult to the Spirit of God (Lk. 12:10).

...There is a sin unto death... (1 Jn. 5:16)

MOTHER OF INVENTION

(1:13)   ...And in the midst of the seven candlesticks one like unto the Son of man...

At this season, we celebrate the birth of Jesus Christ, the eternal Son of God who came into the world, clothed with human flesh, to save us from our sins. Jesus is called both the 'Son of God' and the 'Son of Man', and he is the only one in all of creation who is both God and man. Why did God become man? It was because of the problem of sin. God had created man to worship him, but when Adam sinned, a way was needed to redeem man from sin's curse. The angel Gabriel told Mary, "That holy thing which shall be born of thee shall be called the Son of God" (Lk. 1:35). Jesus is unique, as there can never be another Son of God as he is, being the only begotten Son of God the Father. But, there can also never be another "Son of Man", who came once to save mankind from sin. As Mary was chosen to be the mother of this "holy thing", she also became unique. "Necessity is the mother of invention", as it has been said, and Mary became the mother of Gods invention to deal with man's sin. Jesus referred to himself as "the Son of Man", to remind his disciples that he was that unique invention of God, come to rescue them and all of us from sin. There seems to be no other way that God could have saved us. Christmas is the day we celebrate the birth of the Son of Man as a child who was "born of a virgin", a necessary part of the invention. It was necessary that Jesus be sinless, so he was not born of an earthly father, but it was also necessary that he be human, and so the Son of Man was born physically of a real woman. When John saw "one like unto the Son of Man", he knew he saw the same Jesus he had walked with, but now he was once again in heaven, clothed with glory.

Necessity is the mother of invention.

COME AND SEE

(6:1)   ...the noise of thunder, one of the four beasts saying, Come and see.

The Apostle John records these words, 'Come and see' four times, as each of the first four seals are opened, and at each command a horse and rider come out for John to see. What do you see? The first horse is white, with a rider who comes with a bow and a crown, "conquering and to conquer". Is this Christ or the antichrist – what do you see? Three other horses – red, black and pale – come next as each is introduced with the words "Come and see", and they represent, in order, bloodshed and war, famine, and death. Which of these will the inhabitants of the earth see? And which will you and I see? What you carry in your heart will determine what you will see. When John began his gospel account, he said, "And the light shineth in darkness; and the darkness comprehended it not" (Jn. 1:5). Then, when two of John the Baptist's disciples met Jesus and asked him, "Rabbi,... where dwellest thou?" Jesus answered "Come and see" (Jn. 1:38-9). One of them, Andrew, then brought his brother Simon Peter that he could also see Jesus. When Nathaniel heard the words of Philip, that they had found the Messiah, Jesus of Nazareth, he said, "Can any good thing come out of Nazareth?" Philip saith unto him, "Come and see" (Jn. 1:46). This is our commission from Jesus, just to get others to come and see, and if there is faith to be awakened in their hearts, they will see Jesus as Lord. It is interesting that when "certain Greeks" first came to worship at Jerusalem, they said to Philip, "Sir, we would see Jesus", then Philip and Andrew told Jesus (Jn. 12:20-22). Let us be like them, and tell hungry souls "Come and see Jesus". Which rider will we see when he comes?

Each one sees what he carries in his heart.

TIME AFTER TIME

(10:6) And sware ... that there should be time no longer.

This is spoken by an angel, and he swears this "by him who liveth forever and ever", the God who created and will finally destroy time. Imagine existence without time: no schedules to meet, no alarm clocks to shock us out of our nice dreams, no more John Cameron Swayze (from the old TV commercial) saying, "And the Timex watch is still ticking!" What is time anyway? It is just another creation of God, made to be destroyed with heaven and earth and all of created existence. We can mark the passage of time only by events that happen, like the clockwork motion of the planets around the sun, or rotation of the earth. We may speak of "at the end of time" without thinking what it means. Our history books, including the Bible, record important events, as one succeeds another, but when all will be fulfilled there will be no more need of time, as we will all be in that Eternal Day, worshiping "him that liveth for ever and ever". In God's presence, there will be no boredom, no need of food, or fun or fancy things. He "...who created heaven,...and the earth,...and the sea, and the things which therein are" will far exceed any idolatrous fascination we may have had with any of these things. But what about those who don't go to heaven? For them, sadly, there will also be no time. A Catholic nun, Mother Regia, once told us as children that Hades would have a broken clock that keeps chiming out "never...never... never"; there will be no hope of ever escaping the torments for those who have rejected God's gracious gift of Christ. Everyone there will finally have a "Rolex", and curse it! There will be no more time, after time.

Time is an illusion – Albert Einstein.

SONG OF THE LAMB

(15:3)   And they sing the song of Moses the servant
of God, and the song of the Lamb...

What is "the song of the Lamb"? A good place to find out is to read the song of Moses, as they are the same basic story, one being a foreshadowing of the other. Notice how the plagues nearly coincide, and how people continue to harden their hearts instead of repenting. Moses' song was one of victory over the army of Pharaoh, who oppressed God's people, an ante-type of Satan's defeat. The Lamb's song is an eternal one, and is a celebration of a much more eternal victory, in a conflict that has continued on from creation. Only the redeemed will be able to sing that song. Moses' song changed somewhat in Deuteronomy 32, from the one in Exodus 15. The second was concerned not only with Pharaoh's sin, but now also with Israel's sin, and with God's forgiveness and faithfulness to these stiff-necked, rebellious people. Likewise, the Lamb of God deals not only with those who never repented and finally had to be cast into outer darkness, but also with God's redeemed people who will know for eternity that we don't deserve to be in heaven. It is a song of mercy and grace which the angels will never understand, having never experienced redemption, so even angels can't join in this song. It will be like Solomon's "Song of Songs", a love song to our God, our lover who delights in us. Those who have experienced "the fellowship of his sufferings" (Php. 3:10) will sing the loudest of all, as they will best understand its meaning. We will sing it over and over for eternity, because its theme is our eternal praise to Jesus for his victory on our behalf against sin.

Is anyone happy? Let him sing songs of praise.

GRADING TESTS

(20:4)   *I saw thrones on which were seated those who*
           had been given authority to judge. (NIV)

In a dream last night I saw someone grading my test, and I was given a "D-" on one page. (Why not an "F"? Who gets a "D-"?!) It was for three meaningless "infractions", all excused as <u>not</u> mistakes by the final judge. But I pronounced to the one who gave it to me, "So shall you be judged" (Mt. 7:2). Jesus will be the final judge of all things, and the "accuser of our brethren" (Rev. 12:10) will be judged <u>by us!</u> People will be judged, as well: "I will judge you by your own words, you wicked servant!" (Luke 19:22 - NIV). The Final Exam will be completely fair. God wants to forgive us, if we will forgive others, and confess our own sins. God's Kingdom is established as we submit to him in all areas, and those who are found trustworthy will be given a charge to judge others (as in a court system, with a supreme court). Who will pass the Final Exam? Those with no apparent infractions? No, but those who have their sins washed clean in the blood of Christ's sacrifice. God won't compare our test paper with anyone else's, except the perfect test score of Jesus: 100% true! Only by Christ's righteousness can we judge others with equity. We try to bring others down to make ourselves look better, but God is not fooled. Judgment will be swift and final. Only a perfect score will pass, and only sins washed in Christ's blood are forgiven. So now, "It is done. I am Alpha and Omega" (21:6), says Jesus. Today is the end of a year, but the beginning of a new year. I've learned that it is by making reasonable, timely and measurable small goals that I also get the larger ones done. Judge yourself and trust in the grace of the Final Judge, and press on to the end! Happy New Year!

"Yes, I am coming soon". Amen.
Come, Lord Jesus. (22:20)